AF505905

Heather Grabbe
THE EU'S TRANSFORMATIVE POWER

Eva Gross
THE EUROPEANIZATION OF NATIONAL FOREIGN POLICY
Continuity and Change in European Crisis Management

Hussein Kassim and Handley Stevens
AIR TRANSPORT AND THE EUROPEAN UNION
Europeanization and its Limits

Katie Verlin Laatikainen and Karen E. Smith (*editors*)
THE EUROPEAN UNION AND THE UNITED NATIONS
Intersecting Multilateralisms

Esra LaGro and Knud Erik Jørgensen (*editors*)
TURKEY AND THE EUROPEAN UNION
Prospects for a Difficult Encounter

Ingo Linsenmann, Christoph O. Meyer and Wolfgang T. Wessels (*editors*)
ECONOMIC GOVERNMENT OF THE EU
A Balance Sheet of New Modes of Policy Coordination

Hartmut Mayer and Henri Vogt (*editors*)
A RESPONSIBLE EUROPE?
Ethical Foundations of EU External Affairs

Philomena Murray (*editor*)
EUROPE AND ASIA
Regions in Flux

Daniel Naurin and Helen Wallace (*editors*)
UNVEILING THE COUNCIL OF THE EUROPEAN UNION
Games Governments Play in Brussels

David Phinnemore and Alex Warleigh-Lack
REFLECTIONS ON EUROPEAN INTEGRATION
50 Years of the Treaty of Rome

Sebastiaan Princen
AGENDA-SETTING IN THE EUROPEAN UNION

Palgrave Studies in European Union Politics

**Series Standing Order ISBN 978–1–4039–9511–7 (hardback) and
ISBN 978–1–4039–9512–4 (paperback)**

You can receive future titles in this series as they are published by placing a standing order. Please contact your bookseller or, in case of difficulty, write to us at the address below with your name and address, the title of the series and one of the ISBNs quoted above.

Customer Services Department, Macmillan Distribution Ltd, Houndmills, Basingstoke, Hampshire RG21 6XS, UK

Coping with Accession to the European Union

New Modes of Environmental Governance

Edited by

Tanja A. Börzel
Professor of Political Science
Freie Universität Berlin, Germany

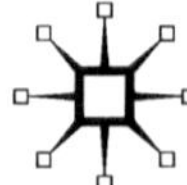

First published 2009 by
PALGRAVE MACMILLAN

Palgrave Macmillan in the UK is an imprint of Macmillan Publishers Limited, registered in England, company number 785998, of Houndmills, Basingstoke, Hampshire RG21 6XS.

Palgrave Macmillan in the US is a division of St Martin's Press LLC, 175 Fifth Avenue, New York, NY 10010.

Palgrave Macmillan is the global academic imprint of the above companies and has companies and representatives throughout the world.

Palgrave® and Macmillan® are registered trademarks in the United States, the United Kingdom, Europe and other countries.

ISBN: 978–0–230–57551–6 hardback

This book is printed on paper suitable for recycling and made from fully managed and sustained forest sources. Logging, pulping and manufacturing processes are expected to conform to the environmental regulations of the country of origin.

A catalogue record for this book is available from the British Library.

A catalog record for this book is available from the Library of Congress.

10   9   8   7   6   5   4   3   2   1
18 17 16 15 14 13 12 11 10 09

Printed and bound in Great Britain by
CPI Antony Rowe, Chippenham and Eastbourne

Contents

Figures

Abbreviations

BAT	best available technology
BATNEEC	best available technology not entailing excessive costs
CCDRs	Commissions of Regional Coordination and Development (Portugal)
CEE	Central and Eastern European
CIS	Common Implementation Strategy
DEH	Public Electricity Corporation (Greece)
DWD	Drinking Water Directive
EBRD	European Bank for Reconstruction and Development
EC	European Community
ECJ	European Court of Justice
ECL	Licenses Management Entity (Portugal)
EIA	Environmental Impact Assessment
EIAD	Environmental Impact Assessment Directive
EIS	Environmental Impact Statements
ENGOs	environmental nongovernmental organizations
ELVs	emission limit values
EPER	European Pollutant Emission Register
EU	European Union
FFHD	Fauna, Flora. Habitats Directive
IBAs	Important Bird Areas
IPPC	Integrated Pollution Prevention and Control
IPPCD	Integrated Pollution Prevention and Control Directive
IRAR	Institute Regulating Water and Waste (Portugal)
ISPA	Instrument for Structural Policies for Pre-Accession
LCP	Large Combustion Plants
LCPD	Large Combustion Plants Directive
LEPAs	Local Environmental Protection Agencies (Romania)
MMDD	Ministry of Environment and Sustainable Development (Romania)
MOE	Ministry of Environment (Poland)
NAPA	National Agency for Natural Protected Areas (Romania)
NGOs	nongovernmental organizations
OMC	Open Method of Coordination
PPPs	Public-private partnerships
pSCIs	potential Community Interest Sites

RBMCs	River Basin Management Committees (Romania)
RD	Real Decreto (Spain)
REIs	Regional Environmental Inspectorates (Hungary)
REPAs	Regional Environmental Protection Agencies (Romania)
SACs	Special Areas of Conservation
SCIs	Sites of Community Importance
SEARN	State Secretariat for the Environment and Natural Resources (Portugal)
SPAs	Special Protection Areas
TAIEX	Technical Assistance Information Exchange Office
WFD	Water Framework Directive
YPEXODE	Ministry of Environment, Urban Planning and Public Works (Greece)

Acknowledgments

This book summarized the major findings of a joint research project 'Coping with the Challenge of Accession' (COPA), which explored how transition countries in Southern Europe as well as in Central and Eastern Europe coped with the challenge of accession to the EU. The research was part of the Integrated Project 'New Modes of Governance in Europe', funded by the sixth Framework Programme of the European Union and coordinated by the European University Institute. Funding by the European Commission is gratefully acknowledged.

The project was conceived and implemented in a truly European spirit bringing together researchers from five different countries in the South, East and West of Europe. Noble ideas of Brussels often tend to get dashed in the administrative grindings of the EU's multilevel bureaucracy. Special thanks, therefore, go to Ingo Linsenmann, administrative coordinator of NEWGOV in Florence, and Kaja Kreutz and Astrid Timme, who managed the project at the Freie Universität Berlin. Without their management skills, patience and endurance, our scientific adventure would have turned into a bureaucratic nightmare.

The endless hours spent on filling hundred of pages for annual activity reports, management and implementation plans and financial statements were largely compensated by the intellectual leadership of and personal friendship with Adrienne Héritier and Martin Rhodes, the two scientific coordinators of NEWGOV, as well as Helen Wallace and Stefano Bartolini, who subsequently acted as heads of the Steering Committee.

The ultimate recipe for success of a transnational research project is personal relationships. While academic excellence may be the necessary condition, personal commitment and mutual trust are crucial in creating synergies among brilliant minds and turning their scientific input in a joint output. After more than four years of hard work and at times heated debates between Athens, Barcelona, Berlin, Bucharest, Centennial (WY), New Haven (CT), Paris and Vienna, we can honestly say that we reached a new level in our professional and personal relationships. This volume is a true joint venture.

Our project benefited from invaluable input of many colleagues. We thank Stefano Bartolini, Elena Belokurova, Michael Blauberger, Lena

Bobinska, Susana Borrás, Liliana Botcheva-Andonova, Laszlo Bruszt, JoAnn Carmin, David Coen, Thomas Conzelmann, Adam Fagan, Gerda Falkner, Mateusz Falkowski, Mike Fichter, Tomasz Grosse, Jürgen Grote, Niam Hardiman, Adrienne Héritier, Ingmar von Homeyer, Elena Iankova, Klaus Jakob, Beate Kohler-Koch, Amelie Kutter, Davin Lane, Sandra Lavenex, Dirk Lehmkuhl, Zdenka Mansfeldova, Alina Mungiu-Pippidi, Sabine von Oppeln, Diana Panke, Guy Peters, Heiko Pleines, Martin Rhodes, Thomas Risse, Bo Rothstein, Fritz Scharpf, Waltraud Schelkle, Susanne K. Schmidt, Philippe Schmitter, Miranda Schreurs, Uli Sedelmeier, Beate Sissenich, Carina Sprungk, Imogen Sudberry, Máté Szabó, Mark Thatcher, Oliver Treib, Vera van Hüllen, Jelle Visser, Helen Wallace, Wolfgang Wessels and Nicole Wichmann.

Katrin Bergholz, Marta Cantijoch, Meritxell Costejà, Marina Dimasso, Adam Hildebrandt, Tomasz, Jerzyniak, Henrike Knappe, Rafael Köhler, Iwona Podrygala and Carrie Romero worked as research assistants for the project and were particularly helpful in preparing and conducting the numerous interviews we did.

We are grateful to the three editors of the Palgrave European Studies Series. Michelle Egan, Neil Nugent and William Paterson gave us terrific comments and suggestions making us try ever harder to improve the quality of the manuscript.

We also owe tremendously to Carina Breschke, Farina Ahäuser, Mathias Großklaus, Nicole Helmerich and Lisa Thormählen for their relentless help in the formal editing of the manuscript.

Finally, we would like to thank Alison Howson, Amy Lankester-Owen and Gemma d'Arcy Hughes who made the publishing of this book with Palgrave a real pleasure

Tanja Börzel, Aron Buzogány, Ana Mar Fernández, Nuria Font, Sonja Guttenbrunner and Charalampos Koutalakis.

Athens, Barcelona, Berlin, Centennial (WY), New Haven (CT), Vienna, April 2009.

Contributors

Tanja A. Börzel is Professor for Political Science and holds the Chair of European Integration at the Otto-Suhr-Institute for Political Science, Freie Universität Berlin. Together with Thomas Risse, she directs the Research College 'The Transformative Power of Europe'.

Aron Buzogány is research associate at the Otto-Suhr-Institute for Political Science, Freie Universität Berlin, and currently holds a Fox Fellowship at Yale University. He is about to complete his PhD thesis on the Europeanization of social movements in Central and Eastern European countries.

Ana Mar Fernández is assistant professor of political science at the Universita Autonoma de Barcelona. Her research interest lies with the process of European integration and the analysis of the European institutional system with a focus on the EU Council Presidency.

Nuria Font is professor of political science at the Universita Autonoma de Barcelona. She has done research on environmental policy, EU institutions and public participation.

Sonja Guttenbrunner is EU project manager for a nonprofit company with focus on research coordination. She is completing her PhD thesis on civil society and accession in Poland.

Charalampos Koutalakis is a lecturer at the Department of Political Science and Public Administration, University of Athens, Greece. His current research focuses on governance in states with weak regulatory capacities with emphasis on pharmaceutical and environmental policies.

1
Introduction

Tanja A. Börzel

In recent years, the literature on governance within and beyond the state has focused on a specific mode of governance based on nonhierarchical coordination and the involvement of private actors in the formulation and implementation of public policies. In the 1970s, the comparative policy and politics literature already showed that nonhierarchical modes of governance might help to overcome problems of state failure (for a good overview of the literature see Mayntz and Scharpf, 1995a; Scharpf, 1997). The direct participation of nonstate actors in public policy making would improve both the quality of public policies and the effectiveness of their implementation, since target groups could bring in their expertise and their interests. Twenty years later, this argument was reintroduced into the governance literature by students of International Relations and European Politics, who discuss 'new modes of governance' as functional equivalents to the traditional top-down, command-and-control approach of hierarchical steering (Rosenau and Czempiel, 1992; Jachtenfuchs, 1995; Héritier, 2002; Risse and Lehmkuhl, 2007).

This book explores the role of new modes of governance in helping future member states to cope with accession to the European Union (EU). To what extent have nonstate actors assisted the governments of Southern and Central and Eastern European (CEE) accession countries in adopting and adapting to the *acquis communautaire*? In order to assess the importance of new modes of governance for coping with the challenge of accession, the country chapters take a broader view on new policy developments and seek to give a fuller account of how EU environmental policies have been implemented in Southern European and CEE accession countries.

New modes of governance and accession to the EU

New modes of governance seem to be particularly appropriate for the European Union. Unlike within the nation state, EU policymakers can hardly rely on majoritarian decision making and coercive power to make effective and legitimate policies (Hix, 1998; Kohler-Koch and Rittberger, 2006). Yet, empirical research on new modes of governance in Europe demonstrates that nonhierarchical coordination and the involvement of nonstate actors are far less prevalent in European policymaking than the limited powers of the European Union would lead us to expect. Moreover, new modes of governance do not necessarily increase the effectiveness and the legitimacy of public policymaking either. These findings also hold for the previous enlargements of the EU to Southern, Central and Eastern Europe, which appear to be the most likely cases for the emergence of new modes of governance. On the one hand, the EU cannot hierarchically impose the *acquis communautaire* on accession countries. Before they join, their relationship with the EU remains in the realm of classic diplomacy and international negotiations. The EU's supranational institutions do not even cast a shadow of hierarchy, yet, since the supremacy of EU law and its direct effects, which empower domestic courts to enforce EU law without the consent of national governments, takes effect only after accession. On the other hand, the Southern European and CEE countries have been limited in their capacity to coordinate the adoption of and adaptation to the *acquis* hierarchically. The implementation of the *acquis communautaire* created an enormous policy load, which met with limited resources (expertise, money and personnel) that were already strained by managing the transition from authoritarian and socialist rule. Given the limited capacity of both the EU and the accession countries, it would only be rational for public actors to seek cooperation with private actors in order to share or shift the burden by pooling resources and delegating certain tasks. Private actors, in turn, could exchange their resources for influence on the policies that would significantly affect them. Finally, the European Commission strongly encouraged accession countries to involve nonstate actors in the adoption of and adaptation to the *acquis* in order to ensure both greater effectiveness and legitimacy of the accession process.

The governance literature leads us to assume that new modes of governance could compensate for the weak hierarchical steering capacity of both the EU and the accession countries in the implementation of EU policies, since private actors can provide the governments of the accession countries with important resources (money, information, expertise and support) that are necessary to make EU policies work. Yet, as our empirical studies show there is only limited evidence for the emergence of new modes of governance in the accession process. Adoption of and adaptation to the *acquis communautaire* ran into serious problems when the high costs involved in the implementation of EU policies met with the weak capacities of the accession countries. Funding was usually insufficient; public administrations were seriously understaffed and lacked the necessary expertise to apply and enforce EU policies. Moreover, administrative responsibilities were highly fragmented and were combined with weak coordination mechanisms that did not allow the pooling of competencies and resources across different ministries and levels of government.

State actors, however, have only barely taken recourse to nonstate actors in order to pool resources and share the costs in the implementation of EU policies. If at all, we find nascent forms of cooperation between state and nonstate actors that hardly go beyond consultation and the delegation of technical tasks that some might not even consider as particularly new. Moreover, new modes of governance are most likely to emerge if EU legislation explicitly requires the involvement of the public. Overall, however, traditional command-and-control approaches prevail in Southern European and CEE accession countries.

Explaining new modes of governance

To address the puzzle and explain why new modes of governance played at best a marginal role in the accession of Southern European and CEE countries to the EU, we argue in this book that the literature has neglected an important finding in the early research on political steering. The work of Renate Mayntz and Fritz Scharpf, in particular, has shown that nonhierarchical modes of governance may produce better policy outcomes – but only if policymakers have the option to impose policy hierarchically, that is if they have the capacity to adopt and enforce it without the involvement of, and against opposition from, private actors (Mayntz and Scharpf, 1995b; Scharpf, 1997; Héritier, 2003). This 'shadow of hierarchy' has a crucial impact on the incentives for both public and private actors to engage in nonhierarchical coordination (Héritier and Lehmkuhl, 2008; Börzel, forthcoming-c) and helps to explain why we have found so little evidence on new modes of governance in accession countries. Their state capacities have often been too limited to cast a credible shadow of hierarchy that would provide sufficient incentives for nonstate actors to cooperate. Moreover, state actors that command only limited resources have themselves been reluctant to cooperate with nonstate actors for fear of agency capture. Finally, weak states are mirrored by weak societies – like state capacities, the degree of societal organization is significantly lower in Southern European and CEE countries compared to the liberal democracies in Northern and Western Europe. Nonstate actors often simply lack the capacity to engage with state actors and have little to offer in return for access to the policy process.

In a nutshell, this book argues that the accession countries of the Southern and Eastern enlargements have lacked two fundamental preconditions for the emergence and effectiveness of new modes of governance: state and nonstate actors with sufficient resources to engage in nonhierarchical coordination in order to improve the effectiveness of public policy. This 'governance capacity' has largely been taken for granted by the governance literature since it has almost exclusive focused on Western democracies.

The structure of the book

The book presents the findings of a four-year joint research project that explored how transition countries in Southern Europe as well as in Central and Eastern Europe coped with the challenge of accession to the EU. The research was part of the Integrated Project 'New Modes of Governance in Europe', funded by the 6th Framework Programme of the European Union and coordinated by the European University Institute.[1] It provides the first systematic comparison of Southern and Eastern enlargement from the perspective of the candidate countries.

The first chapter, by Tanja A. Börzel, lays out the empirical puzzle and the theoretical challenge it poses to the literature on (new modes of) governance. The second chapter, again by Tanja A. Börzel, discusses the specific challenges that accession countries face in adopting and adapting to the *acquis communautaire* in the field of environmental policy. It also explains the research design of the empirical study and provides the analytical framework that guides the comparative case studies.

The six empirical chapters systematically compare how Southern European and CEE countries coped with the challenge of accession. More specifically, they analyze the role of new modes of governance in the adoption of and adaptation to selected EU water, air pollution and nature protection policies. Placing new modes of governance in the broader context of EU policymaking, each of the country chapters gives a fuller picture of how accession countries implemented these policies and which problems they had to confront.

The country studies by Ana Mar Fernández, Nuria Font and Charalampos Koutalakis provide a comparative analysis of the implementation of EU environmental policies in the three Southern European countries that joined in the 1980s. They show that Greece, Portugal and Spain faced huge costs in the adoption of and adaptation to the environmental *acquis* that met with relatively weak capacities. Yet, both state and nonstate actors had initially been too weak to pool resources. Only when EU membership helped to strengthen state capacities and transformed political opportunity structures for nonstate actors did new modes of governance start to emerge. These, however, present only 'timid deviations' from the traditional command-and-control approach that still prevails in all three Southern European countries.

The country studies by Aron Buzogány and Sonja Guttenbrunner on Hungary, Poland and Romania find as limited empirical evidence for the emergence of new modes of governance in the Eastern enlargement process as the three case studies on Greece, Portugal and Spain at the time of their accession. The capacities of Hungary, Poland and Romania have been weaker than those of their Southern counterparts in the 1980s. Poor funding, insufficiently qualified personnel and administrative fragmentation proved as much of a problem for the effective implementation of EU environmental policies as it did in Greece, Portugal and Spain. However, the demands on state capacity were even higher in the CEE countries since the *acquis* had in the meantime doubled and EU conditionality imposed strict pressure both in terms of time and compliance. As expected, new modes of governance are scarce and have emerged only where state actors possessed sufficient capacities to remain in charge of the policy process.

In the concluding chapter, Tanja A. Börzel summarizes the major findings of the comparative case studies and discusses their implications for the literature on (new modes of) governance. Despite, or rather because of, serious capacity problems, new modes of governance hardly emerged in Southern and Eastern Europe. If they did, they hardly went beyond consultation with stakeholders and delegation of technical tasks – rather old-fashioned forms for the involvement of nonstate actors in public policymaking. The double weakness of transition countries results in a serious dilemma for governance research and practice alike – the stronger the need for nonhierarchical modes of governance, the less favorable are the conditions for their emergence and effectiveness. In order to escape the low capacity trap, the capacities of both state and nonstate actors need to be strengthened. While the EU has developed a sophisticated toolbox for capacity building, its financial and technical assistance favors an asymmetrical empowerment of state actors. This appears to be particularly problematic for current accession countries in the Western Balkans and the EU's Eastern neighborhood, where states are not only weak but often lack the stable democratic institutions that would grant civil society sufficient autonomy to use the opportunities offered by accession and approximation to the EU, respectively, while avoiding their constraints.

Note

1. http://www.eu-newgov.org (last access: 25 November 2008).

2
New Modes of Governance and Accession: The Paradox of Double Weakness

Tanja A. Börzel

Accession is both a blessing and a curse to transition countries aspiring to become members of the EU. On the one hand, the implementation of the *acquis* supports their transformation from authoritarian regimes with state-controlled economies into liberal democracies with market economies, while on the other hand, accession countries face great difficulties in restructuring their economic and political institutions in order to meet the conditions for EU membership. The adoption of and adaptation to the *acquis* run into serious problems concerning both the effectiveness and the legitimacy of EU policies. Since these countries are 'weak' states that often lack absorption capacity rather than willingness to implement EU policies effectively, accession problems cannot simply be solved through hierarchical coordination (command-and-control). Alternative or 'new' modes of governance based on nonhierarchical steering that systematically involve private actors in policymaking could be more effective in helping to ensure the adaptation of and adoption to the *acquis*.

New modes of governance – what are they?

There is a Babylonian variety of definitions and understandings of what new modes of governance are and what makes them really new compared to traditional modes. Part of the confusion is related to the existence of both broad and a narrow understandings of governance, the latter of which is identical with what is usually understood as 'new' modes of governance. This is not the place to rehearse the entire debate (for an overview see Börzel, 2010b). For the purpose of studying the role of new modes of governance in EU enlargement, we adopt the following definition. New modes of governance refer to the making and implementation of collectively binding decisions (based or not based on legislation) that

- are *not hierarchically* imposed, that is, decisions are adopted and complied with on a voluntary basis (actors cannot be bound against their will) and
- systematically involve *private actors*, for-profit (e.g., firms) and/or not-for-profit (e.g., nongovernmental organizations (NGOs)) in policy formulation and/or implementation.

Nonhierarchical coordination is constitutive for new modes of governance. It is 'governance without government' (Rosenau and Czempiel, 1992), which refers to a mode of political steering that does not authoritatively impose policies but is based on voluntary cooperation. We can distinguish between two forms of nonhierarchical steering or modes to *voluntarily* engage actors in a particular action deemed necessary to address a policy problem:

- the setting of positive and negative incentives, for example, through side payments, linkage of issues or sanctions, which changes the cost-benefit calculations of actors in favor of the desired behavior, without affecting their preferences over outcomes and
- nonmanipulative persuasion and social learning through which actors are convinced to change their preferences over outcomes in a way that accords with the desired behavior.

Understanding new modes of governance as the involvement of private actors in public policymaking through nonhierarchical coordination covers a variety of potential arrangements. It ranges from consultation and cooptation, delegation and coregulation/coproduction to private self-regulation in and outside the shadow of hierarchy cast by public actors. In order to avoid conceptual overstretch, however, certain forms remain outside this definition (Figure 2.1). We exclude the lobbying and pure advocacy activities of nonstate actors aimed at governments, supranational and international organizations (cf. Börzel and Risse, 2005). Private actors who are not active participants in governance arrangements or negotiating systems pose few challenges to existing concepts and theories in political science and International Relations. Also excluded are those arrangements among

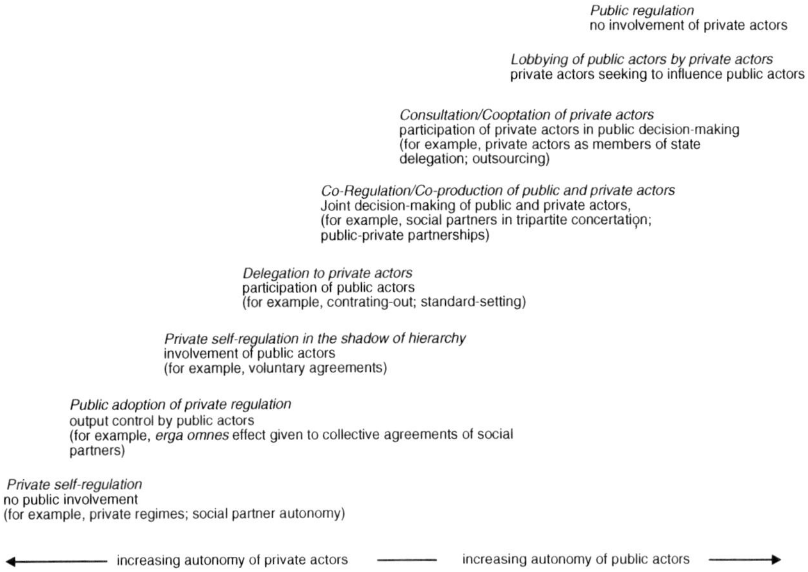

Figure 2.1 New modes of governance – the nonhierarchical involvement of private actors.

Source: Based on Börzel and Risse, 2005.

private actors that

- are based on self-coordination and do not aim at the provision of common goods and services (markets) or
- produce public goods and services as unintended consequences (e.g., rating agencies) or provide public 'bads' (mafia, drug cartels and transnational terrorism).

New modes of governance in the EU: not new but different

The nonhierarchical involvement of private actors in public policy-making is not new but a well-known phenomenon of domestic politics that has been thoroughly studied by the research on corporatism (Lehmbruch, 1982; Streeck and Schmitter, 1985), policy networks (Börzel, 1998; Rhodes, 1997) or the 'negotiating state/administration' (Czada and Schmidt, 1993; Voigt, 1995). Yet, while new modes of governance in Europe may not be necessarily new in *strictu sensu*, they are still different from both international and domestic politics.

Unlike most international organizations, the EU has the capacity for hierarchical steering. It can adopt policies against the will of individual member states, for example, when the Council decides by qualified majority voting (cf. Börzel, 2011). Unlike a state, however, the EU has no power to enforce its policies but ultimately has to rely on the voluntary compliance of the member states. Thus, the EU is a most likely case for new modes of governance. Some consider it even as a prototype of new modes of governance or 'network governance' (Kohler-Koch, 1996b), where the authoritative allocation of values is negotiated between state and societal actors (cf. Kohler-Koch and Eising, 1999; Ansell, 2000; Schout and Jordan, 2005).

Yet, if we define new modes of governance as the nonhierarchical involvement of business and civil society in public policymaking, the EU is still largely dominated by supranational decision making and intergovernmental negotiations. Where new modes of governance have emerged, they operate under a strong shadow of hierarchy cast by supranational institutions (cf. Börzel, 2011).[1]

Consultation and cooptation of economic and social actors certainly abound in the EU, particularly in the committees and working groups of the Commission and the Council (Christiansen and Piattioni, 2003). *Coregulation*, by contrast, is almost impossible to find. While nonstate actors are regularly involved in EU policymaking, they are hardly engaged on 'a more equal footing' (Kohler-Koch, 1999: 26). A rare exception is the partnership principle in structural policy, which explicitly requires the involvement of social partners in inter- and transgovernmental negotiation systems. Their representatives are members of the management committee of the European Social Fund, in which the member state governments are also represented and which is chaired by the European Commission (Art. 147 ECT). There are also several EU regulations providing for the participation of social and economic partners at the various stages of programming under the Social and the Regional Development Funds (1260/99/EC: Chapter IV, Art. 8). Moreover, a recent regulation extends the partnership principle to include civil society (1083/2006/EC). The extent to which business and civil society are actually involved, however, is contested in the literature and varies significantly across the member states. Overall, it seems that they still have a marginal role compared to national, regional and local governments (cf. Börzel, forthcoming-d).

Nonstate actors are equally marginalized in the Open Method of Coordination (OMC), the epitome of new modes of governance in the EU. OMC was first applied in EU employment policy. It emerged as an innovative way to implement the so-called Lisbon Strategy, which the European Council adopted in 2000 in order to promote economic growth and competitiveness in the EU (cf. Armstrong, Begg and Zeitlin, 2008). OMC has allowed to coordinate national policies in areas where member states have been unwilling to grant the EU political powers and additional spending capacity, particularly in the field of economic and social policy (Hodson and Maher, 2001). In the meantime, it has traveled beyond Lisbon and is applied in justice and home affairs (Caviedes, 2004; Lavenex, 2009), health policy (Smismans, 2006), environmental policy (Lenschow, 2002) and tax policy (Radaelli and Kraemer, 2008). OMC is in principle open to the participation of nonstate actors. Yet, in practice, they are neither involved in the formulation of joint goals at the EU level nor in their implementation at the national level (Hodson and Maher, 2001; Borrás and Jacobsson, 2004: 193–194; Rhodes, 2005: 295–300; Büchs, 2008). This is not too surprising since it is precisely the intergovernmental and voluntaristic nature that makes OMC an acceptable mode of policy coordination for the member states in sensitive areas.

Delegation is somewhat more prominent in the EU, although it has been around for quite some time, at least when it comes to technical standardization. The setting of EU technical standards is mostly voluntary since supranational harmonization of health and security standards is confined to national regulations concerning the public interest (Gehring and Kerler, 2008).For other areas, the Council has delegated the task of developing technical standards to three private European organizations, which are composed of representatives from the member states. Since national standardizing organizations, however, are mostly public, self-regulation is not only governed by the EU and subject to the control of the member states through comitology, but involves mostly public actors.

This also holds for other areas of risk regulation, where regulatory networks have emerged in response to liberalization and privatization in the Single Market. These market-making processes require some form of re-regulation at the EU and national levels in order to ensure fair competition and correct or compensate undesired market outcomes. Since the member states have been reluctant to transfer regulatory powers to supranational institutions, particularly in the area of economic regulation, market-creating and market-correcting competencies are usually delegated to independent regulatory agencies or ministries at the national level (Coen and Héritier, 2006). To fill the 'regulatory gap' at the EU level, national regulatory authorities have formed informal networks to exchange information and develop 'best practice' rules and procedures to address common problems (Coen and Thatcher, 2008). We find these networks in an increasing number of sectors, such as pharmaceuticals and food stuffs, but also beyond risk regulation, including competition, public utilities, financial services or data protection and law enforcement. While these regulatory and operational networks may be open to participation by private actors (e.g. providers and consumers), they are transgovernmental rather than transnational in character.

The strongest form of delegation in the EU is the Social Dialogue (Art. 138–139 ECT). In selected areas of social policy, the social partners have the right to conclude agreements, which can then be turned into European law. Moreover, the EU cannot take legal action in these areas without consulting the social partners. If the latter abstain from collective bargaining, however, the EU is free to legislate. While this form of Euro-corporatism is unique, the negotiation procedure under the Social Dialogue has hardly ever been invoked (Rhodes, 2005). Despite qualified majority voting in the Council, member states still are too diverse to agree on EU legal standards. In the absence of a credible shadow of hierarchy, employers have had little incentive to negotiate with the trade unions. Moreover, the social partners themselves have faced problems in reaching agreement among their members, since industrial relations are still organized along national lines. As a result, delegation has hardly been used in social policy.

Other forms of delegated or regulated private self-regulation in the shadow of hierarchy are equally rare. While voluntary agreements at the national level abound, they have been hardly used by European business organizations to prevent EU regulation. If at all, they are found in the area of environmental and consumer protection (cf. Héritier and Eckert, 2008).

Private self-regulation without any public involvement, finally, is almost impossible to find at the EU level. Private actors may coordinate themselves without having a mandate from or being under the supervision of supranational institutions. The EU is crowded with a multitude of nonstate actors, representing both civil society and business. They have organized themselves at the EU level in umbrella organizations. The so called Euro-groups have the ability to take binding decisions for their members, e.g. by adopting codes of conduct, negotiating voluntary agreements and monitoring compliance, but they have seldom embarked on collective action – and if they do, the shadow of hierarchy looms. The few voluntary agreements at EU level have been negotiated in order to avoid stricter EU regulation (Héritier and Eckert, 2008). Rather than engaging in private interest government, business and civil society organizations focus on individual and collective lobbying of decision makers, at both EU and national levels (Coen, 2008). The emergence of private interest government is further impaired by European peak associations and umbrella groups organized around and often divided along national lines, which in turn renders consensus among their members difficult.

To conclude, new modes of governance have proliferated far less in the EU than the ever growing literature would lead us to expect. Business and civil society do play a role in EU policymaking, but political decisions are taken and implemented largely by inter- and transgovernmental actors. Delegation and private self-regulation in and outside the shadow of hierarchy are both equally rare. The dominance of public actors distinguishes European governance from both governance within and beyond the state. At the member-state and international levels, private actors do play a much more prominent role in policymaking than in the EU (cf. Börzel, forthcoming-d).

Turning the inside out? New modes of governance and accession

The relationship between the EU and the accession countries is even less governed by hierarchy than is policymaking within the EU. Until the candidate states become members, their relations with the EU fall into the realm of international diplomacy. The EU's supranational institutions do not even cast a shadow of hierarchy, yet, since the supremacy of EU law and its direct effects, which empower domestic courts to enforce EU law without the consent of national governments, take effect only after accession. Conditionality has provided the EU with considerable leverage over accession countries (Schimmelfennig and Sedelmeier, 2004; Vachudova, 2005; Schimmelfennig, Engert and Knobel, 2006;). However, the provision of negative and positive incentives is still based on nonhierarchical coordination. Conditionality seeks to manipulate the cost-benefit calculations of governments but leaves them a choice – unlike under a hierarchy. The relationship between the EU and accession countries may be asymmetrical in terms of the distribution of power but the EU has no legal or physical means of imposing its will upon accession countries.

The capacity of the accession countries for hierarchical steering is constrained, too. The CEE accession countries faced the tremendous task of implementing more than 10,000 legal acts before joining the EU. While the challenge for the three Southern European countries was less formidable, they still ran into huge problems of policy overload, particularly in areas where they had hardly had any legislation in place, such as the environment.

The challenge of 'downloading' vast numbers of policies met with weak capacities of the accession countries. State actors often lacked the necessary resources, the capacity to mobilize them and/or the autonomy to introduce policy changes that would allow them to cope effectively with the *acquis*, as a result of which their capacity for hierarchically imposing EU policies was severely constrained. As we will see in the next section, the governance capacity of the Southern European and CEE accession countries has been considerable weaker than those of the Northern and Western European member states (see below).

Because of, on the one hand, the enormous policy load that the implementation of the *acquis* placed on the accession countries and, on the other, their limited absorption capacities, public actors, at both European and national levels, may promote and seek the cooperation with private actors to share or shift the burden of implementing and applying the *acquis* but which capacities are actually necessary to implement EU policies?

State capacity: an elusive concept?

As with 'new modes of governance', the concept of 'state capacity' is not used uniformly in the literature and its operationalization differs as well. First of all, we can distinguish between, on the one hand, performance- or output-related concepts and, on the other, input-oriented concepts (cf. Honadle, 1981).[2] The former focus on the ability of the state to formulate and implement policies that pursue collective interests, for example, economic growth, environmental protection or public health care (DEMSTAR, 2002: 7). State capacity is treated as the dependent variable, defined as the effective policy output of a state and measured in terms of performance indicators such as Gross Domestic Product (GDP) or per capita GDP, economic growth rates, public deficits, crime rates or the level of environmental regulation (*inter alia* Hellman, Jones and Kaufmann, 2000; DEMSTAR, 2002; Fritz, 2004; Colton and Holmes, 2006). The political science literature largely discusses state capacity as a product of state institutions and of the relationship between state and society. The debate centers on the question whether an 'insulated' or 'embedded' state is the better performer.[3]

Even though the EU has adopted a more performance-related approach (cf. Dimitrova, 2002; Sissenich, 2007), equating state capacity with the effective implementation or absorption of EU policies, exploring the causal relationship between state capacity and new modes of governance in European enlargement requires a different, input-oriented concept. This concept conceptualizes state capacity as a factor that explains the success and failure of accession countries in adopting and adapting to the *acquis communautaire* effectively. Treating state capacity as a means to reach certain ends (independent variables) avoids the fallacy of circular reasoning to which many studies tend to fall prey when they equate state capacity with state performance. Moreover, it allows controlling for alternative explanations not related to state capacity that may account for effective policy implementation, such as competitive market pressure or societal and industrial norm entrepreneurship. Input-oriented concepts can be organized around three different prongs, focusing on different dimensions of state capacity.

Resource-centered approaches define capacity as a state's ability to act, that is, the sum of its legal authority and financial, military and human *resources* (Przeworski, 1990; Zürn, 1997; Haas, 1998; Simmons, 1998). In order to implement EU policies effectively, accession countries need sufficient and adequately qualified personnel. State actors must have legal knowledge of the precise behavioral requirements that result from regulations as well as the technical expertise on the practical application of the law and the monitoring of compliance. Financial resources do not allow only for the acquisition of additional personnel, expertise and technical equipment. They can also help to pay off the delegation of implementation tasks to third actors (outsourcing) and compensate potential losers of a policy (cf. Börzel, 2003a). Yet, even if a state has sufficient resources, its administration may still have difficulties in pooling and coordinating them, particularly if the required resources are dispersed among various public agencies (e.g., ministries) and levels of government. We therefore introduce a second, resource-centered capacity variable that relates to the efficiency of a state bureaucracy to mobilize and channel resources into the implementation process (Mbaye, 2001; Hille and Knill, 2006; Börzel et al., 2007).

Neo-institutionalist approaches, by contrast, argue that the domestic institutional structure influences the degree of a state's capacity to act and its *autonomy* to make decisions (Katzenstein, 1978; Olson, 1982; Evans, 1995;). Domestic veto players can block the implementation of international rules because of the costs they have to (co-)bear (Putnam, 1988; Duina, 1997; Haverland, 2000). A high number of veto players reduces a state's capacity to make the necessary changes to the *status quo* for the implementation of costly rules (Alesina and Rosenthal, 1995; Tsebelis, 2002). At the same time, however, the implementation literature has argued that the involvement of those affected by public policies in decision making may increase compliance and effectiveness by accommodating diverse interests and fostering the acceptance of the policy (Mayntz, 1983; Franck, 1990; see also Lijphart, 1998; Héritier, 2003;). Another critique of the concept of state autonomy, or the 'insulated state', comes from the more recent development studies literature, which points to the differential success of authoritarian, that is, 'insulated', regimes in promoting economic growth (East Asia vs. Latin America, cf. Amsden, 1989; Evans, 1995).

The critique has resulted in the development of a third concept of *embedded, enabling* or *engaging* state capacity. It refers first of all to the capacity of states 'to penetrate society, regulate social relationships, extract resources, and appropriate or use resources in determined ways. Strong states are those with high capabilities to complete these tasks, while weak states are on the low end of a spectrum of capabilities' (Migdal, 1988: 4–5).[4] State actors embed themselves in tight networks with societal àctors that provide information and help implement public policies (Evans, 1995; Weiss, 1998; Pierre and Peters, 2000; Howard, 2002). Note that this concept of capacity bears the danger of circular reasoning by blurring state capacity and new modes of governance – the way embedded or engaging capacity is defined comes very close to what we understand to be new modes of governance. Thus, we have to define carefully what exactly it is that enables state actors to embed themselves in and engage with society.

While embedded state capacity is indeed almost synonymous with new modes of governance, enabling state capacity focuses more on the capacity of states to provide 'rooms that enable and encourage deliberative processes' (Zürn, 1998: 281). The underlying assumption is that networks between state and societal actors enable the state to tap into the resources of nonstate actors and to foster reasoned argumentation, mutual understanding and common values, as a result of which decision making may proceed beyond self-interested bargaining (Scharpf, 1993: 76–77). The state needs to create deliberative arenas to enable the exchange of information, collect expertise, create trust, and profit from the emergence of issue-related problem-solving coalitions. It also enables, facilitates and encourages the existence and flourishing of societal organizations (Hall, 1999; Levy, 1999; Padgett, 2000). This requires the capacity for strategic reflection, internal consensus building and the formal assignment of resources that can facilitate the coming together of policy actors to deliberate in an impartial and informed way on specific issues (Blaug, 1997; Palincsar, 1998; White, 2005). This more deliberative type of state capacity may also be relevant for the other two types of state capacity: autonomy and resources. It can help state actors to pool and coordinate the resources required for effective policymaking, but dispersed among various public agencies (e.g., ministries) and levels of government. The same is true for inducing nonstate actors to cooperate and offer their resources. Regarding autonomy, state actors can exert 'integrated leadership' persuading actors not to invoke their veto power (Börzel, 1999; Héritier, 2001).

With the exception of government autonomy, the Southern European and CEE accession countries score significantly lower than their Northern and Western European countries regarding their state capacity (see Figure 2.2).[5] Case studies confirm that our accession countries lacked the capacities to adopt and enforce public policies effectively (cf. Baker and Jehlicka, 1998; Paraskevopoulos, Panagiotis and Rees, 2006; Sissenich, 2007). The prospect of membership for the three Southern European countries and accession conditionality for the CEE canditate states , respectively, increased government autonomy at least in the legal implementation of EU policies. Yet, state actors often did not have the necessary resources or effective coordination mechanisms to mobilize them and/or extract them from nonstate actors in order to cope effectively with the *acquis*. As a result of this, their capacity for hierarchically applying and enforcing EU policies was severely constrained.

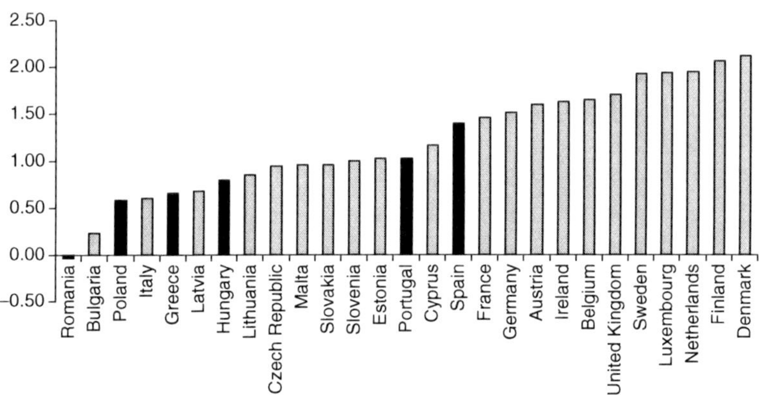

Figure 2.2   State capacity in the EU 27 compared (2005).
Source: Kaufmann, Kraay and Mastruzzi, 2005.

Capacity, new modes of governance and accession

Governance literature does not regard capacity only as a crucial condition for the effective implementation of (environmental) policies of both domestic and international origin (Mayntz, 1983; Chayes and Chayes, 1995; Jacobsen and Weiss Brown, 1995; Jänicke, Weidner and Jörgens, 1997; Haas, 1998; Börzel et al., 2007). It is also a major factor in explaining the emergence and effectiveness of new modes of governance.

Governance research has drawn heavily on resource dependency approaches to explain the emergence of new modes of governance (cf. Scharpf, 1978; Mayntz, 1997; Rhodes, 1997). To make policies, state actors become increasingly dependent upon the cooperation and joint resource mobilization of nonstate actors, which are outside their hierarchical control. New modes of governance allow state actors to establish 'webs of relatively stable and ongoing relationships which mobilize and pool dispersed resources so that collective (or parallel) action can be orchestrated toward the solution of a common policy' (Kenis and Schneider, 1991: 36). Public actors can mobilize resources in situations where they are widely dispersed among public and private actors at different levels of government, international, national, regional and local (Kenis and Schneider, 1991; Marin and Mayntz, 1991; Kooiman, 1993; Mayntz, 1993; Le Galès, 1995; Wolf, 2000). Private actors offer public actors information, expertise, financial means or political support, which the latter need to make and collectively enforce binding norms and rules. In exchange, private actors receive substantive policy influence, since public actors are unlikely to adopt and implement policies that are against the interests of the private actors upon whose resources they depend. In addition to providing public actors with additional or necessary resources to make 'good' policies, the involvement of private actors in the policy process helps to ensure effective implementation. The more the actors affected by a policy have a say in the decision-making process, the more likely they are to accept the policy outcome to be implemented, even if their interests may not have been fully accommodated. In short, new modes of governance can significantly strengthen the capacity of state actors in public policymaking (cf. Héritier, 2003). The main incentive for nonstate actors to get involved in public policymaking is the exchange of their resources for influence on the policies by which they are affected.

Given the huge implementation load and the weak capacities of the accession countries, new modes of governance could compensate for the weak hierarchical steering capacity of the EU and the accession countries in the *implementation* of EU policies, since private actors may provide the governments of the accession countries with important resources (money, information, expertise and support) necessary for making EU policies work. In return, they can gain influence on the ways in which the new policies are implemented and enforced.

In the adoption of and adaptation to the *acquis communautaire*, new modes of governance can help increase effectiveness by

- strengthening the capacity of public actors to transpose European directives into national law and to build up the administrative and judicial institutions (norms, rules and procedures) to practically apply and enforce EU policies and by
- fostering voluntary compliance with EU policies by involving those affected in the policymaking process.

While the pooling of resources and the sharing of implementation costs provide a very important incentive for state actors to enlist non-state actors in the policy process, the governance literature also points to major countervailing factors that may make state actors shy away from new modes of governance. If state actors feel weak because they lack important resources (information, expertise, personnel and support), they are far more reluctant to seek the cooperation with nonstate actors. The fear of agency loss (autonomy) or even agency capture is a powerful disincentive for resorting to new modes of governance (Hellman, Jones and Kaufmann, 2000). Moreover, the interest of nonstate actors in participating in the policy process depends on the capacity of state actors to impose a policy unilaterally and turn a joint agreement into a formal decision, respectively (Mayntz and Scharpf, 1995b; Scharpf, 1997; Héritier, 2003).

This 'shadow of hierarchy' is so important for new modes of governance because it generates major incentives for cooperation for both state and nonstate actors (cf. Mayntz and Scharpf, 1995b; Scharpf, 1997). Nonhierarchical coordination entails high transaction costs for the actors involved. If the policy outcome does not fully correspond to their preferences, it requires the threat of a hierarchically imposed decision to change the cost-benefit calculations in favor of a voluntary agreement (Héritier and Lehmkuhl, 2008a). This is particularly true for the self-coordination of nonstate actors. Business associations or societal networks rarely have sufficient sanctioning capacities to deter opportunistic behavior of their members in the implementation of voluntary agreements (the free-rider problem). Therefore, we hardly ever find societal self-coordination without the involvement of state actors that have the capacity for taking and enforcing unilateral decisions.

If the shadow of hierarchy provides an important incentive for non-state actors to cooperate, their willingness to engage in new modes of governance should increase with the degree to which state actors are capable of resorting to hierarchical modes of governance. For state actors, it is exactly the reverse – the higher their capacity for hierarchical policymaking, the fewer incentives they have to cooperate with nonstate actors. In order to avoid falling prone to what Renate Mayntz called the 'functionalist fallacy of governance research' (Mayntz, 2004: 71, author's translation), we must assume that state actors seek to increase, or at least to maintain, their autonomy as well as their problem-solving capacity in the policy process. Since the cooperation with third (non) state actors entails a significant loss of autonomy, they are willing to engage in new modes of governance only if they (re)gain problem-solving capacity compared to using hierarchical modes of governance. The 'strength of weakness' (Kohler-Koch, 1996b), which is also referred to as the 'neue Staatsräson' in International Relations literature (new *raison d'état*, Wolf, 2000; Grande and Risse, 2000) is a core feature of the modern state (Scharpf, 1991; Mann, 1993; Mayntz, 1993).

In sum, the shadow of hierarchy provides both state and nonstate actors with an important incentive for cooperation, albeit in opposite ways (see Figure 2.3).

State actors have to possess sufficient capacities in terms of both resources and autonomy in order to cast a credible shadow of hierarchy, so that nonstate actors have an incentive to cooperate and the state

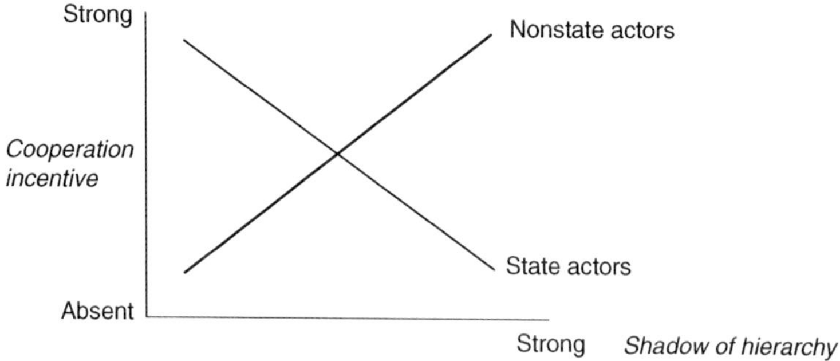

Figure 2.3   The shadow of hierarchy and reverse incentives for cooperation for state and nonstate actors.

actors are not afraid of being captured. But at the same time, these state capacities must not be so strong that they provide a disincentive for the state actors to seek cooperation with nonstate actors.

Sufficient resources and autonomy are also deemed necessary but not sufficient in themselves for the state to engage with or embed itself in society (Evans, 1995; Weiss, 1998; Migdal, 1988). The literature identifies at least two other necessary conditions. First, an administrative or state culture is required that renders the cooperation with nonstate actors an appropriate means to ensure good governance (Kohler-Koch, 2000). Thus, new modes of governance may not always be compatible with the dominant view of state actors on how to make effective and legitimate policies. This is particularly true for countries with an authoritarian legacy and no sustained tradition of institutionalized state-society relations (Linz and Stepan, 1996; Börzel, 2003a). But even consolidated democracies differ significantly with regard to state tradition and policy style (Richardson, 1982; Knill, 2001). Moreover, in postsocialist countries, new modes of governance are often seen as undemocratic since they circumvent the parliamentary arena and are prone to corruption and state capture. NGOs appear to be particularly skeptical of new modes of governance, equally because they do not want to be seen by their supporters as being co-opted by the state. In Southern Europe and Central and Eastern Europe alike, civil society largely emerged in opposition to the authoritarian state. Many civil society organizations still see themselves as 'watchdogs' rather than partners of the state in public policymaking (Fagan, 2004: chapter 4; Obradovic and Alonso Vizcaino, 2007). Finally, it has been argued that precisely because postcommunist states are weak, they should build up their institutional capacity and autonomy rather than give their powers away to nonstate actors (Dimitrova, 2002; Jerre, 2005). This argument resonates well with considerations about the 'shadow of hierarchy' as a scope condition for the emergence of new modes of governance.

Second, nonstate actors must also have the necessary collective action capacity and autonomy to engage in new modes of governance. On the one hand, they need sufficient personnel, information, expertise, money and organizational resources in order to make strategic decisions, to act as reliable negotiation partners and to offer state actors something in exchange for becoming involved in the policy process. On the other hand, nonstate actors have to have the necessary autonomy in order to act free of political control (Mayntz, 1993; Mayntz, 1995: 157–158). While the autonomy of societal actors is no longer the issue in Southern European and CEE countries, civil society is still weak

(Rose, 1994; Mudde and Kopecky, 2002; Glenn and Mendelson, 2002). Protest in the late-1980s was highly politicized in Central and Eastern Europe; but civil society organizations lost their political edge with the democratization of their societies. Membership in organizations and interest in civil rights and the environment dwindled during the 1990s. As a result of the post authoritarian heritage and the dynamics of economic and political transition, the potential for concerted collective action is still small; membership in voluntary associations (except for trade unions) is on average still lower than in the Northern and Western European countries in both Southern and Central and Eastern Europe (Linz and Stepan, 1996; Howard, 2003; Sissenich, 2007; USAID, 2008). The same applies to the number and strength of organized interests in general, the scope of protest actions and willingness to engage in voluntary work (Howard, 2003; Rose-Ackermann, 2007; Lane, 2007). The various indicators for the strength of civil society are highly correlated. Citizens who engage in voluntary work, join civil associations and also participate in protest events (Sissenich, 2010).[6]

In-depth case studies on the strength of civil society in Southern and Central and Eastern Europe corroborate the patterns found in the statistics, although they contend that civil society in Greece is weaker, not stronger, than in the other postauthoritarian countries (Sidjanski, 1991; Baker and Jehlicka, 1998; Eder and Kousis, 2001; Ghellab and Vaughan-Whitehead, 2003; Zimmer and Priller, 2004; Paraskevopoulos, Panagiotis and Rees, 2006; Kohl and Platzer, 2007a). Evidence shows that civil society organizations in Southern and Central and Eastern Europe (still) suffer from serious capacity problems. Being chronically underfunded, NGOs have difficulty in getting qualified personnel. Experienced activists find better-paid jobs in the private sector and the largely project-based funding schemes hardly allow for nonpermanent contracts. Moreover, social recognition for civic engagement is still low.

Some studies, however, paint a more optimistic picture. They argue that the 1990s saw a far-reaching process of institutionalization and consolidation within civil society. Crucial for this development have been the increasing specialization and differentiation of NGOs (Stark, Vedres and Bruszt, 2006). Political participation measured at individual level may be low, but there is a rapid growth of civic organizations, some of which demonstrate high mobilizing capacities (Petrova and Tarrow, 2007).

While there is no doubt that civil society has been gathering strength, its impact on policymaking remains weak and its activities are mostly oriented toward the local level. Moreover, professionalization has kept their membership base low, and civil society organizations have become detached from their root constituencies. Finally, their agenda tends to be determined by the funding priorities of their donors. One may therefore question whether accession to the EU has helped to empower civil society in transition countries or had a more ambivalent effect circumcising the action repertoire of civil society organizations (Fagan, 2004; Börzel, 2010a). As a matter of fact, NGOs often act as implementation agencies rather than autonomous representatives of civil society (Baker and Jehlicka, 1998; Fagan and Jehlicka, 2001; Fagan, 2006a, 2006b). They can help to increase the effectiveness of EU policies, but this may come at the price of undermining the legitimating function of civil society (Figure 2.4).

In sum, accession countries have suffered from weak governance capacities. State and society are on average weaker in the Southern European and CEE countries than in Northern and Western European member states. The East-West and North-South capacity gap is not only systematic. State and societal weakness appears to be highly correlated (Sissenich, forthcoming). Weak states face weak societies. According to the statistics, only Spain and Greece do not fit the pattern. Spain looks like a comparatively strong state with a weak society, while Greece presents the opposite case, a weak state with a rather strong society. If we discard the assessment of qualitative studies, these two outliers pose an

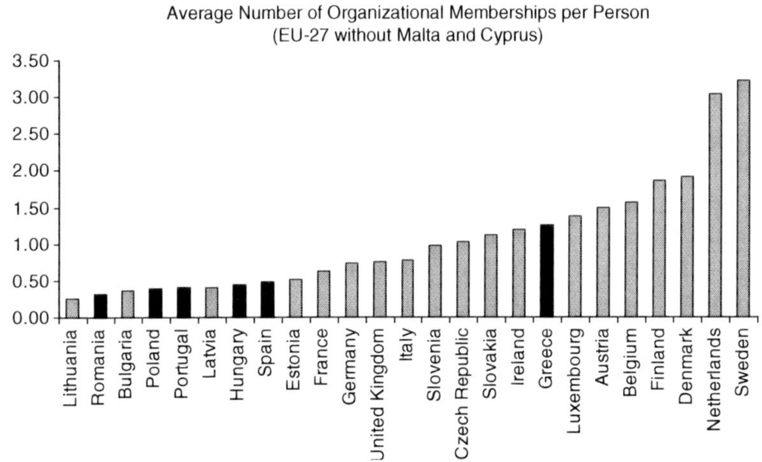

Figure 2.4   Strength of civil society compared (2005).
Source: Own compilation based on Sissenich, 2007: 163.

interesting puzzle for research on the relationship between state and society. Yet, the conditions for the emergence of new modes of governance remain unfavorable, particularly in case of Greece, where the likelihood for state capture would appear to be high.

The overall weakness of both state and society results in a serious governance dilemma for accession countries. On the one hand, state actors often lack the capacity to adopt and adapt effectively to the EU *acquis communautaire*. As a result, they should have an incentive to seek cooperation with nonstate actors in order to share and shift the burden of implementation. On the other hand, however, state actors also tend to be too weak to cast a credible shadow of hierarchy in order to provide important incentives for nonstate actors to engage in cooperation. At the same time, nonstate actors also face capacity problems. Not only may they lack the necessary resources to serve as reliable cooperation partners in public policymaking, but their relations with state actors are often characterized by (mutual) distrust. Given the weak governance capacities of Southern European and CEE accession countries, new modes of governance should be far less likely to emerge here than resource dependency approaches would lead us to expect. This is all the more so the case since these countries share a legacy of authoritarian statism that is hardly compatible with new modes of governance.

The double weakness of state and nonstate actors is likely to impair the emergence of new modes of governance. But is there really no escape from the 'low equilibrium trap' (Bruszt, 2008), in which accession countries seem to be caught? After all, European enlargement is about drawing neighboring countries closer to the EU by supporting their transformation into full-fledged Western-style democracies and market economies (Vachudova, 2005; Grabbe, 2006).[7] Political and economic liberalization should not only foster the modernization of societies (Mayntz, 1993). With its enlargement policies, the EU has sought to influence both the willingness and the capacity of candidate countries to adopt and adapt to the *acquis communautaire*. Thus, the Europeanization of domestic policies and institutions may help to overcome some of the problems created by the weak governance capacities of accession countries. The strengthening of state and societal actors should eventually foster the emergence of more cooperative and inclusive modes of governance.

EU push and pull

Nonstate actors are not the only source of capacity building (see Figure 2.1). The EU has made significant efforts to help strengthening the governance capacities of accession countries. The transfer of money and expertise through Community programs and twinning processes provides state as well as nonstate actors with additional resources that they can exchange (cf. Grabbe, 2006: 80–89). Thus, to help the accession countries implement the *acquis*, the EU's preaccession instruments, such as PHARE (Poland and Hungary: Aid for Restructuring of the Economies),[8] ISPA (Instrument for Structural Policies for Pre-Accession) or SAPARD (Special Accession Program for Agricultural and Rural Development), provided significant financial and technical assistance (cf. Sissenich, 2007: 54–57). Between 1998 and 2003, the PHARE programme alone earmarked around 1.5 billion euros per year of financial assistance to prepare the candidates for institution building, with stress on training public servants, adopting EU policies and implementing Structural Funds after accession (cf. Bailey and Propris, 2004). Technical assistance was organized though the 'Twinning Programme', by which member states supported accession countries with legal and administrative expertise, and TAIEX, the EU's Technical Assistance Information Exchange Office (Dimitrova, 2005).

Participation in EU preaccession programs in the 1990s has strengthened the capacities of municipalities, firms, NGOs and universities to participate in national and regional development programs after accession (Bruszt and Vedres, 2008). The three Southern European countries were not subject to systematic European Community (EC) capacity building before accession. However, unlike their CEE counterparts later, Greece, Portugal and Spain were not expected to take on board the entire *acquis communautaire*, which at the time was much smaller, in order to join the EC (cf. Chapter 3). For them, the challenge of making EC policies work started mostly after accession. In order to help them cope, the Structural Funds provided financial assistance that went far beyond what the CEE accession countries have received since they joined the EU in 2004 and 2007, respectively. Thus, the Cohesion Fund and other EU environmental programs (e.g., LIFE) covered up to 75 percent of the costs entailed in the implementation of environmental directives in the Southern European accession countries (cf. Börzel, 2003a).

Likewise, transnational regulatory networks, such as the Pan-European Regulatory Forum in Pharmaceuticals, the 'Seville Process' under the Integrated Pollution Prevention and Control Directive or the Network for the Implementation and Enforcement of Environmental Law, have fostered the building up of technical knowledge as well as trust among regulatory authorities, firms and consumer and health organizations from accession countries, both in the South and East of the EU (Sissenich, 2008; Koutalakis, 2008a; Koutalakis, 2008b).

In addition to financial and technical assistance, the EU also provides state actors of accession countries with additional legitimacy to enact certain policies. The strong domestic consensus in favor of EU membership allowed state actors to neutralize domestic veto players, despite the high costs incurred by EU policies. Strict accession conditionality and the strong emphasis on 'absorption capacity', such as the capacity of accession countries to spend EU funds, have strengthened the role of the executive to the detriment of parliamentary oversight and societal pressures (Goetz, 2005: 272; Grabbe, 2006: 207) or territorial decentralization (Bruszt, 2008).

The EU has not only directed its capacity building efforts toward state actors but has also sought to support civil society organizations, on the one hand, and companies, on the other (Andonova, 2003; Börzel, 2003a; Sissenich, 2007; Iankova, 2009).

NGOs have received direct funding from the EU. From 1992 on, for instance, the EU made a small amount of preaccession funds directly available to NGOs and professional organizations (e.g., PHARE democracy, LIEN and the Partnership Programme). The programs include extensive references to 'participation' and 'common ownership' and seek to strengthen, *inter alia*, the democratic and organizational structure of NGOs. For the postaccession period, the EU established a temporary funding line in 2005 for 'Action in support of civil society in new EU member states'. Between 2005 and 2007, the EU dedicated about 4 million euros to projects fostering dialog and cooperation between the EU and civil society in new member states.[9]

NGOs could also apply for short-term project grants to work on local issues related to the implementation of EU policies. In the early years of transition, external donors, such as the United Nations, Western governments and US-based foundations and charities were among the main funders of civil society organizations. From the mid-1990s, however, EU funds increasingly became the main financial resources for NGOs from the region. In the three Southern European countries, civil society organizations and business have benefited from similar support under the Structural Funds, EU Sectoral Programmes or the Rural Development Policy within the Common Agricultural Policy (Paraskevopoulos, Panagiotis and Rees, 2006).

To enable them to access its funding, the EU has offered seminars to train NGOs how to submit applications for projects on the setting up of sectoral dialogs and multistakeholder fora or for training in communication, mediation and language skills (Kutter and Trappmann, 2010). In the business sector, PHARE financed projects to strengthen the capacity of social partners. Likewise, the *Consensus* Programme, which was launched in 1995, was to assist the social partners and other NGOs in preparing for accession in the field of social policy (Sissenich, 2007: 54–57). Moreover, a network of Euro-Info Centres was designed to provide logistical support to local firms in accession countries and help them to cope with the challenges of accession (Iankova, 2009). Similarly to the case of the Southern enlargement, the European Commission and nonstate actors from the old member states encouraged the participation of NGOs and business associations from CEE accession countries in transnational networks and European umbrella organizations (Euro-groups) to learn how to shape and implement EU policies (Sidjanski, 1991; Obradovic and Pleines, 2007; Sissenich, 2008; Iankova, 2009).

While the EU has made significant efforts to strengthen the governance capacities of accession countries to pull them closer to the *acquis*, it has also exerted pressure on state actors in pushing them toward using new modes of governance in order to cope with the challenge of accession. Before candidate countries join, the EU has only limited enforcement powers. However, 'accession conditionality' has given the Commission a powerful tool to pressure candidate countries toward effective implementation of the *acquis communautaire* (cf. Schimmelfennig and Sedelmeier, 2005). After accession, the infringement proceedings of Article 226 provide the European Commission with a potent means of exercising external pressure on new member states trying to renege on their obligations (Börzel, 2003b). Finally, with Eastern enlargement, the EU created special safeguards that allow for suspension of some of the benefits of the internal market during the first three years of membership.

The EU often explicitly requires the involvement of private actors in the implementation of EU policies. With regard to accession of the CEE countries, the European Commission insisted that the social partners (business and labor) were included in the preparation of the government positions on the various chapters of the *acquis*. Representatives from employers' organizations, chambers of commerce, trade unions, farmers associations and consumer, environmental and women's groups also participated in the 30 working groups to facilitate accession negotiations between the EU and the candidate countries (Iankova, 2009). In addition, the European Commission encouraged the creation of economic and social councils in the accession countries, modeled after the European Economic and Social Council, to facilitate civic dialog on economic and social development, respective national legislation and strategic planning (Iankova, 2009). Governments were also asked to use bipartite social dialog in order to support social partners in developing capacities to implement the *acquis* (Sissenich, 2007: 57).

Moreover, preaccession funding was made subject to the partnership principle that the Commission had introduced in the 1980s to open up bilateral relations between the national governments and their regions at the domestic level, seeking to turn structural policy into a process of multilevel cooperative policymaking (Heinelt and Smith, 1996; Hooghe, 1996; Ansell, Parsons and Darden, 1997; Bache, 1998). National and sub-national governments of accession countries have been asked to coop-erate with business and NGOs to achieve development goals (Bruszt, 2008). As with the Structural Funds, working groups and commissions were created for the joint monitoring and control of SAPARD, ISPA and PHARE grants. In order to mobilize the cofinancing required by EU funds, the European Commission recommended public-private part-nerships (Iankova, 2009).

Finally, there are important EU policies that explicitly require the establishment of new modes of governance. Social and environmental policies, in particular, contain procedural regulation meant to empower nonstate actors in the policy process (see Chapter 3). Overall, it might have been rational for state actors to apply new modes of governance in order to gain access to EU funding or to avoid negative consequences of noncompliance, such as delays in the accession process (accession conditionality) or infringement proceedings after accession.

Beyond setting positive and negative incentives in the accession pro-cess, the European Commission has promoted new modes of governance as a general paradigm for EU policymaking (Kohler-Koch, 1996a) seeking to socialize accession countries into the 'EU way of doing things'. The White Paper on Governance advances 'modern forms of governance', which systematically involve civil society, as the most appropriate way to address problems of the declining effectiveness of EU policymak-ing and its persistent lack of democratic legitimacy (Schout and Jordan, 2005: 201–205). The EU has externalized this governance paradigm to its enlargement policy, asking accession countries to bring society in to make the *acquis* work (Sissenich, 2007). Its 'intensified preaccession strategy' of 1999 explicitly sought to enlist the help of NGOs in 'pulling in' (Jacoby, 2000: 210–211) EU policies and drumming up support for EU accession referenda (Raik, 2004).

While accession conditionality and infringement proceedings allow the EU to push accession countries toward new modes of governance, NGOs and companies can use the EU to exert additional pressure on public authorities (cf. Börzel, 2003a: chapter 3; Börzel, 2006). They can lobby national policymakers for a correct and complete transposition into national law. When it comes to practical application and enforcement, citizens and societal groups are an important source of information for the European Commission, which lacks proper monitoring capacities. Moreover, societal actors, in alliance with the media, often launch public campaigns to shame their government in the case of serious instances of noncompliance. Finally, societal actors play a major role in the decentralized enforcement of European law through national courts after accession. Given its supremacy and direct effect, European legislation confers rights to any affected individual to challenge noncompliance before national courts. Business actors, in particular, have made use of litigation to get market access. Companies tend to be less supportive of market-correcting regulations, such as environmental protection. Yet, green industry and multinational corporations have realized that common standards at the European level may be preferable to lower average standards that vary from one country to another and are subject to unpredictable changes. Moreover, companies operating in countries with higher environmental standards may benefit from rising general standards because they are already in compliance. Likewise, lax implementation and enforcement in other countries can cause them significant competitive disadvantages.

Legal or political pressure may not only force state actors to open up the policy process. They may themselves seek to involve societal and business actors in order to avoid litigation or conflict with other stakeholders in the first place. Thus, EU push and pull factors can empower domestic actors, increasing their capacity and willingness to cooperate in the adoption of and adaptation to the *acquis*. Figure 2.5 summarizes the different ways in which EU push and pull may foster the emergence of new modes of governance.

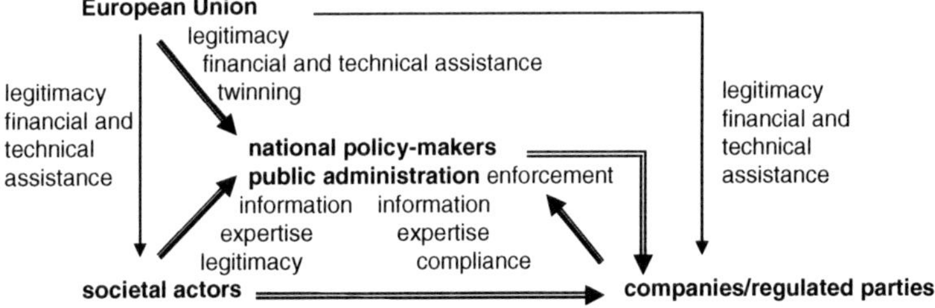

Figure 2.5   EU push and pull.

The empirical case studies on six accession countries in Southern and Central and Eastern Europe will explore whether the paradox of double weakness has resulted in a governance dilemma for accession countries and to what extent EU push and pull factors have helped them to escape the capacity trap. Before that, however, the next chapter outlines the challenges of accession in the field of environmental policy and explains the research design of the book.

Notes

1. For a broader understanding of new modes of governance that lead to a more prominent role in EU and national policymaking see Héritier and Rhodes 2010.
2. There is an abundant literature on state capacity (for a good overview see Pierre and Peters, 2000). For reasons of scope and the particular focus of this book, I concentrate on the literature on the transition countries in Central and Eastern Europe.
3. *Inter alia* Evans, Rueschemeyer and Skocpol, 1985; Katzenstein, 1985; Putnam, 1993; Evans, 1995; Stark and Bruszt, 1998; Weiss, 1998; Bruszt, 2002.
4. The notion of embedded or engaging capacity comes close to what Michael Mann defined as infrastructural power as opposed to despotic power or state autonomy (Mann, 1986).
5. The capacity indicators of the World Bank measure the quality of public services, the quality of the civil service and the degree of its independence from political pressures, the quality of policy formulation and implementation, and the credibility of the government's commitment to such policies. While they provide a rather crude measurement of state capacity that is more output-oriented, we always find the same capacity gap irrespective of the data and indicators we use. Despite variation within each group (compare Greece and Spain for instance), the East–West gap remains significant (for a statistical analysis see Sissenich, forthcoming). While the capacities of all states have increased over time, their relative ranking has not changed much. We acknowledge, however, that the capacity of a state may vary significantly across both time and policies (Howlett and Ramesh, 2003). Moreover, individual policies may require different types of capacity. Finally, we are aware that it is not always easy to distinguish between capacity and willingness. 'Cunning states' (Randeria, 2003) may use their weakness as an excuse to avoid the implementation of costly policies.
6. We are concerned with the relevance of the capacity of state and nonstate actors for the emergence of new modes of governance. We do not make any claims about whether and how weak governance capacities affect democracy (for a good overview of the debate see Sissenich, 2007).
7. This also applies to the European Neighbourhood Policy, by which the EU seeks to induce its Southern and Eastern neighbors to adopt the entire governance package enshrined in the Copenhagen criteria and key parts of *acquis communautaire* without providing a membership perspective (Kelley, 2006; Magen, 2006; Magen and Morlino, 2008).

8. Initially meant to help Poland and Hungary make the transition to a market economy, PHARE was quickly extended to other transition countries to help in preparing them for EU membership.
9. See http://ec.europa.eu/justice_home/funding/support_ngo/funding_support_en.htm, (last access: 23 January 2009).

3
Environmental Policy and the Challenge of Accession

Tanja A. Börzel

Accession significantly reinforced the processes of democratic transition and socioeconomic modernization in the Southern and Central and Eastern Europeancountries that had applied for EU membership. The conditions for accession, however, differed significantly between the Southern and Eastern enlargements. The *acquis communautaire* doubled over the 20 years that laid between the two accession processes. When Greece, Portugal and Spain joined the EC, there was no enabling legislation related to the completion of the Single European Market, not to mention the Common Currency, political cooperation on Justice and Home Affairs or the Common Foreign and Security Policy. Moreover, accession conditionality was introduced only with the Eastern enlargement. Finally, the EC was much more generous in granting temporary derogations than the EU. Despite these differences, Southern and Eastern candidate countries faced similar challenges in coping with accession because of their limited governance capacities. Greece, Portugal and Spain only felt the main burden after they had joined the EC. The CEE countries, in contrast, had to do their homework first before they were allowed in. The time elapsed in the case of the three Southern accession countries allows for a more dynamic perspective tracing of changes over time, particularly with regard to the impact of EU push and pull factors.

This chapter examines the particular challenges the Southern European and CEE accession countries have been facing. We focus on the field of environmental policy as an area of positive, market-correcting integration that imposes significant costs in the implementation rather than in the decisionmaking stage (cf. Majone, 1996). The challenge at the EU level is for the member states to agree on common standards to reduce and prevent environmental pollution traveling across national borders and to avoid market distortions. As environmental latecomers, Southern European and CEE countries have not just suffered from increasing environmental pollution as a negative externality of striving for economic growth. Before accession, t heir lower levels of environmental regulations gave them a competitive advantage over EU member states whose industry has had to heavily invest in abatement technologies to meet EU environmental standards. If, however, strict EU environmental regulations are now adopted, the latecomers face huge implementation costs in having to adapt their legal and administrative structures and help industry cope with the necessary investments (cf. Börzel, 2003a).

The greening of the South: The EC meets the 'Mediterranean Syndrome'

As with the postsocialist countries of Central and Eastern Europe, applying for EC membership meant a 'return to Europe' for Greece, Portugal and Spain (Paraskevopoulos, Panagiotis and Rees, 2006). Accession allowed the CEE and three Southern states to 'lock in' their transition processes. Committing themselves to the political and economic principles of European integration helped their governments to consolidate democratic and economic reforms (Pridham, 1991b; Morlino, 2002; Royo, 2003). At the same time, accession entailed serious challenges. The three Southern states were economically in a similar position to the CEE accession countries in the 1990s, although their GDP per capita at around 60 to 70 percent of the EU average was still twice as high as the GPD per capita of their CEE cousins.[1] Macroeconomic constraints and profound political, institutional and administrative weaknesses appeared to be at odds with economic and legal harmonization with the EC member states. Yet, political considerations prevailed over concerns regarding the capacities of the three Southern newcomers to catch up with Europe. Thus, the EC set only some broad political criteria as conditions for membership, including respect for human rights and democracy (cf. Pridham, 1991a; Curzon Price, 1999).

Consequently, accession negotiations for the three Southern European candidates focused on a number of sensitive areas of interest to both sides. They were mostly about agriculture, and fisheries in case of Spain, because of the scale of agricultural output, which was expected to exacerbate competitive pressures on existing member states, particularly France and Italy. To facilitate approximation, the EC awarded transition periods, for example for the establishment of a common market in industrial (textile) and agricultural products (Roy and Kanner, 2001; Maraveyas, 1994). Interestingly, the accession negotiations with Greece went not only considerably faster (1976–79 as compared to 1978–85 for Spain and Portugal), but Greece received a much shorter transition period of five to seven years, while the other two newcomers were granted up to ten years (Tovias, 2002, 171).

Market-correcting policies, such as regarding the environment, received little attention, although it was in the areas of regulatory policy that the economic and administrative capacities of the three Southern countries were the weakest regarding effective harmonization with EC standards. Nor did the EC evaluate the institutional and administrative capacities of Greece, Portugal and Spain to implement the *acquis*. Only slowly did they adjust their domestic institutions to the requirements of EC membership. The Europeanization of environmental policy epitomizes the challenges with which Greece, Portugal and Spain had to cope.

When Greece, Portugal and Spain joined in the 1980s, their environmental policies were only weakly developed. While they had regulated some aspects of water management, air pollution and nature conservation, environmental legislation had remained largely ineffective (Börzel, 2003a). Accession thus became the determining factor of their environmental regulatory structures, mainly through the downloading of EC policies. While the environmental *acquis* at the time was much smaller, it challenged the administrative traditions and regulatory structures of the three Southern European transition countries. They quickly ran into serious compliance problems and earned themselves the reputation of being the environmental laggards of Europe (Börzel, 2003a). Capacity shortcomings largely impaired the effective adoption of and adaptation to the environmental *acquis* during the years following accession. A strong preference for generating economic growth and employment put environmental policy at the bottom of the political agenda and severely restricted funding for building up environmental governance structures (Pridham, 1994). There was not enough money and policy expertise to ensure the correct and complete transposition of often highly complex EU environmental laws, the integrative problem-solving approach and participatory policy instruments of which were alien to regulatory traditions characterized by reactive, legalistic and command-and-control patterns of policymaking (Aguilar Fernández, 1994; Börzel, 2003a). The institutionalization of environmental policy used to be weak and fragmented. Only in the

1990s did the three Southern European countries follow the example of other EU member states and establish environmental ministries to help coordinate environmental responsibilities across different sectors and levels of government (Fernández, Font and Koutalakis, 2008). But financial, administrative and cognitive resources to enable them establish new administrative units, procedures and technologies for the practical application and enforcement of European policies remained weak. Understaffed environmental administrations lacked the expertise to interpret technical EU environmental regulation, which became ever more complex. At the same time, formal and informal patterns of interest intermediation were largely absent and public participation in environmental policy almost nonexistent (Pridham, 1996; Fernández, Font and Koutalakis, 2008). This has not just created additional pressure in adapting to EU requirements for public involvement. Closed political opportunity structures and low levels of socioeconomic development have resulted in weak public support for environmental issues and tended to discourage societal mobilization in favor of environmental protection (Börzel, 2003a, 51–53).

The poor performance of the three Southern European countries, and Italy, with regard to the adoption of and adaptation to the (environmental) *acquis* became so prevalent that a debate emerged in the literature on the extent to which the EU was suffering from a peculiarly 'Southern problem' (Pridham and Cini, 1994). Insufficient administrative capacity, a civic culture inclined to individualism, clientelism and corruption, together with a fragmented, reactive and party-dominated policy process are believed to undermine the willingness and capacity of Greece, Portugal, Spain and Italy to implement EU environmental law effectively. Some have even gone so far as to argue that the Southern European member states suffer from a particular disease called the 'Mediterranean Syndrome', which renders their political systems and societies largely unable to engage in collective action (La Spina and Sciortino, 1993; for a discussion of the argument see Börzel, 2003a). A civic culture that is characterized by 'amoral familism' (Banfield, 1958) and is void of social capital (Putnam, 1993) renders both state and non-state actors unlikely to engage in mutual cooperation to provide collective goods, such as a clean environment. While our theoretical model agrees with part of the diagnosis, we reject the cultural determinism underlying the Mediterranean Syndrome. Whatever the sources of the weak governance capacities may be, comparison with the CEE countries shows that there is nothing endemic to the capacity problems of Southern Europe.

Do your homework first: avoiding the 'Southern' problem?

Like in Southern Europe, Europeanization significantly reinforced the processes of democratic transition and socioeconomic modernization in the CEE accession countries (Schimmelfennig and Sedelmeier, 2005; Vachudova, 2005; Grabbe, 2006). But unlike in the cases of Greece, Spain and Portugal, the CEE states had to adopt the whole body of EU law before their accession date. Thus, the opening of accession negotiations in 1993 made the adaptation of the overall EU legislation a top priority for CEE policymakers (Börzel and Sedelmeier, 2006). The *acquis* was far more comprehensive than in the early 1980s, essentially covering all areas of state activity. Moreover, the asymmetric relationship between the EU and the accession countries was reinforced by the strict accession conditionality of the EU and its distinctive emphasis on the development of administrative capacities in the CEE states (Dimitrova, 2002). The candidate countries not only had to implement EU policies into law but also to prove that they were able to put in place the necessary administrative infrastructure to apply and enforce them. Moreover, the so called 'fifth' Copenhagen criterion required them to demonstrate the administrative capacity to adopt and adapt to the *acquis* by making sufficient progress in implementing it. In its reinforced preaccession strategy, the European Commission undertook regular assessments of the progress made by the candidate countries.[2] This is in stark contrast to the approach that the Commission had taken toward the three Southern European countries. Even after their accession, it did not systematically monitor and enforce the *acquis*. This occurred only in the early 1990s, when the Commission and the European Court of Justice started to pursue a more aggressive enforcement strategy in order to ensure the effective completion of the Single European Market (Talberg, 1999; Börzel, 2003b).

As a result of the different institutional heritage and the complex transition processes in the CEE countries, some parts of the *acquis* have harmonized better than others with the domestic structures and policy aims of domestic policymakers. In general, market-making policies, aimed at deregulation and economic liberalization, have been more in line with domestic reforms. By contrast, policies attributed to the field of market-correcting or positive integration have required more comprehensive changes (Andonova, 2003). As in the case of the three Southern European states, environmental policy has proven to be particularly challenging for the governance capacities of the CEE accession countries.

The adoption of and adaptation to the EU environmental *acquis* met with a multifaceted environmental situation in Central and Eastern Europe. On the one hand, the CEE countries enrich the EU with vast areas of pristine wilderness, large spots of untouched nature and a high degree of biodiversity. At the same time, they suffer from the socialist legacy of forced and intensive industrialization, which created a significant number of environmental hotspots in the region (Turnock, 2001; Auer, 2004). After the postcommunist regime changes and during market liberalization, most CEE countries witnessed a period of 'natural clean-up' caused by the breakdown of the state economy. With economic growth taking off in the second half of the 1990s, however, they started to experience similar environmental problems as the old member states did decades before (Pavlinek and Pickles, 2000). While some of the CEE countries had developed environmental regulations back in the 1970s, their effectiveness remained limited and did not meet the requirements of the environmental *acquis* (Jehlicka and Tickle, 2004; Schreurs, 2004b). Environmental policymaking was largely carried out by using reactive 'end-of-pipe' approaches, which seek to remove contaminants rather than to prevent their formation in the first place, and generally drew on command-and-control regulation resonating well with the long standing traditions of an authoritarian state (Caddy, 2000; Archibald, Banu and Bochniarz, 2004).

In the accession process, the CEE countries were confronted with the challenge of implementing some 200 environmental directives. This transfer of EU environmental policy has imposed heavy costs on their weak fiscal capacities, swallowing 2–3 per cent of their GDP (DANCEE, 2001; Homeyer et al., 2001; Schreurs, 2004a).[3] In 1995, PHARE, the major EU assistance program, estimated that the CEE countries would need ECU 300 billion and at least 15 years to make the substantial improvements to their environment necessary to comply with most of EU environmental law (Kolk and Van der Weij, 1998: 55). In addition, accession entailed implementing regulations that were mostly alien to their political and economic systems as they clashed with the legacies of the socialist period (Pavlinek and Pickles, 2005).

In addition to the immense financial burden imposed, the adoption of the green *acquis* and the adaptation of national law required comprehensive administrative capacity as well as scientific and technical expertise in order to transpose EU requirements, expertise often based on the best available technology (BAT), and to ensure their practical application, monitoring of compliance and enforcement on the ground (Baker and Jehlicka, 1998; Börzel, 2003a; Paraskevopoulos, Panagiotis and Rees, 2006). Given their overall weak resources, which were already largely consumed by the managing the transition process, the accession countries faced a serious capacity gap (cf. Carmin and Vandeveer, 2004). Not only did they lack funding to acquire additional personnel, expertise and technical equipment, but state actors were also unable to compensate potential losers of a policy, for example, companies that had to invest heavily in green technology to meet EU air pollution standards. Similarly to Greece, Portugal and Spain, industrial and agricultural plants in CEE countries had used outdated production and abatement technology causing serious problems of air and water pollution. Public administrations have also suffered from difficulties in pooling and coordinating the scarce existing resources (ECOTEC, 2000), particularly where these have been dispersed among various public agencies and levels of government (Nunberg, Barbone and Derlien, 1998; Goetz and Wollmann, 2001; Lippert, Umbach and Wessels, 2001; Zubek, 2001). As in Southern Europe, these capacity problems have been aggravated by the inherently weak standing of environmental administrations within frequently changing governments, most of which prioritized economic development (Archibald, Banu and Bochniarz, 2004).

Finally, the implementation of often costly EU environmental policy has also lacked the support of its target groups. While in several CEE countries, most notably in Hungary, the degree of environmental mobilization was high during the 1980s, the level of environmental engagement (Greenspan Bell, 2004b; Hallstrom, 2004; Hicks, 2004) and awareness of environmental problems remained low and even decreased in the early 1990s (Homeyer, 2004). As in Southern Europe, citizens have been more concerned with socioeconomic issues, such as employment and income security (Lee and Norris, 2000; Gerhards and Lengfeld, 2006). Finally, green industry and transnational companies already in compliance with EU environmental standards have only recently started to settle in CEE countries.

Coping with accession: South and East compared

While there are significant differences between the Southern and Eastern enlargements, accession posed similar challenges to the – equally weak – governance capacities of the Southern European and CEE candidates.

To explore how accession countries have coped with the challenge of adopting and adapting to the EU environmental *acquis*, we compare six candidate states. While our sample covers all three Southern European countries that joined the EC in the first half of the 1980s, we selected Poland and Hungary as representatives of the accession states that became members in 2004 and also included Romania, which joined in 2007. Since the Southern European countries only started to feel the burden of accession after their admission, we decided to extend the time period of our analysis to the postaccession stage, which also allows for a more direct comparison with the CEE countries and an assessment of postaccession compliance (Epstein and Sedelmeier, 2009).

Overall, the countries were chosen because they have the most diverse systems. The six countries differ significantly with regard to their political, social, economic and cultural institutions. The three Southern European countries made their transitions from dictatorship to democracy in the mid-1970s. In all three cases, economic transition preceded political transition. The common starting point for economic transition was state capitalism complemented by family-based small and medium enterprises. The economies of Spain, Portugal and Greece were agrarian based and dominated by private land ownership. Nevertheless, the three Mediterranean countries followed different transition paths, giving rise to different political and social institutions (Chilcote et al., 1990). In Spain, the 'pacted democratization' (Whitehead, 1991: 56) resulted in a quasi-federal state with a multiparty system, while Greece and Portugal remained highly centralized and became dominated by two parties. All three pursued economic modernization, but Spain was much faster in catching up with Western European countries. Of the two small economies, Portugal, a founding member of EFTA, benefited considerably from EU membership, whereas Greece experienced more than a decade of economic decline after accession, putting 'social modernization first' and rapidly expanding its public services and social policies (cf. Markou, Nakos and Zahariadis, 2001; Tovias, 2002; Royo, 2007).

The three CEE countries examined here share a socialist legacy of a common ideology, state-controlled economies and single-party systems, although they balanced domestic concerns and Soviet demands in different ways. Like their Southern cousins, the three EU candidates embarked on different paths of political and economic transition and have also adopted different strategies of adapting and adopting to EU policies (cf. Vachudova, 2005; Grabbe, 2006). While Hungary established a parliamentary system with a strongly bi-party structure, Poland and Romania feature semi-presidential systems and rather fluid party structures. At the same time, Poland displays a stronger degree of territorial decentralization than Hungary and Romania. Economically, both Poland and Hungary were among the fast movers regarding the dismantling of state socialist heritages, even though they differed in speed and openness toward foreign investors (Bohle and Greskovits, 2001). But while Hungary consistently pursued a strategy of rapid adaptation to EU requirements, Poland was more 'combative' (Grabbe, 2006: 111), often dragging its feet because of domestic conflicts. Romania, in turn, embraced economic liberalism rather reluctantly only in the mid-1990s and also lagged behind in the implementation of the *acquis,* suffering from persistent problems of corruption, organized crime and economic underperformance (Gallagher, 2005; Cernat, 2006; Pasti, 2006).

What the six have in common, however, is that they were accession countries whose governance capacities were, and still are, much weaker compared to the Northern and Western European states (see Chapter 2). While state and nonstate actors are weak overall, the governance capacities of Spain and Hungary appear to be on the higher end while Greece and Romania are laggardly, being the least likely cases for the emergence of new modes of governance.

The dual weakness of state and nonstate actors might be traced back to a joint legacy of state authoritarianism. But this is not the concern of our study and is only relevant to the extent that our six countries share an administrative culture that is hostile to the involvement of nonstate actors in public policymaking. Rather, we seek to find out how the weak governance capacities of the six accession countries have influenced the propensity of new modes of governance to emerge and to what extent EU push and pull factors have shaped the governance capacities of accession countries. Finally, we explore what role new modes of governance, if they emerged in the first place, have played in making EU policies more effective in accession countries.

EU environmental policy and new modes of governance

When the CEE countries opened accession negotiations in 1999, the *acquis communautaire* in the environmental field comprised some 460 pieces of legislation, mostly in the form of directives.[4] Some directives establish explicit limit values, other focus on environmental goals and define procedures by which such goals are to be attained. All of these requirements must be transposed into national legislation, which allows the member states some room for interpretation and flexibility in adopting EU requirements to national conditions.

In the implementation, directives often oblige member states to follow standardized procedures for monitoring environmental quality and discharges of pollutants and for reporting the results to the Commission. Some directives establish mechanisms for issuing permits for activities that may damage the environment. Others specify procedures for enforcing the rules. EU environmental standards often require industries and other nonstate bodies to make substantial investments. In such cases, the government's role is to set clear rules, ensure that firms make the investments and monitor and report the results.

We concentrate on directives (as opposed to regulations) because national governments can decide individually how the directives are transposed into national law and implemented. Our comparative case studies cover three main sectors of environmental policy: water management, air pollution control and nature protection. Within each of the three sectors, we look at two sets of policies:

1. Traditional command-and-control policies, such as the directives on Drinking Water (DWD; 80/778/EEC; 98/83/EEC) and Large Combustion Plants (LCPD; 88/609/EEC; 2001/80/EEC). These policies impose considerable costs of domestic adaptation, especially on firms that have to internalize compliance costs to their production. Thus, both public and private actors may have an incentive to cooperate in order to share or shift the costs.
2. New environmental instruments, such as the directives on Fauna, Flora and Habitats (FFHD; 92/43/EEC), Wild Birds (79/409/EEC), Environmental Impact Assessment (EIAD; 85/337/EEC; 97/11/EEC), Integrated Pollution Prevention and Control Directive (IPPCD; 96/61/EEC) and Water Framework Directive (WFD; 2000/60/EEC). The application of these directives may stipulate the emergence of new modes of governance because their procedural regulations directly provide for private actors' participation in the policy process.

Irrespective of whether the directives entail new or old instruments, they are the most likely cases for the emergence of new modes of governance. They all impose significant implementation costs and require substantial governance capacities, creating incentives for state actors to involve nonstate actors in order to share or shift the burden. The emergence of new modes of governance becomes even more likely if directives explicitly require the involvement of private actors.

The remainder of this chapter gives an overview of the general requirements of the six policies and the kind of challenges they pose to accession countries in their implementation, particularly with regard to governance capacities.

Water management

The DWD: Directive 98/83/EEC on the quality of water intended for human consumption amends the older DDWD from 1980 (80/778/EEC), which was considered outdated in respect to its scientific/technical basis and the managerial approach. Council Directive 80/778/EEC contained quality standards required of water intended for human consumption, both directly after abstraction and after its purification. The new Council Directive 98/83/EC introduced requirements for another nine substances and imposed more stringent quality standards for those that were already controlled earlier. Both Directives follow a reactive, end-of-pipe approach (as opposed to the more precautionary polluter-pays principle). While largely entailing command-and-control regulations on water quality, the Directives also prescribe some requirements for how often and by what means the monitoring of water quality is to be carried out. They also give reference to a method of analysis for each parameter. Member states have to invest in sufficiently qualified personnel and new measuring technology in order to monitor compliance with the conditions of authorization and the effects of discharges on groundwater, to keep an inventory of authorizations and to supply the European Commission with any relevant information at the latter's request. Moreover, if water services are not privatized, governments have to make sure that the distribution systems are up to standards.

The WFD: Directive 2000/60/EEC, establishing a framework for the Community action in the field of water policy, provides an integrated framework for the protection of inland surface waters (rivers and lakes), transitional waters (estuaries), coastal waters and groundwater. It is designed to ensure the responsible and sustainable exploitation of water and the reaching of a 'good water status' until 2015. The Directive requires the member states to establish river basin districts and to formulate for each of these a river basin management plan. The member states need personnel with sufficient expertise and information to design the river basin districts, analyze the characteristics of each river basin district, review the impact of human activity on the water, conduct an economic analysis of water use and set up a register of areas requiring special protection. All bodies of water used for the abstraction of drinking water also have to be identified. Governments then have to prepare river basin management plans, implement them and review them every six years. In order to set up and manage the cyclical process, public authorities have to coordinate their competencies and activities across different levels of government and policy sectors. Finally, the procedural regulations of the Directive also require the active participation of all stakeholders in both the elaboration of the River Basin Management Plans and their periodical revisions and updates. This will not only ensure transparency of water policies but also help to increase the effectiveness of the management plans by drawing on the expertise, support and monitoring capacities of non-state actors. The Common Implementation Strategy (CIS), which in meant to support member states in achieving the goals of the WFD, also encourages the involvement of nonstate actors and the diffusion of best practices through peer review. Thus, the WFD clearly promotes the idea of new modes of governance.

Industrial air pollution

The LCPD 2001/80/EEC amending 88/609/EEC: The Directive on the limitation of emissions of certain pollutants into the air from large combustions plants was adopted in 2001 amending the 11-year old existing Directive 88/609/EEC from 24 November 1988. The Directive sets emission standards, which must be applied to every new large combustion plant ('new plant') and directs member states to establish programs for reducing total emissions of pollutants (sulfur dioxide (SO_2), nitrogen oxide (NO_X) and dust) from existing large combustion plants ('existing plant'). The overall aim of the Directive and its predecessor is to reduce the emissions of acidifying pollutants and ozone precursors, which are carried over very long distances and damage human health, leading to ground level ozone episodes and deposits in the form of 'acid rain'. The LCPD predominantly relies on command-and-control regulation. Like the DWD, however, it entails some procedural requirements encouraging the application of the best available technology not entailing excessive costs (BATNEEC) to reduce emission and to in monitor compliance. While the compliance costs largely rest with industry, member states have to muster capacities to develop national emission reductions plans in which the timetable and implementing procedures for the total emission reduction of the relevant gases are set out. The LCPD defines national emission ceilings (bubbles) for each member state, which leave some flexibility in defining differing emission standards for existing plants. This does not only require expertise and information, but working relations with industry to identify individual emission targets and to help cope with the necessary investments. Moreover, public authorities have to set up monitoring and enforcement procedures using measurement technology that complies with BAT standards.

The IPPCD 96/61/EEC: The directive was adopted in 1996 as a new and integrated approach to reducing and preventing pollution from industrial and agricultural activities. These activities require an integrated permit that is to be issued by one competent authority if certain environmental conditions are met, including the use of BAT. To issue one integrated permit, member states have had to coordinate authorization competencies across different levels of government and sectors of environmental administration. Moreover, they must have sufficient qualified personnel to evaluate the entire environmental performance of industrial and agricultural installations and their compliance with BAT requirements. While the European IPPC Bureau in Seville's role is to help the member states and their companies to define BAT, governments have to adapt the reference documents (BREFs), formulated by the Technical Working Groups at the European level, to the conditions on the ground. Identifying what is technically and economically available to an industry to improve its environmental performance does just not require technical expertise. Public authorities should also cooperate with industry to determine what BAT demands on a case-by-case basis. The IPPCD explicitly requires the participation of nonstate actors. The public has a right to participate in the licensing process, receives access to permit applications and can issue statements. The European Pollutant Emission Register (EPER) makes the emissions data reported by the member states publicly available. Like the WFD, the IPPC strongly encourages the use of new modes of governance in its implementation.

Nature protection

The FFHD/Wild Birds Directive92/43/EEC: The directive on the conservation of natural habitats and wild fauna and flora was adopted in 1992 to protect biodiversity in Europe from human activities. The FFHD provides a comprehensive protection scheme for a wide range of animals and plants as well as for a selection of habitat types. To meet the FFHD objectives, the member states have to prepare and propose a national list of sites for evaluation in order to form a European network of Sites of Community Importance (SCIs). Once adopted, these are designated by the member states as Special Areas of Conservation (SACs), and, along with Special Protection Areas (SPAs) classified under the Wild Birds Directive (79/409/EEC), form a network of protected areas known as Natura 2000. This process requires the setting up of an authority (ministry or agency) to carry out measures and set standards. These authorities need to pool competencies usually allocated across different ministries and levels of government. Public authorities also have to have sufficient qualified personnel and the necessary information to draw up inventories of habitats, animals and plants that are covered by the Directive. The European Commission also requires the member states to report on the implementation of the FFHD every six years, formally starting in 2001. The national reports have to include information about the status of the listed habitats and species and about the implementation and effect of applied management measures. Based on monitoring results, the status and the effect of management measures are assessed. Furthermore the authority must provide the public with information and obtain the opinions of stakeholders, particularly with regard to the national list of protected habitats, animals and plants and the national implementation reports. The stakeholders should also be involved in the management of the protected sites. Thus, the FFHD includes provisions fostering the emergence of new modes of governance.

The EIAD 97/11/EEC: The directive amending 85/337/EEC on the assessment of the effects of certain public and private projects on the environment prescribes a procedure to ensure that the environmental consequences of projects are identified and assessed before authorization is given. The public can give its opinion and all results are taken into account in the authorization procedure of the project. The public is informed of the decision afterward. The EIAD outlines which project categories shall be made subject to an EIA, which procedure shall be followed and the content of the assessment. The importance of the EIAD lies in its preventive, multidisciplinary approach. This directive intends to align the provisions on public participation in accordance with the Aarhus Convention on public participation in decisionmaking and access to justice in environmental matters. Since the EIAD regulates the authorization of activities with potentially harmful effects on the environment, it is relevant to the FFHD and also the IPPCD. Thus, the EIA procedure is often made an integral part of their implementation. It requires similar governance capacities as the FFHD and the IPPCD, particularly with regard to expertise and administrative coordination.

Assessing the implementation of EU environmental policies

All six EU environmental policies have required substantial governance capacities from the Southern and CEE countries. Since the directives that predate the Eastern accession process (DWD, LCPD and EIAD) have been revised and updated in recent years, their implementation does not impair a South-East comparison.

Our case studies analyze how the six countries have coped with the challenge of adopting and adapting to these policies, which capacities they have required for their effective implementation and to what extent these capacities have been available to state actors. Do public authorities have sufficient staff power with the necessary legal and technical expertise and information on the situation on the ground to transpose and apply the EU policy correctly? Is there enough funding to invest in and expand the administrative and technical infrastructure to monitor and enforce compliance as well as to help the rule targets cope with the compliance costs (*resources*)? Has the public administration been able to coordinate the competencies and other resources required to make the EU policy work (*efficiency*)? Has implementation met the resistance of powerful domestic veto players (*autonomy*)? How far can public authorities draw on existing relations with nonstate actors and deliberative arenas to tap into their resources and neutralize their opposition (*embeddedness*)?

In cases where state capacities have been wanting, we investigate whether state actors have sought to enlist the help of nonstate actors and to what extent this has given rise to the emergence of new modes of governance. Do we find stable patterns of cooperation between public administrators, business actors and civil society organizations giving nonstate actors a real say in the policy process (*coregulation/coproduction*)? Do public authorities regularly consult stakeholders or coopt them into advisory and management bodies (*consultation/cooptation*)? To what extent is the implementation of EU policies outsourced, contracted out or delegated to nonstate actors (*delegation*)? Finally, do NGOs and business coordinate among themselves to help make EU policies work (*self-regulation*)?

Adopting a dynamic perspective, we explore to what extent EU push and pull factors have strengthened the governance capacities of accession countries, thus fostering the emergence of new modes of governance. Has the EU provided financial and technical assistance to state and nonstate actors through (preaccession) funds, twinning projects and transnational working groups pulling accession countries toward compliance (*capacity building*)? To what extent has the EU pushed accession countries toward establishing new modes of governance through conditionality and infringement proceedings (*EU pressure*)? Have nonstate actors mobilized, pushing public authorities toward compliance (*domestic pressure*)? How have state actors responded to such pressure from above and below?

Where new modes of governance have emerged, we are also interested in how far they have helped to increase the effective adoption of and adaptation to the environmental *acquis*. Effectiveness relates to the timely, complete and correct implementation of EU environmental legislation. We consider an EU policy to be effectively implemented and complied with if: (1) the directive is completely and correctly incorporated into national legislation and conflicting national rules are amended or repealed (formal implementation); (2) the administrative infrastructure and resources are provided to put the objectives of the policy into practice and to monitor the rule-consistent behavior of the target actors (practical application); and (3) the competent authorities are equipped to encourage or compel rule-consistent behavior of the target actors by effective monitoring, positive and negative sanctions and compulsory corrective measures (monitoring and enforcement).

Our six comparative case studies come to surprisingly similar findings confirming our theoretical expectations. All six accession countries have faced huge costs in the adoption of and adaptation to the environmental *acquis*, not least because of the weak governance capacities in the South and the even weaker capacities in the East. Yet, both state and nonstate actors were initially too weak to pool resources and share the costs. Only when EU membership helped to strengthen state capacities and transform political opportunity structures for nonstate actors did new modes of governance start to emerge. Yet, they present only 'timid deviations' from the tradition command-and-control approach that prevails in South and East alike and casts a strong shadow of hierarchy on any alternative forms of policymaking.

Notes

1. ICRG/IRIS Database, www.countrydata.com, (last access: 22 January 2009).
2. In this context, the Commission evaluates the administrative capacities of accession countries according to indicators such as available resources in personnel and finance, procedures applied to enforcement and monitoring and the overall compatibility of preexisting policy traditions in each policy area. Detailed scrutiny by the Commission is based on the *differentiation principle*, which entails a variable negotiation pace with each applicant.
3. OECD countries spend between one and two percent of their GDP on environmental policy cf. http://www.uni-mannheim.de/edz/pdf/dg4/ENVI106_EN.pdf, (last access: 31 May 2007).
4. Environmental policy was part of Chapter 22 on 'environment, consumers and health protection' and consisted of about 300 legal acts, of which about 80 are directives.

4

Greece: Overcoming Statism in Environmental Governance?

Charalampos Koutalakis

Introduction

Environmental policy in Greece was not a top priority area of public intervention when Greece joined the EC in 1981. Environmental regulation has been largely of a symbolic character and has suffered from a legacy of implementation gaps. Environmental protection has ranged low on the political agenda not least because it has been regarded as incompatible with economic development (Spanou, 1998). Like the other two Southern European member states, Greece faced a set of policy principles that hardly reflected its distinctive environmental concerns during its accession period (Kerameus and Kremlis, 1988; Kazakos, 1999). The mismatch between EU policies and domestic regulatory regimes widened when the adoption of the Single Market Programme fundamentally altered the scope and pace of European integration, posing unprecedented obligations to member states. The EU placed emphasis not only on expanding environmental policy to new areas but also on sustainability and the need to strengthen effective implementation through *shared responsibility* and *partnership* between different levels of government, environmental organizations and business in the implementation process. The poor level of compatibility between the specific environmental concerns of Greece and substantive policies pursued at the EU level generated serious problems with compliance to directives that imposed considerable costs of adaptation to the practically non-existent environmental administration. This is particularly the case with water and air pollution directives, which were barely implemented (Kerameus and Kremlis, 1988).

To what extent has the weak compliance performance of Greece stimulated the emergence of new, more inclusive governance arrangements that depart from traditional hierarchical modes of steering? Have new modes of governance fostered the more effective adoption of and adaptation to the *acquis communautaire*? Given the weak administrative capacities as regards effectively monitoring and enforcing environmental legislation, we would expect that Greek state actors would systematically resort to cooperative arrangements with nonstate actors that could contribute essential resources to the policymaking process in terms of expertise, finance and support. This chapter systematically traces the evolution of domestic modes of environmental governance in water management, air pollution and nature protection. To what extent do state actors resort to cooperation with private actors in order to pool resources and share the costs emanating from the adaptation to the EU environmental *acquis*? Under which conditions do private actors (business, interest groups and NGOs) mobilize their resources in order to compensate for weak state capacities and facilitate effective compliance with EU policies? The following section highlights the fundamental characteristics of environmental policymaking in Greece. During the early period of the country's EU membership, the dominance of command-and-control policy instruments hindered the emergence of cooperative patterns of policymaking between public and private actors. However, during the 1990s, increasing pressure from the Commission and strong public mobilization toward environmental protection acted as enabling factors towards the institutionalization of novel, less hierarchical modes of governance. Section three will systematically trace the gradual diffusion of new policies 'imported' from the EU and their impact on the traditional structures and patterns of policymaking in Greece. The evolution of EU environmental policy from command-and-control to more participatory modes of policymaking has generated significant pressures for adaptation, giving rise to some inceptive forms of new modes of governance.

Environmental policy in Greece

Legislative measures related to environmental policy were introduced in Greece as early as the beginning of the last century, regulating the protection of human health and nuisance from private economic activities. After the collapse of the dictatorship in 1974, the new constitution acknowledged a general state obligation to protect the natural, urban and cultural environments (Art. 24). However, a comprehensive framework legislation covering all facets of environmental degradation was introduced only in 1986, a year after the creation of the Ministry of Environment, Physical Planning and Public Works (YPEXODE). The persistent failure of postdictatorial governments to incorporate environmental and sustainability concerns into the political agenda is attributed to two interrelated factors. First, a dominant public discourse that has perceived environmental regulation as profoundly incompatible with the imperatives of catching up with the EU's more developed member states resulted in a low willingness of powerful industrial actors and state-owned industry to invest in green technologies (Spanou, 1995). Second, the horizontal fragmentation of responsibilities between central government departments with more power compared with YPEXODE and the lack of effective interministerial coordination and conflict resolution seriously weakened the administrative capacity of the Greek government (Spanou, 2000). Air pollution from industrial activities was regulated by the Ministry of Industry as an integral part of industrial permits while monitoring of atmospheric pollution was, until the creation of YPEXODE, a responsibility of the Ministry of Health. YPEXODE shared responsibilities over water regulations with the Ministries of Health and Welfare, Industry, Agriculture, the Interior and National Economy. Likewise, competences over the protection of biodiversity areas were divided between the Ministry of Agriculture (protection of forests and areas of special botanical and ecological value, hunting areas, game reserves and bird breeding stations) and the Ministry of Culture (for recreational parks and forests), while the Ministries of Defense, Development and Merchant Marine, Foreign Affairs and National Economy have been involved in several codecision procedures related to policy formulation and implementation (Spanou, 1998). The lack of effective horizontal coordination between central government actors sharing responsibilities over environmental policies has hindered the mobilization of dispersed administrative resources and capacities to engage in comprehensive planning, monitoring and enforcement.

Despite weak state capacities, the prevailing institutional properties prevented the emergence of participatory modes of environmental governance to tap into the resources of nonstate actors and share the costs of implementation. Administrative fragmentation enabled economic actors to choose their interlocutors strategically. Industrial actors have traditionally been linked to the Ministries of Development and National Economy, which are responsible for permits on industrial installations, while ship owners – the most powerful domestic lobby – are traditionally attached to the Ministry of Merchant Shipping (Weale et al., 2000). Moreover, YPEXODE's General Secretariat for Environment has comparatively fewer resources and less expertise than that of Public Works, which manages all major infrastructure projects. This trend was exacerbated during the 1990s with the implementation of works paid for by EU structural funds, which placed considerable emphasis on large infrastructure projects. As a result, YPEXODE was and still is overstaffed with civil engineers and architects while environmental expertise is lacking (Spanou, 1995: 150). YPEXODE's enforcement capacities were also weak. An environmental inspectorate authority was created in 2001 with a general mandate over all environmental legislation and became fully operational only in 2003. The creation of the inspectorate has strengthened enforcement capabilities, although they still suffer from serious administrative capacity shortcomings and limited staff power.

The 13 Regional Administrations are mostly responsible for territorial planning, with emphasis on regional economic development plans, within the structure of EU community support frameworks and the distribution of funds to environmental protection. However, their involvement in the formulation, monitoring and enforcement of environmental regulations is as a purely advisory role to central administration, especially regarding compiling of environmental information (Presidential Decree, 404/1989; Spanou, 1995).

Local authorities also face serious capacity shortcomings. Law 1650/1986 provides for the transfer of competencies related to the implementation of environmental policies to Local and Prefectural Authorities. However, as of now only limited competencies and resources have been transferred. The 53 Prefects, who since 1992 have been directly elected, share important responsibilities over policy formulation, implementation and enforcement, especially regarding environmental impact assessments, emission limit values on water and air, the designation of protected areas and the imposition of fines to polluters. Their administrative capacity is still weak, since the transfer of the above responsibilities was not accompanied by adequate funding and personnel. The same holds for municipalities, which often lack the capacity and the willingness to monitor and enforce environmental regulations effectively. They are mostly responsible for licensing permissions, waste collection, small-scale environmental projects at the local level, water distribution in areas outside of the country's two largest urban agglomerations (Athens and Thessaloniki) and drainage systems. Local client networks hinder effective monitoring and enforcement of environmental regulations at the local and prefectural level. This is particularly evident in the area of urban planning, where real estate speculative pressures in tourist regions and large cities are perceived to be the main source of corruption.[1]

Societal involvement in environmental policies is far from being institutionalized. Legalism and the dominance of command-and-control policy instruments have hindered the emergence of cooperation between public and private actors. To a large extent, closed opportunity structures elucidate recent trends of high levels of protest activities by environmental groups and NGOs that disconfirm conventional assumptions regarding the weakness of civil society in Greece (Kousis, 2001). Instead of trying to accommodate societal mobilization by more inclusive modes of policymaking, Greek authorities have tended to close up the policy process. The involvement of business interests in environmental policymaking is also rarely institutionalized. Environmental voluntary agreements require effective structures and patterns of interest intermediation that foster mutual understanding and trust between participants. Public authorities and firms are not accustomed to cooperative patterns of interactions. The dominance of small family enterprises based on a rather informal network of interconnections between them hinder the emergence of consensus and trust because of the lack of strong representative associations to serve as credible interlocutors with public authorities (Koutalakis, 2003).

In Greece, the implementation of environmental policies is further hindered by a lack of data on the specific environmental conditions both at the territorial (regional and local) and sectoral levels. This is not just a problem associated with a lack of qualified personnel, but touches upon more fundamental characteristics of Greek public administration, such as its closed nature and the weak integration of scientific expertise in the policymaking process. Patterns of interactions between the scientific community and policymakers are *ad hoc* and depend largely on individual contacts and the political affiliations of certain experts with the political leadership of environmental ministries (Ladi, 2005).

Environmental policy and the challenge of accession

As in the cases of the Central and Eastern European and the other two Southern European countries, Greece's 'return to Europe' provided an indispensable frame of reference and source of cognitive ideas which helped the country to define its political and economic orientation after the collapse of the authoritarian regime in 1974. At the same time, Greece was economically in a similar position as the current Eastern accession countries with a per capita GDP of around 50 percent of the

EU average.[2] Macroeconomic limitations and profound political, institutional and administrative weaknesses were at odds with the process of economic and legal harmonization with EU member states. However, as in the case of the Eastern enlargement, political aspirations prevailed over technocratic considerations (Curzon Price, 1999). This resonated with the EU's approach to Southern enlargement, which focused on the respect for human rights and democracy as the essential criteria for accession.

In stark contrast to the Eastern enlargement, the European Commission did not thoroughly evaluate Greece's institutional capacities to implement the *acquis* prior to accession. Negotiations were mostly about agriculture and the free movement of labor. Greece sought to secure a number of transitional arrangements to protect local industry from competitive pressures emanating from the customs union and regarding state aid, regional policy, social affairs, capital movement and the establishment of common market in industrial (textiles) and agricultural products (Maraveyas, 1994; Iankova and Katzenstein, 2003).

The environmental *acquis* of the EU when Greece joined was tailored to the needs of advanced industrialized economies and the realization that the model of economic growth had reached its environmental limits (Weale et al., 2000). Thus, accession hardly challenged the dominant perception in Greece that environmental protection was difficult to reconcile with economic growth.

While accession did little to change the general policy approach, it had an impact on administrative structure. EU environmental policies provided additional leverage to YPEXODE over other central government ministries sharing responsibilities in environmental policies (Fousekis and Lekakis, 1997; Kazakos, 1999; Spanou, 2000). Compliance pressure by the Commission and the European Court of Justice (ECJ) 'from above' combined with increasing domestic mobilization 'from below' by major environmental non-governmental organizations (ENGOs) fostered the demand for opening up the domestic policy process to nonstate actors (Kousis, 2003; Koutalakis, 2004). Moreover, the systematic incorporation of environmental policy considerations into the EU structural funds provided unprecedented opportunities for Greek public and private actors to strengthen administrative and cognitive capacities to comply with EU legislation. However, EU financial assistance had an ambivalent effect on domestic capacities to comply with environmental legislation effectively. Macroeconomic imperatives for becoming a member of the eurozone placed considerable limitations on regional policies that contradict the aims of economic and monetary convergence. Given the lack of administrative capacity to implement multinational programs for environmental protection, central government departments were reluctant to commit significant financial resources to innovative environmental plans. Party competition has exacerbated this trend. This is a result of central government's concern to secure high absorption rates of EU structural assistance. As a result, the relevant operational programs in the four community support frameworks implemented so far have never exceeded 6 percent of available funding.[3] Moreover, the emphasis on large infrastructure projects limited the potential of EU structural funds for strengthening domestic administrative capacities to implement the *acquis* effectively (cf. Koutalakis, 2003). Finally, the coexistence of public works and the environment in the same ministry had adverse effects on central government's environmental capacities. YPEXODE's prioritization of the rapid completion of large infrastructure projects has led to significant staff reductions in its environmental services. According to data from the ministry from 1993–2005, a significant 20 percent reduction of staff in environmental services took place with a corresponding increase of available staff in the public works services (YPEXODE, 2006).

The following sections examine the evolution of domestic structures and patterns of governance in three policy areas: water management, air pollution and nature protection. In all three policy areas EU requirements have imposed considerable costs of adaptation, which have met with weak capacities of the Greek state to effectively apply, monitor and enforce environmental legislation.

Coping with the challenge of accession

Water Management: balancing quality and quantity

Water policy in Greece is largely shaped by EU legislation. The fundamental characteristic of the domestic regime for water regulation is fragmentation between different central government departments. The main competencies are shared between the YPEXODE's and the Ministries of Health and Welfare, Development, Agriculture, Interior and Economy and Finance. In the country's two largest urban centers, Athens and Thessaloniki, distribution and quality inspections of drinking water are responsibilities of two large state-owned enterprises (SOEs), while in smaller urban areas and villages these are responsibilities of municipal enterprises and prefectural authorities. The lack of effective coordination between the large numbers of actors sharing responsibilities over water management has considerably impeded the capacity of central government to regulate water consumption effectively. Domestic policies have never departed from purely legalistic measures because of the lack of scientific data and expertise for effective quality controls, especially at the subnational levels of government.

The *Drinking Water Directives* (778/1980 and 83/1998) (DWD) are a case in point. The directives' requirements for the renewal of outdated infrastructure for water storage and distribution and the introduction of quality control systems affect a wide range of industrial actors, essentially the food industry and the constructors of water distribution systems that have to comply with quality standards of materials used in their construction. In the Greek case, the application of the directives required considerable public expenditure, especially in small urban areas where distribution systems did not comply with standards related to the consistency of the nonferrous and heavy metals (nickel, copper and lead) that were traditionally used by domestic constructors because of their low cost and durability. The same holds for the domestic producers of machinery used in water abstraction, storage and filtering, who would face considerable problems of in competing with foreign companies as a result of their lack of the expertise needed in order to comply with new product standards. State actors faced considerable additional costs to comply with requirements for monitoring and quality control. Lack of data and expertise in relation to the above-mentioned issues has hindered consultation with the domestic industry (Servos, 2003).

Administrative fragmentation, lack of expertise and, until recently, limited systematic attempts to compensate for weak state resources with the participation of nonstate actors, have not only rendered the implementation of EU water directives ineffective, but have also limited the country's capacity to shape the course of EU water policies and advance its own preferences. During the 1980s, the dominant perception in Greece was that EU initiatives imposing *qualitative* indicators on water resources failed to address the country's acute shortcomings regarding *quantity*, especially during the summer period.[4] When the revision of the DWD was negotiated in the EU, the Greek authorities failed to push for a regulation that would allow for less strict measures related to the management of water sources given the shortage of water, especially in summer. The directive was discussed in the Council of Environmental Ministers. However, in Greece the central government department responsible for monitoring the quality of drinking water is the Ministry of Health. As a result, the latter was only informed about the revision six months before the end of the preparatory phase. The issue was conceptualized as a technical issue with no significant economic implications apart from those related to public health protection. The lack of consultation with the domestic industry, subnational authorities, the scientific community and the public minimized input regarding the economic effects of the directive and, in effect, hindered the adoption of a national position.[5] During the same period Greece was indicted by the ECJ for noncompliance with almost all major EU water directives.[6] These cases demonstrate not only the lack of scientific expertise and financial resources on the part of subnational actors (prefectural authorities) but also profound problems of administrative adaptation to the underlining logic of directives that require the implementation of programs that lay down quality objectives and limit quantities of emissions into water. In this case, Greek authorities have shown considerable rigidity with regards to expanding the range of policy instruments used in the area beyond measures of a legislative nature. Instead of submitting water management programs to the Commission the Greek authorities undertook purely legislative measures, laying down procedural requirements for issuing permits to industry. Given the lack of data, Greek authorities in some areas were unable even to identify the industrial plants that discharge emissions into the aquatic environment.[7]

A turning point in the incremental process of strengthening administrative and engaging capacities of YPEXODE came in the beginning of the 2000s with the introduction of the *Water Framework Directive* (WFD). The Greek government had transposed the directive with a new law (3199/2003), which introduced for the first time institutionalized participatory structures for the elaboration of national water policy and placed all pre-existing fragmented competencies under the coordination of YPEXODE. At the central government level, it establishes a new interministerial coordination committee comprising all of the ministries that share responsibilities for water policy, namely YPEXODE and the Ministries of National Economy and Finance, Development, Agriculture, Health and the Interior. This committee is responsible for the formulation of national plans for water management as well as the overall supervision of compliance with EU law. A systematic involvement of nonstate actors can be observed only in a number of newly created consultation structures. A National Water Council with a consultative role to government comprises a wide range of public and private actors. NGO participants include Greenpeace, WWF-Hellas, the Hellenic Foundation for Nature Protection, Network Mediterranean SOS and the Mediterranean Environmental, Cultural and Developmental Information Office. The major participant from the scientific community is the Institute of

Geological and Metallurgical Research, which has considerable expertise in monitoring the quality and quantity of water resources, and works together with the National Centre of Seawater Research, National Centre of Biotopes, National Centre of Natural Sciences, National Foundation of Agricultural Research, Technical Chamber of Greece and National Environmental Agency. Stakeholder participation included the Consumers Chamber and Public Electricity Company.[8]

However, consultations between domestic actors failed to compensate for the weak capacities of national authorities in fulfilling their obligations under the directive. The lack of preexisting administrative capacities in terms of expertise and access to qualitative and quantitative data related to water management considerable hindered YPEXODE in taking advantage of the willingness of nonstate actors to offer their resources in order to improve implementation. As a result, neither the scientific community nor large professionalized NGOs or subnational actors could offer sufficient expertise to designate water management departments.[9] Lack of knowledge and expertise considerably hindered the absorption of about 19.3 million euros earmarked for the implementation of the directive in the third Community Support Framework's operational programs for Competitiveness, Rural Development, Fisheries and Research and Technology.[10] In sum, neither consultations with nonstate actors nor EU capacity building have helped to improve effective implementation. In January 2008, the ECJ issued a judgment against Greece for not properly applying the WFD, claiming that national measures were of a purely legislative nature rather than comprehensive water management programs.[11]

The failure to compensate for weak administrative capacities, in terms of expertise, required for the implementation of national and regional plans highlights the limits of participatory approaches in Greece. Unlike in the case of the DWD, the introduction of the WFD provided an institutional incentive to overcome domestic institutional rigidities that prevented the emergence of participatory structures and inclusive patterns of policymaking. The creation of several advisory boards at national and regional levels has given rise to patterns of consultation. However, the lack of cognitive capacities on the part of both state and nonstate actors still hinders effective application of the directive.

Air Pollution: defragmenting regulatory areas

Air pollution policies in Greece are largely shaped by attempts since the 1970s to combat the problem of photochemical smog in Athens. Early legislation dealt with the problem by resorting to predominantly urban planning instruments, including regulations that provided for the relocation of most polluting activities outside the Athens metropolitan area and the introduction of air quality monitoring systems (Spanou, 1995). Preventive policies for air pollution were first introduced in 1981 with a Presidential Decree (1180/29.6/6.10.1981) by the (then) Ministry of Industry (now Ministry of Development), which introduced environmental impact assessments as part of the licensing requirements of new industrial installations, the classification of areas according to their pollution conditions and the introduction of emission limit values (ELVs) for industrial installations. The framework law for environmental protection (Law 1650/1986) did not depart from the predominant command-and-control instruments described above. It included a wide range of prohibitions and penalties covering industrial installations (reductions in energy consumption and production), a rotating use of cars in the center of Athens according to their license plate numbers, which is still applied today, and private energy consumption.

The legislation did not depart considerably from the regulatory style of the air pollution directives the EU had adopted in the 1980s. Nevertheless, the *Large Combustion Plant Directive* (LCPD) and its mother directive caused a mismatch with regard to the level of regulatory stringency of ELVs, which had not been elaborated in detail by Greek law. Moreover, Greece was required to implement national programs for the reduction of emissions. While Greece, together with Spain, Ireland and Portugal, successfully pressed for higher emission limits, EU obligations for emission reduction still have imposed direct investment costs to domestic industry, especially to state-owned power plants and the country's major oil refineries (Weale et al., 2000). Consequently, the transposition of the LCPD in Greece and the fulfillment of reporting obligations were delayed for three years and resulted in a conviction by the ECJ (C-1993/304). Likewise, Greece had to stand before the ECJ for violating the emission values provided by Directive 360/1984 for combating air pollution from industrial plants (C-364/2003). Finally, the Commission pursued legal action against Greece in the case of the Directive on National Emission Ceilings for Certain Atmospheric Pollutants (C-2001/81), for which Greece delayed submission of a national program for the reduction of emissions.

The practical application of the directives was considerably impaired by the lack of investment potential of domestic industry. In Greece, the largest pollutant is the Public Electricity Corporation (DEH), which, even today, holds a monopoly on production and distribution of electricity. To a large extent, the negative environmental performance of

DEH has been reinforced by successive governments' policies of pursuing social and economic policy objectives through state intervention in electricity prices. Energy policy has long served the purposes of low inflation, protecting the competitiveness of local industry and regional policy, especially in agricultural areas, where producers pay lower prices. As a state-controlled industry, DEH has little incentive to go against state policy recommendations, since the Ministry of Development has the final decision making powers over important issues such as pricing and investment in new technologies. The imminent opening up of the energy market is expected to foster considerable changes in the balance of power between domestic producers and the state and to create the preconditions for the emergence of novel patterns of regulatory policymaking.

During the 1990s, the introduction of new EU legislation caused additional friction with Greek authorities since these laws departed from traditional command-and-control approaches to industrial pollution abatement. The adoption of the *Integrated Pollution Prevention and Control Directive* (IPPCD) (61/1996) constitutes the most profound case of policy misfit. The directive introduces significant policy innovations related to the policy content and procedures to be applied to the adoption of environmental standards, their monitoring and implementation. It is the first time that EU environmental policies depart from media-specific regulatory approaches to pollution abatement by introducing an integrated approach that incorporates a single permit system covering all polluting activities of industry, water, air and land, as well as the efficient use of energy (Koutalakis, 2008a).

The transposition of the IPPCD in Greece was considerably delayed. It took almost four years after the deadline (30 October 1999) and an ECJ judgment in 2001 (C-64/01) to persuade the Greek government to transpose the directive in 2002 (Law 3010/2002). However, implementing measures were adopted only later through three ministerial decrees issued in 2002 and 2003, defining the detailed requirements for issuing single permits to new and existing industrial installations and the distribution of competencies between central government departments and subnational authorities sharing responsibilities over industrial activities. As with the case of nature protection, the fundamental problem lies with administrative fragmentation. The introduction of a single permit requirement for new and existing installations challenges the domestic distribution of power between several ministerial departments, public services and subnational authorities involved in the preexisting industrial policy regime. As in many other areas of environmental policymaking, the IPPCD empowers YPEXODE as a central coordinating authority in the process of issuing industrial permits.

Although from the 1980s industrial pollution was one of the key competencies of YPEXODE, responsibilities for industrial permits were shared between four different central government departments that issued six different permits. These permits covered a preliminary approval of location issued by either YPEXODE or the General Secretary of the Region according to the size of the proposed industrial installation and the spatial characteristics of the location. Based on this approval, YPEXODE issued an Environmental Impact Assessment Approval, while Solid Waste disposal permits for all installations were issued by the Prefect. Moreover, the prefectural authorities issued permits for waste disposal, the Ministry of Agriculture for agricultural activities and the Ministry of Development for power plants (Koutoupa-Regakou, 2007).

Long before the adoption of the IPPCD, the simplification of the preexisting fragmented system of permits was a key policy demand of industrial associations, mainly the Association of Greek Industrialists and an epistemic community dominated by the Technical Chamber of Greece, with a view to reducing both administrative burdens on industrial investments and costs. During the last decade, Greek governments supported the introduction of 'one-stop shops' for companies and industry that would operate as a front of stage service to coordinate the fragmented permitting system. However, reform plans did not proceed because of administrative inertia and antagonisms between different public services, mainly YPEXODE and the Ministry of Development.[12]

Competing claims of ownership over the IPPCD's requirements for single permits explains the method employed by central government to transpose the directive into domestic law. Law 3010/2002 legally implemented not only the IPPCD but also the *Environmental Impact Assessment Directive* (EIAD). In fact, the implementation of the two directives was fully integrated in an attempt to insulate it from interministerial competition. EIA already had an established system of horizontal and vertical cooperation between central government departments and subnational actors involved in the process. The result of this strategy was the emergence of a permit system that goes beyond the requirements of the IPPCD and fully integrates pollution abatement requirements to spatial planning. However, the lack of horizontal inter-ministerial cooperation between YPEXODE and the Ministry of Development resulted in the emergence of a dual permitting system with considerable overlaps nurtured by the antagonistic relationships between the two ministries.

An even more challenging endeavor for Greek authorities was the practical application of BAT based on ELVs to each industrial plant covered by the IPPCD. Greek public administration has no tradition regarding the flexible definition of BAT-based ELVs. It has also lacked any experience since the BAT requirements of the LCPD were never implemented. One of the key problems that delayed the practical application of the directive was the lack of data on industrial installations. Moreover, enforcement of the directive requires significant expertise and equipment in order to monitor and register the available techniques used by a wide range of industrial sectors and to assess the environmental improvement potential of each industrial plant covered by the directive in relation to local environmental conditions and the economic feasibility for the adoption of BAT. Last but not least, it requires monitoring and enforcement capacities for continual inspections of individual plants' compliance with the permits issued on the basis of the above assessments.

The responsible department in YPEXODE was seriously understaffed with only 12 full time employees (11 engineers and one lawyer).[13] Such limited administrative resources stimulated the emergence of a network of cooperation mainly with public research institutes in the two largest Polytechnic Schools of Athens and Thessalonica and the Institute for Environmental Research and Sustainable Development of the National Observatory of Athens, the Technical Chamber of Greece and the Hellenic Association of Chemical Engineers. Given the lack of data, YPEXODE resorted to using private consultants and delegated studies to them in order to develop an inventory of emissions from statutory pollution sources, the data used for the definition of BAT-based ELVs. The studies were coordinated by the National Observatory of Athens and financed by the operational 'Environment' program of the second Community Support Framework.[14] However, this approach did not prove sufficient. The main problem encountered during the compilation of the inventory was the lack of interest on the part of Greek companies and the lack of trust in any procedure directly or indirectly related to data provision for regulatory purposes. Moreover, small and medium enterprises often lack qualified personnel and data on simple issues, such as their productive capacity.[15]

These limitations led to a change from the delegation of technical and scientific tasks as the main method employed for initializing the implementation of IPPCD in Greece. Although the studies provided essential information for registering IPPC firms, additional strategies had to be employed in order to coordinate the definition of BAT-based

ELVs for domestic facilities in different sectors, which would serve as national reference documents in the Seville process. Intensive consultations between YPEXODE and individual firms and representative organizations have provided an alternative to the traditional command-and-control instruments for the definition of ELVs, monitoring and inspections (Interview, legal expert, 15 December 2006). Numerous conferences and sectoral workshops with major firms have facilitated the gradual deployment of an epistemic community, the generation of trust and mutual exchange of information that serves as a basis for the elaboration of national reference documents.

Not all enterprises were receptive of IPPC single permit requirements, however. Critics have pointed to the additional administrative burdens resulting from the addition of a second permitting procedure that largely overlaps the with existing licensing administered by the Ministry of Development.[16] Moreover, there was a certain degree of uncertainty related to the binding character of BAT requirements for existing installations and costs involved in the upgrade of infrastructure in 2007. Even today, an estimate of the direct financial costs of compliance is missing. However, in order to stimulate trust within the business community as a prerequisite for their active involvement in the process of BAT national reference documents, YPEXODE – in cooperation with the Ministry of Development – formulated a cost containment strategy in order to mitigate private compliance costs for individual firms. These involved the introduction of specific measures and actions that support the adoption of BAT technologies into the operational 'Competitiveness' program of the third Community Support Framework administered by the General Secretariat for Industry, Ministry of Development.[17]

The cumulative effect of cost containment strategies employed by YPEXODE and the Ministry of Development was the gradual emergence of trust between YPEXODE, the epistemic community and individual firms and sectoral associations. This served as a precondition for conducting all preparatory stages in a negotiating mode that was dominated by arguments referred to sound scientific knowledge and the foundation of claims on international literature. In fact, private actors involved in these preparatory stages also participated in various Technical Working Groups in the EIPPC Bureau in Seville (Koutalakis, 2008a).

Environmental groups, in contrast, have remained rather skeptical about the scope of direct business involvement into the definition of BAT-based emission values at both national and EU levels. Clientelistic traditions in relationships between state regulators and the industry and a legacy of weak enforcement capacities have generated controversy over private involvement in environmental policymaking. The latter is often perceived as the institutionalization of privileged access to decision making for powerful industrial groups, and this generates mistrust among other stakeholders and the public. The dominant perception that law enforcement is not negotiable reflects the wider suspicion among the public that new modes of governance are just a refined way of circumventing compliance with legal obligations.[18]

Nevertheless, the introduction of the IPPCD signifies a clear break with past attempts to regulate air quality with command-and-control approaches. Participatory requirements of the directive have opened up opportunities for pooling cognitive resources and formulating common cost containment strategies between industrial associations and the state. The emergence of stable interactions between the YPEXODE and sectoral industrial associations has proved beneficial for the practical application of the directive and the gradual emergence of consensual patterns of interaction in several technical working groups. While the role of nonstate actors is consultative, their technical opinions have had clear effects on the definition of BAT-based ELVs because of their expertise and knowledge regarding the technological status of individual industrial installations.

Nature protection: 'naturalizing' Natura 2000

EU legislation for the establishment of a Natura 2000 network of protected biodiversity areas (Habitats 1992/43 and Wild Birds 1979/409 Directives) is one of the most problematic examples of Greece's weak compliance record with EU environmental law. Both legal transposition and policy application of the directives were considerably delayed and are still incomplete. The two directives represent a case of profound policy mismatch with the preexisting regulatory regime for the protection of biodiversity. The directives impinge on the domestic fragmented distribution of competencies and require the development of comprehensive management plans and the establishment of effective mechanisms and instruments for nature protection and conservation. The main framework law for environmental protection (1650/1986) attributed the general competence over all protected areas to YPEXODE. However, seven other ministries share responsibilities over different types of areas. As a result, YPEXODE was the only national authority that would benefit from the application of Habitants Directives. However, because of its weak position *vis-à-vis* the other ministries, combined with administrative fragmentation and a lack of coordination mechanisms, negotiations between central government departments resulted in a deadlock, especially with the Ministry of Agriculture, which considerably delayed transposition (Andreou, 2004).

In additions to this institutional mismatch, the implementation of the Wild Birds Directive and the FFHD required profound policy changes. The Greek framework law for environmental protection provides for the creation of five different types of protected areas: Areas of Special Protection where no human activity is allowed other than research; Areas of Natural Protection; National Parks including Marine Parks where only limited human activities area allowed, especially those related to recreation, research and conservation; Protected Landscapes; and Areas of Sustainable Development. However, apart from forest areas managed by the Ministry of Agriculture, no other areas were subject to any special protection scheme because of the lack of data regarding the specific types of flora, fauna and habitats prior to the introduction of the directives. Between 1938 and 1974, the Ministry of Agriculture had specified ten national forests enjoying relatively high levels of protection under the Forest Service. Protection of these areas was based onpolicing and the prohibition of several activities. This legacy of command-and-control instruments created considerable tensions and mistrust between the local communities and the forest service that hindered the application of participatory requirements of the Natura 2000 directives.[19] In effect, central administration had neither prior experience nor the necessary information and expertise to prepare specific programs for the management of these protected areas based on scientific evidence, not to mention environmental impact assessments of various activities, information strategies, monitoring or evaluation of regulatory measures (Andreou, 2004).

As a result of the lack of cognitive resources, it took almost four years after the official deadline for the transposition (June 1994), an ECJ judgment and the initiation of postlitigation infringement proceedings to persuade the Greek government to transpose the FFHD.[20] Compliance pressure from the EU gave rise to intense negotiations between central government departments over the allocation of competencies and the compilation of the national inventory list of areas to be covered by the directive. These were conducted between an inner circle of ministerial delegates. The final joint ministerial decree, which essentially translates the original text of the directive, was issued only after the intervention of the Prime Minister's office (Andreou, 2004: 4). Although YPEXODE was made the competent authority for the management of designated areas, their actual establishment required first a presidential decree

(Law 2742/1999) and then a joint ministerial decree (Law 3044/2002), which was issued according to the proposal of all ministries sharing competencies in the designated areas. Thus, administrative fragmentation has prevailed.

Practical application of the directives also proved problematic. It took the Greek government two legislative initiatives (Laws 2742/1999 and 3044/2002) and one conviction from the ECJ (C-103/00) to introduce the necessary legal instruments. Finally, in 2002 the Greek government designated 25 management authorities for protected areas. However, by 2009 management authorities have been established in only 27 out of 360 protected areas. As a result, two more cases came before the ECJ (C-334/04 and C-518/04), both bringing legal actions against the country for failing to designate and establish effective systems of nature protection in several areas. After significant pressure from the European Commission and domestic mobilization for the establishment of a protective regime, the Greek government opened up opportunities for the inclusion of nonstate actors into the policy process. The most pressing problems related to the compilation of the initial national list of areas that would serve as the basis for negotiations with the European Commission. Given the lack of data related to any sites on the flora, fauna and various habitats covered by the directive and the inexperience of YPEXODE staff, the compilation of the initial inventory was delegated to an NGO-funded research group, Greek Biotope/Wetland Centre, which cooperated with the Departments of Biology of the Universities of Athens, Patras, Saloniki and Crete. The project was co-funded by the EU LIFE Nature Programme, YPEXODE and the Ministry of Agriculture. Based on an initial list of 296 sites, covering approximately 18.2 percent of the country's territory, a number of consultations took place between the relevant ministerial departments (YPEXODE and the Ministries of Agriculture, Merchant Marine, Foreign Affairs, Development and Defense) in order to finalize the national inventory of sites. Negotiations led to further compromises regarding the number of areas designated as Natura 2000 sites, which changed several times.[21] Consultations did not involve local communities or local governments in order to avoid deadlocks during the early stages of the application of the directive. At the same time, local politicians were also hesitant about participating in controversial conservation schemes that initially failed to gain approval of local communities, especially in areas of high land value, such as the Loggerhead sea turtle *Caretta caretta* site in Zakynthos.[22]

Nonstate actors' involvement in legal and policy harmonization with the requirements of FFHD is still in a nascent phase, while conflict resolution mechanisms remain largely hierarchical. It is only in the implementation stage ENGOs, local community groups, research centers, local authorities and individuals in managing authorities are included. While the capacities of public actors are severely limited, environmental NGOs, local community groups and research centers have been willing and able to help in the implementation of the NATURA 2000 directives, offering their expertise and support. The involvement of nonstate actors has taken three different forms. First, ENGOs, such as Arcturos and the Society for the Protection of Mediterranean Seal, participate in a national NATURA 2000 committee, with a consultative capacity to YPEXODE. Moreover, the management boards set up by the ministry to oversee the protected sites also consist of representatives of local authorities, social partners and representatives from the scientific community, who share responsibilities with members of YPEXODE and other ministries. These new modes of governance remain weak, however. They hardly go beyond consultation. The traditional top-down, legalistic administrative culture that still prevails in Greece has prevented the delegation of management functions to these multistakeholder bodies. Nevertheless, while they have no right to issue regulations without the consent of YPEXODE, their management plans have normative consequences for the precise types of activities and conservation actions allowed in the designated areas. To that extent, the application of the Natura 2000 directives has brought about novel structures and patterns of policy making that give consultants and scientific experts substantial say. Public authorities were very resistant to the involvement of civil society actors. NGOs gained access to management boards only after persistent activism in nature conservation with campaigns, protest, public appeals and complaints to the EU. Their involvement was also impaired by the ideological opposition of local environmental groups against participating in institutionalized structures of cooperation with the state (Kousis, 2001).

Second, large environmental NGOs, such as the WWF-Hellas, the Greek Centre for Biotopes and Wetland and the Greek Ornithological Society have acted as educators and mediators between the state and local communities. These patterns of consultation have gained considerable value, especially regarding public awareness campaigns that helped both to overcome negative perceptions of past command-and-control conservation measures, based on policing and absolute prohibitions, and to generate trust in local communities.[23] EU funding from the Life-Nature Programme and the third Community Support Frameworks' operational programs for Environment and Rural Development has acted as catalysts for these initiatives (Karpathaki, 2005). Finally, NGOs have established private conservation regimes through the purchase of private property in order to compensate for the absence of state intervention.[24]

Summing up, the weak institutionalization of nonstate actors' involvement in the policy process is indeed a paradox. They have contributed essential cognitive resources that compensate for a lack of experience and knowledge in central government. Moreover, public awareness campaigns by NGOs have fostered the emergence of trust among local stakeholders in protection measures and, in effect, have strengthened the effectiveness and efficiency of the practical application of the directives. Nevertheless, overall, Greek authorities have remained reluctant to involve nonstate actors on a more systematic, institutionalized level. We do find, however, some isolated cases of private self-regulation where NGOs set up private conservation regimes.

Conclusion

Weak state capacities created significant problems for the effective adoption of and adaptation to the environmental *acquis* in Greece's accession to the EU. Yet we find only limited instances of cooperation between state and nonstate actors in pooling resources and sharing compliance costs. Inclusive, nonhierarchical modes of governance are scare and weakly institutionalized in Greece, even if EU legislation explicitly requires public participation in the policy process, as in case of the FFHD, the IPPCD and the WFD. Nonstate actors are barely being more than consulted, although their expertise and capacities for engagement have given them some say in the policy process. In the cases of the Natura 2000 directives, the neutral stance of NGOs has strengthened state actors' capacities to resolve conflicts between affected interests. In the implementation of the IPPCD, industrial actors have added their expertise in and knowledge related to the emission performances of industrial plants covered by the directive and technologies used in their production lines. Yet the contributions of nonstate actors to effective implementation are still contingent upon the capacities of state and nonstate actors. Fragmentation, coupled with the legacy of deficient implementation and low enforcement capacities, generates skepticism and mistrust between important stakeholders and the state regarding the potential benefits of new modes of governance. Since the beginning of the 1990s, EU push and pull factors have provided for an incremental strengthening of the coordinating capacities of central government actors under the auspices of YPEXODE. However, the monitoring and enforcement capacities of YPEXODE remain weak. Paradoxically, weak administrative capacity has been a major impediment rather than a facilitating factor for the institutionalization of nonhierarchical modes of policymaking in environmental policies.

Notes

1. See Annual Reports 1998–2006, Greek Ombudsman, Department of Quality of Life, available at http://www.synigoros.gr/en_who_is.htm (last access date: 30 June 2009).
2. http://stats.oecd.org/wbos/viewhtml.aspx?queryname=316&querytype=vie w&lang=en, GDP → Country comparison tables, (last access: 1 December 2008).
3. www.eper.gr, (last access: 15 February 2008).
4. The most acute problems are related to the concentration of population in coastal areas, which leads to the intrusion of seawater into the depleted underground aquifers, limited water availability on the numerous tourist islands during the summer seasons when the population is literally doubled, overexploitation of water resources and the use of pesticides in agriculture.
5. Interview, academic policy expert, Athens, 27 October 2005.
6. The ECJ has issued four judgments against Greece for violation of various EU water directives. These include the delayed Transposition of Urban Waste Water Treatment Directive (91/271 EEC, C-161/1995); infringements of the Directive on Pollution caused by Dangerous Substances Discharged into the Aquatic Environment (76/464 EEC) (C-232/95, 233/95 and 384/97) and Directive 80/68 on Protection of Underground Waters from Pollution from Dangerous Substances (C-163/03).
7. See cases C-232/95, 233/95 and 384/97. In those cases the Commission referred Greek to the ECJ for the infringement of Directive 76-464 EEC. Greece failed to submit information to the Commission regarding industrial installations discharging emissions, claiming that there are no such installations in Greece.
8. Unpublished proceedings, YPEXODE, 24 November 2004, consultation meeting with stakeholders.
9. Unpublished minutes, YPEXODE, 24 November 2004.
10. Interview, Ministry of National Economy, Athens, 20 October 2005.
11. http://europa.eu/rapid/pressReleasesAction.do?reference=IP/07/394&form at=HTML& aged=0& language=EN&guiLanguage=en#fn3, (last access: 10 October 2008).
12. Interview, Greek Technical Chamber, 7 December 2006.
13. See http://www.minenv.gr/1/11/g1101new3.htm, (last access: 13 May 2007).
14. Interview, YPEXODE, Athens, 5 April 2007.
15. Interviews, EPEM LTD environmental consultants, Athens, 11 November 2006.
16. Association of Greek Industrialists, Conference Bulletin of Technical Chamber of Greece, 11 November 2002.

17. Interview Ministry of Development, Athens, 15 December 2007. Details on specific measures and actions can be found at (last access: 16 December 2007) http://www.antagonistikotita.gov.gr/epan/site/Home/t_section last accessed 29 June 2009.
18. Interviews, YPEXODE and Environmental Consultant, Athens, 20 April 2006.
19. Interview, nature protection expert, WWF-Hellas, Athens, 10 November 2005.
20. See C-83/1997. The directive was transposed in December 1998 by Joint Ministerial Decree 33318/3028/28.12.1998.
21. The initial list included 296 sites, which were reduced to 164 sites of community interest and 29 SPAs after initial consultations and finally increased to 230 SCIs and 52 SPAs after negotiations with DG ENVI (WWF-Hellas, 2003).
22. Interview, policy expert, Nomos and Physis, Athens, 11 November 2005.
23. Interview, YPEXODE, Athens, 8 November 2005.
24. See www.wwf.gr, (last access: 1 December 2008).

5

Portugal: The Challenges of Environmental Governance and the Realities of Government

Ana Mar Fernández and Nuria Font

Introduction

When Portugal became a member of the European EC in 1986, the country faced two major challenges: democratic consolidation and economic modernization. EU membership offered symbolic and material benefits to the country in support of its transition. The country accentuated its efforts to consolidate newly established democratic institutions, attain economic progress and regain international recognition after the collapse of the Salazar's regime in the mid-1970s. However, EU membership also challenged its administrative traditions and policies (Sapelli, 1995; Magone, 1997). This is particularly true for regulatory domains such as environmental policy, in which the Portuguese state had no prior experience of policy and weak capacities for reaching EU standards. In spite of capacity shortcomings, accession did not induce state actors to cooperate with nonstate actors to cope with their weaknesses and share the burden of implementation. Yet, this situation started to change in the late-1990s.

The conditions for the emergence of new, more inclusive modes of governance in order to comply with the environmental *acquis* became more favorable. Internal factors, such as the improvement of the overall macroeconomic performance, the development of new institutional arrangements and an increasing willingness to cope with EU environmental policies rather than avoid the burden of environmental costs, partly influenced this result. The building up of governance capacities has been directly or indirectly driven by the EU. Overall, increasing pressure from the EU to comply with the evergrowing environmental *acquis* and regulatory requirements and the transfer of financial and cognitive resources through EU programs have helped to strengthen the capacities of both state and nonstate actors and, in doing so, to achieve better levels of compliance. This chapter traces the evolution of environmental governance in Portugal across three areas of environment regulation: water, air pollution and nature protection. It seeks to assess the extent to which the strengthening of state actors' capacities has created the conditions for the improvement of effectiveness in the adoption of and adaptation to the environmental *acquis* of the EU.

Environmental policy in Portugal

Environmental policy in Portugal had barely developed at the time of accession to the EC. Environmental issues entered the Portuguese governmental agenda for the first time in 1971 when the interministerial National Commission for Environment was established in order to deal with Portugal's involvement in the UN Stockholm Conference in 1972 (Calder, 1996). Hitherto, environmental protection had never been an issue in itself but rather a complement of other public policies. While the first Portuguese water law was enacted as far back as 1919 (Decree-Law [D-L] 5787), it had no environmental intentions but rather reflected a concern about human health.

Between the mid-1970s and early 1980s, Portugal witnessed several futile attempts to elevate the institutional status of environmental policy, including the creation of the Ministry of Social Equipment and Environment in 1974, which was suppressed the same year in the event of the 'Revolution of the Flowers'; the creation of the Ministry of Life Quality in 1983, which disappeared just one year later (Calder, 1996), and the creation of a State Secretariat for the Environment and Natural Resources (SEARN), which was integrated into the Ministry of Planning and Territorial Administration shortly before accession.

These difficulties in developing a stable environmental institutional structure hampered the domestic promotion of environmental policies. Instability was reinforced by the considerable extent of horizontal fragmentation of environmental responsibilities and the absence of instruments of effective coordination (Magone, 1997; Gonçalves, 2002). The transformation of the SEARN into the Ministry of Environment and Natural Resources in 1990 proved insufficient to overcome the traditional dispersal and low degree of coordination of environmental competencies among ministries, including the Ministry of Industry and Energy and the Ministry of Agriculture.[1] At the same time, the Ministry of Environment and Natural Resources was understaffed and lacked qualified personnel both to interpret and to implement effectively EU regulations in areas for which there was no previous national experience.[2]

In addition to limited national capacities, the requirement of EU environmental policies for the adoption of preventive, horizontal and participatory approaches collided with an administrative culture characterized by command-and-control policy making, low levels of public participation and an inactive civil society (Bruneau and Macleod, 1986; Gonçalves, 2002). Moreover, economic and social priorities dominated the political agenda. Before accession, the buildup of democratic institutions, the control of macroeconomic imbalances, the acceleration of the industrialization and modernization of agriculture and the development of welfare state policies (Magone, 1997), particularly in the education and health sectors, left little room for environmental policy (Cazes, Domingo and Gauthier, 1985; Bruneau and Macleod, 1986; Neves Sequeira, 2001). At the same time, the decolonization of Portuguese territories in Africa, which, *inter alia*, involved the return of half-a-million people to Portugal in the late 1970s, increased the social and economic pressure on the Portuguese government and maintained the low profile of environmental concerns among both the political elite and society (Magone, 1997; Neves Sequeira, 2001). As a result, the country became a policytaker rather than a policyshaper in EU environmental policy.

Environmental policy and the challenge of accession

As with the other two Southern European countries, Portugal's accession to the EU has had a decisive influence in fostering the adoption of environmental legislation (Magone, 1997; Figueiredo, Fidélis and Pires, 2001). Following accession, the political institutionalization of environmental policy was drastically accelerated with the adoption of the Environmental Framework Act in April 1987 (Law 11/87 of 7 April) and the creation of the National Institute for the Environment in 1989 and the Ministry of Environment and Natural Resources in 1990 (Calder, 1996).

However, ineffective implementation as a result of state actors' scarce resources was the rule rather than the exception. Environmental policy was one of the areas of the *acquis communautaire* where Portugal had considerable problems adjusting to the underlying logic and the capacity requirements attached to positive EU integration. Environmental directives required preventive problem-solving approaches, significant investment in infrastructure and the industrial base, effective vertical and horizontal coordination skills, knowledge and expertise. During the years following accession, such requirements challenged Portugal's state capacities. In institutional terms, the environmental administration reproduced patterns of hierarchy, rigidity and centralization (Magone, 2003), with relatively uncooperative relationships between national and local governments (Cazes, Domingo and Gauthier, 1985; D'Oliveira Martins, 1991; Gonçalves, 2002; Jordana, Levi-Faur and Puig, 2005).

Weak administrative capacity met with enormous economic costs imposed by the implementation of the EU environmental *acquis*. At the time of accession, Portugal remained one of the most underdeveloped countries in Western Europe with a per capita GDP of around 60 percent of the EU average. The level of industrialization was weak and agricultural production was particularly inefficient with 28 percent of the economically active population producing 12 percent of the GDP (Cazes, Domingo and Gauthier, 1985; Bruneau and Macleod, 1986; Sapelli, 1995). In this context, Portugal gave priority to addressing the macroeconomic imbalances that had dominated the economic environment during the years prior to accession and the implementation of structural reforms, especially in the field of transport infrastructure and energy supply, in order to converge with its European counterparts (Ramus, 1991). In addition, while there was a gradual increase in public expenditure on education and health, environmental policies lagged far behind. For instance, public expenditure on pollution abatement and control during the years following accession represented just 0.5 percent of the GDP (OECD, 1993).[3]

In spite of capacity shortcomings, state actors did not seek to involve nonstate actors and their resources to facilitate compliance for at least three reasons. First, while Portugal started to adopt environmental regulations after accession, for example the 1987 Environmental Framework Act, the concern of public authorities about complying with EU environmental policy remained weak. Second, nonstate actors often lacked the capacity to become effectively involved in the policy process, particularly in cases of technical directives such as the air pollution regulations, which required a high degree of scientific expertise. In other cases, nonstate actors themselves were unwilling to cooperate with state actors, either. This is particularly true for small and medium size industries, which have shown scant interest in helping to enforce costly policies that, in their view, could harm their competitiveness (Queiros, 2003). Third, the prevailing culture of public intervention, which has been characterized as paternalist and nonpluralistic (D'Oliveira Martins, 1991), together with low levels of environmental activism, hindered cooperation between state and nonstate actors.

This situation slowly changed throughout the 1990s with gradual progress in capacity building. Administrative reforms, which resulted in the creation of the Ministry of Environment and National Resources in 1990, elevated the political profile of environmental policy and improved the capacity for coordination. Along with institutional upgrading, Portugal made considerable improvements in the integration of environmental concerns in the decision-making process which resulted, for instance, in the adoption of the first National Plan of Environmental Policy in 1995.[4] In addition, public expenditure on environmental protection gradually increased and reached 0.85 percent of the GDP in 1996.[5] These internal factors gradually enhanced state capacity and created better conditions for the emergence of new modes of environmental governance.

State actors' increasing dependence on nonstate actors' resources appears to have been the main rationale behind this trend. Increasingly willing to cope with EU environmental policies rather than avoid the burden of environmental costs, state actors became more receptive to the opening of the policy process to nonstate actors. Both compliance pressure from the EU and growing societal mobilization as a result of rising environmental awareness have significantly contributed to this change in attitude (Carter, Nunes da Silva and Magalhaes, 2000). Major changes in governance structures included the creation of new arenas for public consultation, such as the National Council for the Environment and Sustainable Development, which was established in 1997,[6] the occasional adoption of legally binding contracts by which industry committed itself to (over)comply with environmental policies (Cabugueira, 2004) and, above all, the outsourcing of technical aspects of practical implementation, more particularly those related to obtaining scientific knowledge to overcome gaps in knowledge and expertise. However, in all cases, nonstate actors' involvement in the implementation of environmental policies remained limited, steered from the top and selectively applied. State actors maintained their control of the participatory agenda; they involved nonstate actors as long as state capacities have been sufficient to steer the process but insufficient in terms of material and cognitive resources.

The slow emergence of new modes of governance helped to improve the problemsolving capacity for environmental policies. However, other key factors, and in particular the push and pull of the combined pressure of the EU and environmental groups on the Portuguese government, also seem to account for the gradual improvement in effective implementation. On the one hand, EU incentives and constraints – namely resource transfer, legal requirements and infringement proceedings – played a relevant role in the improvement of compliance. EU advice, funds and programs, such as the Cohesion Funds, which involved an environmental input of 1,559.4 million euros for the 1993–99 period (European Commission, 2001), or the EU POLIS or LIFE initiatives, helped to transfer money and expertise to state actors. Besides, since the 1990s, continuous EU compliance pressure, infringement proceedings and judgments by the ECJ have contributed to improving domestic environmental awareness and willingness to comply. On the other hand, the regulatory requirements of certain directives, such as the WFD and the IPPCD, for public involvement strengthened nonstate actors by giving them new opportunities for participation and direct action (Arriscado Nunes, 2004).

Overall, effective adoption of and adaptation to EU environmental policy has improved over the years largely but not solely due to the emergence of new modes of governance. The reinforcement of state capacitiesand increasing willingness to cope with the EU's environmental requirements as a result of the combined pressure on the Portuguese government from above and from below appear to have been crucial and complementary explanatory factors for the achievement of better levels of compliance. They also helped to foster the emergence of new modes of governance by strengthening the capacity of both state and nonstate actors to engage in cooperation.

The following section analyzes the implementation of EU environmental policies in the areas of water, air and nature protection and examines in more detail the role of new modes of governance and other factors influencing the adoption of and adaptation to the environmental *acquis* in Portugal.

Coping with the challenge of accession

Water management: the state remains in control

EU accession marked a major turning point in Portugal's water policy. Before the country joined the EC, this policy sector was barely developed. National legislation on water management and planning was almost inexistent. Shortly after becoming an EU member, the country started to adopt specific regulations in this area. In 1987, different types of protected waters were defined in the Environment Framework Act 11/87.

Apart from being scarcely developed, the prior domestic policy on drinking water was only partially compatible with the requirements contained in the DWD. In particular, the parametrical values and the methods of analysis contained in EU regulations did not match national regulations. In addition, large investments had to be made and a great deal experience and technical capacity were needed to bring the water supply and sanitation sectors up to the standards prescribed in the directive (Thiel, 2004).

The legal transposition of the DWD suffered a significant delay. Financial, cognitive and, above all, administrative capacity shortcomings partly account for this result. The enforcement of the DWD imposed considerable costs of domestic adaptation, in particular as regards the development of more stringent quality standards, parametrical values and methods of analysis. Following accession, these technical and scientific oriented requirements met with limited expertise in the Portuguese administration. The Water Institute, which is the central authority responsible for the implementation of drinking water policy at the Ministry of Environment, was created only in 1993.

The EU directive was first incorporated into national legislation in 1990 (D-L 74/90), eight years after the deadline expired. The EU considered the transposition of the directive to be deficient, and, as a result, the drinking water legislation was corrected in 1998 through D-L 236/98 on the quality of water intended for human consumption.[7] This new regulation established parametrical values and methods of analysis and defined the responsibilities of water suppliers as regards quality controls, instating, *inter alia*, the obligation to report to the Environment Institute the results of analyses and, if needs be, the corrective measures adopted. Inspection tasks, evaluation of compliance with the parameters contained in the water legislation and information collection are responsibilities falling on the Ministry of Environment, with the assistance of the Waters of Portugal Group, a state-owned company in charge of securing the development of public policies and the strategic action for water supply and sanitation.[8] In parallel with this process, Portugal transposed Directive 83/1998 into the national legislation that revised the original DWD in 2001 (D-L 243/2001), modifying the list of parameters and altering some of the parametrical values included in the D-L 236/98. However, in 2005, the ECJ condemned Portugal for incomplete transposition and, in particular, for not complying with a series of drinking water parameters included in the Annex I of Directive 83/1998 (C-251/03). In a matter indirectly related to the DWDs, the ECJ also ruled against the Portuguese government for the infringement of Directive 75/440/CEE for not having created a systematic action plan including a timeframe for the cleaning of surface waters (C-214/97).

Despite deficiencies in legal transposition, effectiveness in the practical application of the DWDs has slowly improved over the years, especially after 2001, when the new, related, legislation came into effect. A national regulatory agency, the Institute Regulating Water and Waste (IRAR), was specifically created in 1997 for the adoption of and adaptation to the 1998 DWD.[9] The transposition of the DWD involved the Ministries of Environment, Agriculture and Industry, as well as a wide range of nonstate actors, including supply companies, associations of municipalities and environmental organizations. Improvement in its practical application has consisted mainly of better interadministrative coordination and relationships with the management entities, which are responsible for water quality control parameters through the IRAR, and a better follow-up of water management processes. This latter development is also partly a result of the tasks carried out by the IRAR, which broadly include the approval and verification of water quality control plans, inspection and follow-up tasks, as well as the elaboration of technical reports on water quality.[10]

However, some management problems still persist. The main limitations in the practical implementation of the DWD are related to the scarce financial resources available to improve distribution facilities and measurement technology, the lack of human and facility resources in order to monitor small supply companies, an insufficient number of water analyses conducted in order to guarantee the fulfillment of the standards for substances contained in water and the lack of capacities to react to insufficient standards.[11] In some cases, the Portuguese administration has relied on nonstate actors to overcome these problems but without this implying a dramatic change in the prevailing state-centered mode of governance. For instance, since 1993, the government has progressively opened the maintenance and operationalization of water supply services, which were previously under the authority of municipalities, to public-private or private companies in order to mitigate shortcomings in terms of municipal resources availability (D-L 379/93).[12] In other cases, slight variations in the domestic patterns of water governance have been shaped by EU funds and programs. Thus, three multimunicipality drinking water projects had been awarded Cohesion Fund financing by June 2006 (European Commission, 2006).[13] Another example was the creation of intermunicipality enterprises for water supply, sewage, waste treatment and final disposal. The EU POLIS Programme inspired the model by which public companies jointly owned by central and local governments were set up (Partidario and Nunes Correira, 2004). This model involved the creation of a commission of representatives of the main stakeholders. However, the experience to date demonstrates that the development of partnerships has been constrained by the weaknesses of the social partners at the local level and the unequal distribution of power between central and local organizations (Syrett, 1997).

The application of the DWDs in Portugal shows some emerging forms of new modes of governance. They mostly consist of the consultation of nonstate actors in both the transposition and the application of the directives, as well as the creation of intermunicipality companies. Other modes, such as self-regulation, voluntary agreements and independent agencies, are, however, nonexistent. Moreover, the slow trend towards privatization in the municipalities is absent at the intermunicipal level. Here, the state administration and, in particular, the Waters of Portugal Group, continues to play the leading role. The management and operation of multimunicipal systems are usually carried out by the state, or delegated to state enterprises and companies where the state is the sole or major shareholder.[14]

The implementation of the WFD has followed more inclusive schemes as regards the involvement of nonstate actors in the policy process. The adoption of the WFD challenged the Portuguese administration in several aspects. The first provisions related to water management and planning were those included in the Environmental Framework Act of 1987. A few years later, in 1994, three decree-laws were successively enacted in order to better regulate this policy sector (D-L 45/94; D-L 46/94; and D-L 47/94). Finally, in 2002, a National Water Plan was enacted through D-L 112/2002. Until the transposition of the WFD, these regulations constituted the main legal provisions for the planning, control and economic regime of the public hydrologic domain in Portugal. Adoption of the WFD entailed at the same time a considerable increase in and a revision of national regulation in this field. In brief, it involved the revision of the design and characterization of 'River Basin Districts', the adoption of an integrated approach as regards the planning and management of water policy, the application of the principle of cost recovery and the promotion of widespread public participation. This latter and explicit requirement contained in the directive is particularly unfitting in relation to the prior domestic legislation. Public participation had been contemplated in national legislation since the late 1990s, namely through the creation of the National Water Council in 1997 and the Commission of Dam Management in 1998. However, public involvement was almost limited to users, with societal actors in general remaining outsiders (Barreira, 2003).

The transposition of the WFD to Portuguese legislation suffered important delays mainly as a result of the significant mismatch between the EU requirements and the preexisting domestic policy, in particular with regard to problem-solving approaches and policy instruments. The application involved an in-depth reform of Portugal's water legislation, which faltered, however, because of the weakness of the technical, fiscal, administrative and engagement capacities necessary to effectively comply with the EU requirements. As a result, in 2004, the Commission launched an infringement proceeding for noncommunication of the transposition of the WFD against Portugal and, furthermore, the ECJ ruled against Portugal (C-118/05) (European Commission, 2007). The WFD was finally incorporated into national legislation through the 'Law of Water' 58/2005 and D-L 77/2006. In accordance with the requirement for an integrated approach stipulated by the WFD, the new Portuguese water law applies to all kinds of water resources, except drinking water and some other specific uses. In order to implement the directive effectively, the former central units of planning and management have been substituted with new demarcations that coincide with natural river basin boundaries. More specifically, ten River Basin Districts have been created.[15]

From the institutional point of view, the three main changes made in order to adapt to the requirements prescribed in the WFD have been the upgrading of the Water Institute at the national level,[16] the appointment of new competent authorities at the river basin level and the creation of new river consultative arenas securing public participation. First, the Water Institute was raised in importance by being given the status of a competent authority at the national level. The Water Institute is the single most important authority responsible for the implementation of water legislation in Portugal and, consequently, the implementation of the WFD. It depends directly on the Ministry of Environment and its main objective is the conservation of national water resources in physical and ecological terms.[17] Second, the implementation of the WFD has involved the appointment of new river authorities, the so-called 'Hydrographical Region Administrations', which are in charge of planning, management and financing, as well as auditing and controlling water policy at river basin level. Last but not least, adaptation to the EU regulation has also meant the creation of river district consultative and advisory institutions. Public participation was not completely new in domestic policy because the National Water Council, a consultative institution representing public administrations and the most important national professional and business organizations, and ENGOs already existed. However, the innovation consisted of establishing a similar structure at the level of the new river demarcations through the creation of the River Basin Councils. This new body, which was made up of representatives from the ministries, other administrative bodies, affected local governments and stakeholders, aimed especially at enhancing public participation in river-basin-specific issues.[18]

With the adoption of these measures, Portugal came into formal compliance with the EU law. However, an assessment of the degree to which these legal and institutional innovations have helped to ensure effective implementation reveals an uneven picture. The effective implementation of the WFD would have required changes concerning the institutional model of hydrological management and water administration in order to offer the necessary administrative authority and technical and economic capacities (Vieira, 2003). However, the capacities mobilized to implement effectively the requirements of the directive have been less than sufficient. Generally, the Portuguese government appeared to have scant concern for the need for a significant increase in human and fiscal resources in order to enforce the WFD. For instance, at the hydrographical basin level, the implementation of the directive has hardly been accompanied by the reinforcement of qualified technical staff and financial resources in order to apply the proper methodologies and to develop efficient monitoring systems.[19]

Another aspect that has met with difficulties in regards to effective implementation is the promotion of public participation. The involvement of nonstate actors has been formally improved through the National and River Basin Water Councils. However, two types of deficiencies have been identified in the functioning of these forums. On the one hand, nonstate actors have shown a rather passive attitude to participation in these consultative arenas. They often do not see the added value of taking part in the policy process through these channels.[20] On the other hand, operative deficiencies, in particular at the level of the River Basin Councils, have been observed, namely the difficulty of obtaining information and the poor and irregular participation of the representatives of water users (Barreira, 2003). Overall, state actors have shown little concern for the systematic implementation of consultative procedures. Likewise, nonstate actors have had hardly any means of influencing the policy process. Given the low expectations on both sides, the Tajo Basin Council, for instance, has not met since 2000 in spite of national legislation establishing a minimal periodicity of three months for the calling of meetings.[21]

In addition, gaps in information and organizational skills also constitute major problems in securing the practical implementation of the WFD. Both the EU, through the creation of working groups involving Portuguese and European experts, and nonstate actors, such as universities, have been involved in the process of practical implementation in order to counteract informational shortcomings and, in particular, the lack of know-how regarding the deployment of integrated hydrological methodologies. The scientific community, for instance, participated in the design of the River Basin Districts and is expected to maintain its privileged role when it comes to monitoring implementation.[22] However, as societal actors and ENGOs in particular have complained, in other cases, and especially at the river-basin level, significant deficiencies still persist. In the Guadiana Basin, for instance, public authorities have used a different nomenclature than stipulated in the WFD.[23]

Overall, water policy is one of the subfields of EU environmental regulation, in which the patterns of implementation are significantly influenced by the different problemsolving approaches and policy instruments promoted by the directives. The DWD is rooted in a traditional command-and-control approach. It gives a prominent role to state actors and leaves little room for the emergence of new modes of governance. On the contrary, the principles upon which the WFD is based explicitly require the opening of the policy process to nonstate actors, and in consequence, encourage, albeit timidly, the development of less hierarchical modes of governance. The consultation of nonstate actors partly accounts for the improvements in effective implementation since state actors have been able to draw on the resources offered by NGOs and policy experts to compensate for their weak capacities.

Industrial air pollution: squaring the circle

At the time of accession, Portugal's regulations on air pollution were quite limited. The main legislative act on air quality was the Environmental Framework Act, which was enacted in 1987. This established the general principles on which the Portuguese environmental policy had to be based and included, *inter alia*, the idea of an environmental license for the construction and operation of contaminating activities. When the LCPD and its 'mother' directive on Industrial Plant (IPD) were adopted, domestic legislation on reduction in the emission of pollutants from large combustion plants was almost nonexistent. In addition to a lack of prior experience, air protection and control were not priorities for the Portuguese government when it joined the EU. Throughout the 1980s, the main objective of the country was to catch up economically with its

European counterparts and, especially, to overcome its late industrialization. Portugal was dependent on coalfired energy for its development,
and, for this reason, wanted to maintain its consumption of high-sulfur
coal (Ramus, 1991).

Although Portugal had been allowed to increase emissions in order
to catch up with the economic development of Western industrialized states, the implementation of the LCPD still asked for a review of
political priorities, an assumption of significant economic costs and the
internalization of new technical procedures. In particular, it required
the adaptation of the whole energy production system and the development of a national emission reduction strategy for atmospheric pollutants (SO_2, NOX and combustion particles) from existing installations
(licensed before 1 July 1987) based on the use of BAT. Since Portugal
had no experience with precautionary and highly technology-based
policies, these requirements significantly challenged its financial and
technical capacities. Legal transposition did not suffer much delay.
Portugal incorporated the LCPD in 1990 (D-L 352/90).[24] However, effective application and enforcement were problematic, especially during
the early period (1990–2003).

Between 1990 and 2006, three successive emission reduction plans,
fixing emissions limits for eight of the 13 large combustion plants in
Portugal affected by the directive, were developed. It took several years
to draw up the first one, which was adopted in 1996, no fewer than six
years after the incorporation of the EU regulation into domestic law.
A second plan was developed in 2004. However, this did not meet the
expectations of the European Commission and led to the presentation
of a third plan in June 2006 (Ministry of the Environment and Ministry
of Energy and Innovation, 2006). This last plan, which came into force
on 1 January 2008, defines the national emission objectives for the
period 2008–15.

Apart from the initial reluctance to comply with a directive whose
economic cost, in particular as regards the installation of BAT, appeared
to be too high, during the years following accession both public administration and companies lacked technical knowledge on how to achieve
compliance. In particular, the difficulties in both interpreting the technical requirements of the directive and developing a national emission reduction plan hampered effective enforcement (Ramus, 1991).
However, this situation has slowly improved over the years.

The Portuguese administration has come under increasing pressure
from industrial operators seeking explanations and presenting their
concerns about technical aspects of the directive (Rodrigues et al.,

2004). As a result, the Portuguese government has started to rely on the scientific community's expertise in coping with the challenge of implementing highly technical directives without any correspondence at the national level. Until recently, the interpretation of the directive and implementation of the national emission reduction plan were mainly the responsibility of the LCP working group, which was created in 1990 under the umbrella of the Environment Institute and brought together representatives of the Environment Institute, the Ministry of Energy and Innovation and the operators of large combustion plants. In recent years, new actors, such as scientific experts, have become involved in the implementation process. Yet, the state administration still plays a central role and the participation of nonstate actors is limited to classical forms of consultation and advice. For example, in 2004 the University of Aveiro prepared a policy paper to lay down the foundations of a Portuguese emissions reduction strategy, encompassing the different EU directives on air protection and control (1999/13/EC, 2001/81/EC and 2001/80/EC), as well as Portugal's other international commitments (the Kyoto and Gothenburg Protocols). It closely collaborated with the Ministry of the Environment (Environment Institute Air Department) and also received input from industrial operators. The study served as the starting point for the adoption of a new legislative instrument on emissions control in April 2004 (D-L 78/2004) (Rodrigues et al., 2004).

The EU has also helped to improve implementation. Rather than exerting compliance pressure, it provided technical advice and financial support. In particular, the cooperation of Portuguese authorities with the European Commission on the methodology and guidelines to be applied in the design of the national emissions reduction plans have helped to internalize new energy production standards and, in doing so, to improve effective enforcement of emission policies.[25]

While the implementation of the LCPD did not involve a drastic departure from the Portuguese prevailing policy paradigm, the adoption of and adaptation to the IPPCD required major changes in Portuguese environmental policy. The content of the policy, the problemsolving approach and the policy instruments included in the IPPCD were completely new to Portugal. The country had neither a prior tradition of applying environmental parameters to the construction and operation of industrial installations, nor previous experience in the use of policy instruments, such as BAT, since Portugal had not implemented the relevant parts of the IPD and the LCPD.

According to the experts' evaluation report to the European Commission of June 2004, the implementation of the IPPCD could be assessed as 'fairly effective', considering the lack of previous or comparable experience. With state actors increasingly willing to comply with EU environmental law, the legal transposition of the EU directive into national legislation occurred without serious delay. It took place in 2000 (D-L 194/2000).[26] The EU requirements were incorporated without any substantial modifications and with a profusion of details of practical procedures (European Commission, 2004a). However, in terms of practical application, the balance is somewhat mixed. The transposition of the directive gave rise to a single environmental permit for those industrial installations specified in Annex I of the directive. In the case of Portugal, nearly 600 industrial installations were affected by the new environmental license (European Commission, 2004a).

In order to apply and enforce the IPPCD, a complex and fragmented administrative system was put into place within the Ministry of Environment, through the appointment of three different competent authorities for the different stages of the permit procedures: coordination, public consultation and issuance of the licenses. The competent authority for the coordination of the overall permit procedure is the so-called 'License Management Entity' (ECL),[27] which is also responsible for giving technical support and information on BAT to industry, while the competent authority for the issuing of environmental licenses is the Environment Institute. The Commissions of Regional Coordination and Development (CCDRs) are the regional interfaces between the ECL and the Environment Institute. These bodies are also responsible for public consultation and, in particular, for guaranteeing the availability of information on permit applications, in accordance with the requirements of the directive. This complex organizational distribution is a potential source of delays and problems regarding consistency, 'unless the communication and coordination between them is very effective' (European Commission, 2004a: 116). In addition, compliance monitoring tasks are also fragmented through the potential intervention of three authorities: the ECLs, the CCDRs and the Environment Institute, despite the prominence given to the General Inspection of the Environment (IGA) in this field.

In addition to lacking coordination capacities, even by 2007 the Portuguese government had not been able to set up a BAT system. The development of specific national guidance literature had not been completed mainly as a result of a lack of technical capacities at the domestic level. As a result, for the follow-up, promotion and publication of BAT criteria, Portugal then used only the BREF documents produced at the EU level. These guidelines were translated into and included in permit documents as an information source without any specific binding effect.[28] Moreover, the lack of prior experience in the implementation and use of BAT made it difficult even to interpret these European documents. At the end of 2001, Portugal created a specific commission, the Advisory Commission for Integrated Pollution Prevention and Control (CCPCIP) with the aim of studying and promoting the use of BAT as defined in the BREFs. In addition, working groups comprising individual experts, industrial associations, universities, technological centers and NGOs were constituted in 2002 in order to deal with the specific difficulties of six branches of activity (agrofoodstuffs, cement, metal, pulp and paper, chemicals and glass).[29] Thus, the Portuguese government built up new channels of consultation with external actors in order to overcome technical and informational shortcomings and, in particular, to interpret and select BATs as defined at the European level.

The EU has also helped to strengthen state actors' cognitive capacities. In particular, information and technical support from the European Commission have been key features of what our interviewees have called a good relationship based on reciprocal trust between the national and European levels.[30] Yet there have been and still are serious problems of interpretation at the operator level.[31] In spite of the information provided by the Portuguese government, the affected industrial and agricultural installations are still experiencing difficulties in assimilating the new environmental quality standards. Moreover, most of them share a certain resistance to a new and costly law that, from their point of view, might harm their competitiveness.[32] The fact that affected sectors have been kept out of the overall design of the transposition process is partly responsible for this. Public participation and, above all, the involvement of industry during the transposition stage were quite limited. As a result, familiarization with the principles and procedural requirements of the IPPCD and the overall effectiveness of implementation have been undermined. In January 2007, of the 670 installations affected, only 143 – some 25 percent – had the integrated environmental permit.[33]

Overall, air pollution is another sector of EU environmental regulation in which the modes in which directives are implemented vary. The comparative study of the LCPD, which is based on a classical command-and-control approach, and the IPPCD, which explicitly prescribes more inclusive modes of governance, reflects differences regarding the involvement of nonstate actors in the policy process. In the case of the LCPD, the implementation follows a traditional top-down scheme. The participation of nonstate actors is almost nonexistent, except in regard to some aspects of practical enforcement, where we found forms of consultation. In contrast, the implementation of the IPPCD reveals a more profile with more nonstate engagement. Here both consultation and some types of delegation have been employed. In both cases, the opening of the policy process to nonstate actors has helped to improve implementation.

Nature protection: upgrading biodiversity

Before accession, Portuguese legislation on nature conservation had barely been developed. The first reference to this question dates back to the 1970s when Portugal formally endorsed the Environment Declaration adopted at the UN Conference in Stockholm in 1972, which included nature conservation among its objectives. Shortly before accession, Portugal introduced some provisions on fauna conservation in the Hunting Act of 1985. However, national legislation standards were considerably below those of the EU and in the pre-accession period hardly any measures were taken in order to adapt to and adopt the Wild Birds Directive. First steps were taken only in 1988, when the Portuguese government developed its first list of SPAs for birds. Later on, in 1991, the Wild Birds Directive was incorporated into national legislation (D-L 75/91), while the FFHD was transposed into domestic law in 1997 (D-L 226/97), five years after the adoption of the directive by the EU. The lack of previous policies, scarce financial resources and poor expertise, combined with a low concern for nature conservation, appear to be the main reasons behind this lengthy delay.

Effectiveness in the adaptation to the Wild Birds Directive and FFHD has improved in recent years, in particular with regard to the growing number of protected areas. Tellingly enough, in 2008, Portugal designated nine new SPAs for steppic birds and two for Bonelli's Eagle (*Hieraaetus fasciatus*), enabling the Commission to close infringement cases opened in 1999 for noncompliance with nature protection legislation.[34] However, effective implementation seems still to be deficient. Some of the difficulties relate to insufficient financial resources devoted to protection of threatened species and a deficient governmental implementation strategy. Funding devoted to the implementation of the FFHD is almost nonexistent. Thus, while more SPAs have been designated, they are not properly protected in practice. The national government has been considering the possibility of transferring the management responsibilities to third-party actors, including municipalities and environmental groups, in order to save on enforcement costs.[35]

However, progress has been observed in other domains. For instance, in administrative terms, communication has improved between the Ministry of the Environment, and in particular the Institute for the Conservation of Nature, which is responsible for the implementation of the directives, and the Ministry of Agriculture, which is in charge of developing awareness of nature conservation in rural areas, where EU regulations such as Natura 2000 are usually badly perceived because of their potential impact on economic development.[36] Moreover, state actors have increasingly involved nonstate actors in the policy process. Even though the centralized structure of the state prevents a systematic delegation of functions to societal actors, consultations between public administration and environmental groups have been developed. The emerging patterns of collaboration between state and nonstate actors are partly EU driven and mainly consist of the provision of *expertise*. Environmental organizations, such as the Portuguese Society for the Study of Birds, received EU LIFE funds to coordinate the development of an inventory on marine birds in order to implement the Wild Birds Directive. Another EU LIFE project has enabled the same organization to coordinate the recovery of the habitat of the Azores Bullfinch (*Pyrrhula murina*) within an SPA. The project has been carried out in partnership with the Azores Regional Directorate of Forest Resources, the Regional Secretary of Environment and Sea, the Azores University and the RSPB.[37]

Interestingly, environmental groups have often pursued a dual strategy of cooperation and confrontation towards the Portuguese administration in order to pull it towards compliance with EU law. Thus, while the Portuguese Society for the Study of Birds has conducted studies and protection tasks towards the implementation of the Wild Birds Directive and FFHD, at the same time, it has filed several complaints to the European Commission denouncing the Portuguese administration for failing to meet the objectives of the two directives.[38]

In other cases, the European Commission has acted on its own initiative in opening infringement proceedings, for example when it recently sent a letter of warning to the Portuguese government asking it to comply with the ECJ ruling condemning Portugal for building a motorway linking Lisbon and the Algarve through the Castro Verde Special Protected Area (C-239/04). In response to the verdict, the Portuguese government initiated consultation with stakeholders to define nature compensation measures, although they still appear to be at an early stage.[39] Environmental groups fear, however, that EU compliance pressure may have unintended consequences that are detrimental to the environment. For example, the Portuguese government might decide not to declare new SPAs, before settling current infringement proceedings.[40]

Overall, EU push and pull factors have played a central role in the improvement of the effective implementation of the Wild Birds Directive and FFHD. On the one hand, the EU has put pressure on the Portuguese government by opening infringement proceedings. On the other hand, EU funding of projects for better implementation of nature conservation regulation and the consequent threat to national administrations of the suspension of EU funds for bad implementation, have been key in the slow improvement of effectiveness.

The EIAD, the implementation of which in Portugal is largely related to nature protection, presents similar patterns. Before the transposition of the EIAD into Portuguese national law in 1990 (D-L 186/90), the only legal provisions concerning the *ex ante* evaluation of the environmental consequences of investment projects were those included in Articles 30 and 31 of the Environment Framework Act of 1987. Article 30 laid out the procedural aspects of the evaluation process, while Article 31 specified the minimum components of the environmental impact assessment studies, namely, an analysis of the state of the environment and of the modifications involved in the project as well as the measures to be adopted to reduce and compensate for potential environmental damages. In this respect, environmental impact assessment was not completely new in Portuguese legislation. However, existing provisions were hardly developed in the first, very general and basic Portuguese environmental law of 1987. In this sense, the legal transposition and practical implementation of the EIAD involved a significant challenge for the Portuguese administration and, especially, for the Ministry of the Environment, which was in fact created the same year in which the EIAD was transposed into domestic law. The implementation of the EU regulation involved substantially upgrading environmental protection concerns and superimposing them onto investment project strategies; developing new institutional arrangements and, in particular, reinforcing interadministrative coordination in order to deal with cross-media regulation; improving technical evaluation skills and institutionalizing new forms of public participation. At the time of accession, Portugal lacked the qualified staff, scientific expertise and administrative capacities to cope with this multifaceted challenge.

The legal transposition of the EIAD resulted in some delays and followed a somewhat shaky path. The complexity of this cross-media

EU regulation and its impact on economic operators have been partly accountable for this situation.[41] Portugal incorporated the EU regulation into national law in 1990 (D-L 186/90), although the EU deadline was 1988. This law was first modified in 1997 (D-L 172/97) and a second modification was introduced in 2000 (D-L 69/2000) in order to add a provision concerning the binding character of the decisions of the Ministry of the Environment as regards the declaration of environment impact. The last modification took place in 2005 (D-L 197/2005) with the basic aim of improving transparency and enhancing public participation.

According to D-L 69/2000, the overall environmental impact assessment procedure encompasses six phases: selection of the projects, definition of the domain affected, study of the environmental impact, technical evaluation of the EIA study, decision and postassessment. The institution in charge of the overall process and, in particular, of the technical evaluation of the projects at the national level is the Environment Institute, whereas the CCDRs are involved at the regional level, mainly through the elaboration of notes aimed at harmonizing the interpretation of the EU regulation.

In order to meet the EU's requirement as regards public consultation, the Portuguese government created the Advisory Council of Environment Impact Assessment (CCAIA) in 2000.[42] This council is composed of representatives from civil society, industry, the scientific community and ENGOs, as well as representatives of the Environment Institute. Apart from public participation, its main function consists of giving technical support to the Ministry of the Environment. In addition, public participation is also channeled through the 'EIA Portuguese Association', which is a forum for dialog integrated by technical experts, members of the administration, environmental advisors, operators and ENGOs. This forum plays a significant role both as an arena for deliberation and as a think tank for the Ministry of the Environment.[43] Overall, a large group of actors is taking part in the enforcement of the EIAD, reflecting the increasing willingness of the Portuguese government to develop a consensual approach with regards to both transposition and practical implementation of the EU regulation. Apart from state actors' willingness to involve nonstate actors in order to compensate for a lack of capacities, one of the main rationales behind this involvement was to accommodate conflicting interests. In this sense, initiatives are still steered from the top and framed within a command-and-control approach.

In terms of effectiveness, the implementation of the EIAD was initially hindered by a double administrative weakness. On the one hand, the relative lack of scientific input and the absence of institutionalized forms of scientific advice for public administration and channels of public participation limited the scope of discussion with regards to the practical enforcement of the EIA regulation (Magone, 1997). This situation, along with a relatively inactive civil society, helped to maintain the *status quo* of traditional administrative practice, which is most typically centralized and hierarchically organized (Gonçalves, 2002). On the other hand, the separation between planning and EIA, the non-binding nature of final recommendations before the reform of 2000 and the absence of effective control mechanisms during the construction of projects were additional domestic impediments to the effective enforcement of the directive (Pinho, 1997). According to some studies, about 22 percent of EIAs in Portugal contain incomplete information, while no EIAs were found to cover all information requirements (Canelas et al., 2005).

However, over the years, the quality of the EIAs has been considerably ameliorated, especially during the period 1998–2003 (Canelas et al., 2005). Patterns of public consultation also improved throughout the 1990s and after the last legal reform of 2005. Changes include the adoption of mechanisms to incorporate scientific expertise into decisionmaking as well as the institutionalization of new forms of citizen participation, which appear to be greater than EU requirements (Gonçalves, 2002). Meetings between the Environment Institute, the operators and representatives of the local areas affected not only during the EIA procedure but also during the design of the project have also helped to strengthen mutual trust. Consultation procedures during the transposition stage and the delegation of cognitive-related tasks during practical implementation, as well as growing transparency, have increased environmental awareness both among state and nonstate actors, diminished conflicts and improved overall compliance with the EIAD.[44] One of the indicators that reveals the gradual improvement of effective enforcement is the growing number of operators asking for information before starting their projects.[45] The overall balance is therefore quite positive, as compliance has everywhere improved with respect to the first period. However, deficiencies still persist. For example, significantly, 282 EIA procedures initiated between May 1995 and September 2007 were still in the process of evaluation at the end of the latter year.[46] In practice, such administrative delays can dissuade investment projects.

The willingness of state actors to improve compliance with the EIAD, not least through seeking cooperation with nonstate actors, has been fostered by combined pressure from above and from below. On the one hand, the Portuguese government has come under continuous compliance pressure from the European Commission and the ECJ. Infringement proceedings have often originated from complaints lodged by environmental organizations. For instance, the three main Portuguese ENGOs – Quercus, the Liga para a Protecçao da Naturaleza (the League for the Protection of Nature) and GEOTA – denounced the Tagus bridge (Vasco da Gama) project (a project benefiting from EU funding) in 1995 for violating the EIAD. The Portuguese government reacted in June 1996 by asking the three ENGOs to compose a memorandum on the necessary measures to be applied in order to minimize and compensate for the environmental impact (Calder, 1996). Growing pressure from ENGOs has helped to increase the exposure of environmental issues in the media and, as a result, to raise public environmental awareness (Carter, Nunes da Silva and Magalhaes, 2000). In other cases, the European Commission has been actively involved on its own initiative. For example, the Commission referred Portugal to the ECJ for allowing the construction of a tourist complex including residential units in the area of Cascais-Sintra without a prior EIA and as result, in April 2004, the ECJ condemned Portugal for failing to comply with the requirements of the EIAD (C-117/02).

To sum up, both the FFHD and EIAD present some similarities with regards to the key factors accounting for the improvement of effective implementation. In both cases, the involvement of nonstate actors mainly through consultation has played an important role in fostering better levels of effective implementation.

Conclusion

The accession of Portugal to the EC in 1986 entailed significant costs regarding the adoption of and adaptation to the environmental *acquis*. EU directives require preventive problem-solving approaches, investment, interadministrative coordination skills, knowledge and expertise. During the years following accession, such requirements significantly challenged Portugal, which lacked the necessary capacities to cope with EU environmental regulations. Despite their lack of capacities, state actors did not resort at this time to cooperation with nonstate actors in order to compensate for their weaknesses and share the burden of implementation.

However, this situation started to change in the late 1990s. Over time, the Portuguese government has gradually improved its capacity to interpret environmental directives, identify cognitive gaps, adapt administrative structures, coordinate processes and mobilize key actors and networks providing information and scientific knowledge in order to address the technical complexity of EU environmental regulation. Induced by compliance pressure from both above and below, and faced with persistent deficiencies regarding capacities to cope with the burden of environmental costs, state actors have become more inclined to open the policy process to nonstate actors, mainly through the development of channels of consultation and the delegation of expertise-related tasks.

Yet, the emergence of new, more inclusive modes of governance has been uneven and unsystematic. Nonstate actors have provided information and expertise but only if state actors have been able to control the policy process, as has been the case for the EIAD and FFHD. The implementation of the other EU directives shows less engagement of nonstate actors. Particularly where there are more traditional command-and-control policies, such as the LCPD and DWDs, the Portuguese government has limited participatory schemes to the creation of working groups involving state and nonstate actors. The specific legal EU requirements for enhancing public involvement in each case largely account for such variations.

The slow emergence of new modes of governance has helped to improve the effectiveness of implementation by strengthening state capacities. The combined push and pull by the EU and ENGOs have not only increased the willingness and capacity of state and nonstate actors to cooperate with each other, but have also directly impacted on the gradual improvement of effectiveness. EU and domestic pressure to comply with the environmental *acquis* and financial and technical assistance through EU funds and programs have helped to strengthen the capacities of state actors and, in doing so, to promote effective implementation.

Notes

1. Interview, Ministry of the Environment, Lisbon, 7 December 2006.
2. Interview, Ministry of the Environment, Lisbon, 23 March 2006.
3. By way of comparison, EU funding represented 4.7 percent of GDP in 1993. See Drain, 1994.
4. OECD Environmental Performance Review of Portugal. http://www.oecd. org, (last access: 11 June 2007).
5. http://epp.eurostat.ec.europa.eu/portal, (last access: 11 June 2007).
6. Decree-Law 221/97.

7. D-L 236/98.
8. http://www.maotdr.gov.pt/, (last access: 6 December 2007).
9. Decree-Law 230/97.
10. http://www.irar.pt, (last access: 27 March 2008).
11. Interview, Ministry of the Environment, Lisbon, 7 December 2006.
12. http://ec.europa.eu/environment/env-act5/chapt2-4.htm, (last access: 26 March 2008).
13. http://ec.europa.eu/environment/env-act5/chapt2-4.htm, (last access: 24 February 2008).
14. http://ec.europa.eu/environment/env-act5/chapt2-4.htm, (last access: 26 March 2008).
15. Minho and Lima; Cávado, Ave and Leça; Douro; Vouga, Mondego, Lis and Ribeiras do Oeste; Tajo; Sado e Mira; Guadiana; Ribeiras do Algarve; Açores; Madeira. It must be taken into account that more than half of the hydraulic resources in Portugal belong to Portuguese-Spanish rivers (Minho and Lima, Douro, Tajo and Guadiana), with their management being shared with Spain.
16. In April 2007, the Environment Institute and the Waste Institute were merged into the new Portuguese Environment Agency (APA).
17. http://www.inag.pt, (last access: 25 March 2008).
18. http://www.inag.pt, (last access: 25 March 2008).
19. http://iberaqua.com.sapo.pt, (last access: 6 December 2007).
20. Interview, Ministry of the Environment, Lisbon, 7 December 2006.
21. http://iberaqua.com.sapo.pt, (last access: 6 December 2007).
22. Interview, Ministry of the Environment, Lisbon, 7 December 2006.
23. http://iberaqua.com.sapo.pt, (last access: 6 December 2007).
24. The updated directive (2001/80/EC) was incorporated into national law in 2003 (D-L 178/2003).
25. Interview, Environment Institute, IPPC Department, Lisbon, 7 December 2006.
26. Modified by D-L 69/2003 and by D-L 233/2004.
27. In 2007, the number of ECLs was 24.
28. European Union Network for the Implementation and Enforcement of Environmental Law, Implementation and Use of BREF, Final Report, 18 April 2005.
29. http://www.iambiente.pt, (last access: 26 March 2008).
30. Interview, Environment Institute, IPPC Department, Lisbon, 7 December 2006.
31. Interview, Environment Institute, IPPC Department, Lisbon, 7 December 2006.
32. Interview, Environment Institute, IPPC Department, Lisbon, 7 December 2006
33. Source: Ministry of Environment, Territorial Planning and Regional Development, http:www.maotdr.gov.pt, (last access: 23 January 2007).
34. New designated SPAs for steppic birds (Great Bustard *Otis tarda*, Little Bustard *Tetrax tetrax* and Lesser Kestrel *Falco naumanni*): Vila Fernando, Veiros, Sao Vicente, Piçarras, Monforte, Reguengos, Evora, Cuba/Alvito and Torre da Bolsa. New SPAs for Bonelli's Eagle *Hieraaetus fasciatus*: Monchique and Caldeirao. http://europa.eu/rapid/ (IP/08/1803), (last access: 4 December 2008).

35. Interview, SPEA, Lisbon (http://www.spea.pt), December 2006.
36. Interview, Ministry of Environment, Lisbon, December 2007.
37. http://www.spea.pt, (last access: 11 June 2007).
38. Interview, Portuguese Society for the Study of Birds, Lisbon, 7 December 2006.
39. http://europa.eu/rapid/ (IP/07/393), (last access: 11 June 2007).
40. http://www.spea.pt/, (last access: 11 June 2007).
41. See the preamble of D-L 69/2000.
42. D-L 69/2000, modified by D-L 197/2005.
43. http://www.apai.org.pt, (last access: 26 March 2008).
44. Interview, Ministry of Environment, Lisbon, 23 March 2006.
45. Interview, Environment Institute, Lisbon, 22 March 2006.
46. Environment Institute, www.iambiente.pt, (last access: 16 December 2007).

6

Spain: When Government Welcomes Environmental Governance

Nuria Font and Ana Mar Fernández

Introduction

When Spain entered the EC in 1986, the country was a young democracy facing institutional consolidation and confronting the challenge of economic stability and growth. Membership of the EU has provided ideational and material benefits by acknowledging Spain's newly established democratic institutions, supporting the process of economic modernization and offering international acceptance following the breakdown of the Franco regime in the mid-1970s. However, EU membership also entailed significant administrative and political costs, especially in regulatory domains such as the environmental sector, which, at the time of accession, was not a priority on the domestic agenda. Spanish environmental policy was weakly institutionalized and most of the time did not fit EU environmental policies and principles. Administrative, technical and financial capacities, required to meet EU environmental standards, were lacking, with compliance problems being the rule rather than the exception. Despite capacity shortcomings, state actors did not systematically adopt cooperative schemes involving nonstate actors that would allow them to pool resources and share the burden of compliance. The legacies of a hierarchical and state-centered administrative culture impaired the emergence of more cooperative modes of governance.

During the 1990s, conditions for the emergence of more inclusive governance arrangements became more favorable. A combination of internal and EU-driven factors largely accounts for these transformations. Internally, gradual improvement in the macroeconomic situation, the building of institutional arrangements and increasing readiness to implement EU environmental policies rather than avoid them were of crucial importance. Together with internal factors, most of the changes were primarily driven by EU push and pull. The EU has considerably influenced the implementation of directives by adopting a combined strategy of increasing pressure for compliance, building technical and financial capacities and imposing legal requirements for the involvement of nonstate actors. Based on systematic analysis of environmental policies in the areas of water, industrial air pollution and nature protection, this chapter traces conditions favoring the emergence of new modes of governance and assesses the extent to which they have helped to improve the effective adoption of and adaptation to the environmental *acquis*.

Environmental policy in Spain

The beginnings of Spanish environmental policy date back to the early 1970s. Preparing for participation in the 1972 UN Conference on the Environment and in an attempt to improve the excessive fragmentation of environmental management, the Spanish government created the Inter-departmental Commission on the Environment. In addition, in 1972, it enacted regulation of air pollution (Font and Morata, 1998). However, these measures proved insufficient to boost environmental policy in the following years. In the late 1970s and 1980s, the transition to and consolidation of democracy, as well as the need to face major social and economic challenges, were given much greater importance. Thus, at the time of EC accession in the mid-1980s, domestic environmental issues ranged low on the domestic political agenda in relation to other political, economic and social priorities (Font and Morata, 1998). With massive unemployment and a comparative stagnation of per capita income, the main priorities of successive governments centered on achieving macroeconomic stability and growth (Boix, 1998; Alberola, 2001;), the initiation of a cautious liberalization process (Molina, 2001), increased flexibility of labor policy combined with the adoption of wage restraint measures (Aguilera, 2001) and the reorganization of an obsolete and uncompetitive industrial base (Saro, 2001). Moreover, the implementation of core welfare policies, and in particular the creation of educational, health and pension systems, was among the major concerns of the government.

In addition to the achievement of macroeconomic stability and social modernization, the implementation of the 'State of the Autonomies', which created 22 regional authorities and implied a deep transformation of the national power structure towards a quasi-federalstate, was, and has been since the early 1980s, a major political issue. The Spanish constitution distributed powers between the national, regional and local administrations in a number of policy areas, including education, health, agriculture, housing, public works, transport and environmental protection. With regards to the environment, the national administration retained competences over planning and the adoption of framework legislation, whereas the autonomous communities were responsible for the specification and implementation of these laws. At the same time, local authorities had a wide range of environmental competences.

The transfer of environmental powers to regional administrations throughout the 1980s and early 1990s was accompanied by a national reorganization of environmental policy. On the one hand, most environmental competences, and in particular those on nature conservation, which had traditionally been assigned to the Ministry of Agriculture, were progressively transferred to other parts of the state administration. Yet, those changes hardly contributed to the mitigation of interdepartmental rivalries (Font, 2001a). On the other hand, the successive upgrading of the highest rank of environmental administration, which rested with a General Directorate of the Environment within the Ministry of Public Works at the time of accession, began in 1990 and concluded with the creation of the Ministry of the Environment in 1996.

The gradual but slow institutionalization of environmental policy after accession broadened the opportunities available for direct participation by nonstate actors in the policy process and served as a catalyst for political action, although their access was limited and scarcely institutionalized (Börzel, 2003a) and it was not until 1994 that the National Environmental Council was established. Over recent years, such relationships have evolved into more inclusive patterns and, in particular, nonstate actors with economic interests retain informal contacts with state actors, especially at the regional level. The scientific community has progressively become more involved in the formulation and implementation of technical policies, while at least until the late 1980s, environmental groups were perceived as radical activists (Jiménez, 2001). Broadly speaking, state actors' capacities for engagement have been enhanced since the mid-1990s as they have gradually been less reluctant to mobilize key actors into providing information and scientific knowledge. In turn, both industry and environmental groups have recently adopted a more cooperative strategy.

Environmental policy and the challenge of accession

Spanish accession to the EC confronted the national administration with the challenge of incorporating and effectively implementing a huge number of environmental directives. While specific aspects of air pollution and nature conservation were already regulated prior to accession, environmental policies had remained largely ineffective (Weale et al., 2000). Following accession, it soon became clear that Spain was one of the member states least adapted to the task of implementing EU environmental directives (European Commission, 1992) and would be unable to comply effectively with EU environmental legislation (Christiansen and Tangen, 2002). Unlike in the case of the Eastern enlargement, the European Commission did not at first exert much compliance pressure on the Spanish government despite a significant deficit in implementation (Börzel, 2003a).

State actors' financial, administrative, cognitive and engagement capacities were too weak to deal with the huge costs that the implementation of environmental directives entailed. With a per capita GDP well below the EU average (OECD, 1998), limited financial resources and a clear preference for socioeconomic development, Spain committed a comparatively low part of public expenditure to comply with EU environmental regulation. For instance, expenditure on pollution abatement and control during the years following accession represented about 0.5 percent of GDP, while in most European member states it reached between 0.7 and 1 percent (OECD, 1993).

In addition to financial shortcomings, the country's administrative capacities were too weak to cope with the challenge of accession. The absence of an environmental ministry capable of elaborating long-term plans and coordinating environmental policies was the most visible, but not the only, limitation following accession. Upgrading of the institutional rank of the environmental administration between 1990 and 1993 gave rise to the creation of the Ministry of Public Works, Transport and the Environment. However, such institutional changes continued to leave environmental policy largely dependent on a ministry with few environmental concerns. The epistemic community within the ministry, which was responsible for most environmental questions until the mid-1990s, was dominated by civil engineers whose technical orientation made them largely hostile to societal engagement.[1] In addition to internal pressures against environmental protection, the long-standing rivalries between the Ministry of Public Works, Transport and the Environment and the Ministry of Agriculture undermined effective implementation, particularly in the case of nature conservation directives (Aguilar Fernández, 2003).

In spite of limited capacities, state actors were not ready to involve nonstate actors in order to obtain the resources necessary to adapt to EU environmental requirements. First, environmental protection was not a salient issue in the political agenda and, as a result, national administrations did not prioritize compliance with EU directives (Font and Morata, 1998). Second, domestic administrative traditions were characterized by an overwhelming use of command-and-control, legalistic and reactive patterns of policymaking (Börzel, 2003a), with pluralistic arenas for public participation almost nonexistent (Pridham, 1994). Finally, nonstate actors had limited technical, cognitive and economic resources for effective involvement in the implementation process. In this respect, the long-standing absence of adequate administrative structures was aggravated by understaffed environmental administrations facing difficulties in interpreting the technical requirements contained in EU environmental regulation (Molina, 2000).

However, this situation was gradually transformed throughout the 1990s as environmental protection gained budgetary and political . On the one hand, public expenditure on the environment rose from 1.78 percent of total public expenditure to 2.39 percent between 1987 and 1992.[2] On the other hand, the creation of the Ministry of the Environment in 1996 ended long-standing interdepartmental conflicts and sought to make environmental protection a more cohesive policy area (Aguilar Fernández, 2003). In spite of the institutional upgrading, the Ministry of the Environment's position has been relatively weak *vis-à-vis* other ministries, which have been reluctant either to transfer powers or to incorporate environmental considerations into sectoral policies.

Increasingly willing to meet EU environmental requirements, state actors were gradually persuaded of the benefits of cooperating with nonstate actors. Throughout the 1990s, new participatory arrangements were created in order to obtain crucial resources for implementation. These generally entailed consultation, delegation and outsourcing. Yet, the involvement of nonstate actors in environmental policies has been relatively weak and top-down, with state actors being unwilling to give up control over the policy process.

The emergence of more inclusive modes of environmental governance such as it has been, is largely accounted for by the pull and push factors resulting from both domestic environmental mobilization and EU strategies aimed at improving implementation records.

On the one hand, environmental groups have found new regulatory resources as well as access points to the policy process. On the other hand, EU regulatory, distributive and sanctioning activities have contributed to the reshaping of Spanish environmental policy. First, the participatory requirements contained in many environmental directives have encouraged national administrations to create participatory institutional arrangements. Second, EU technical and financial capacity building mechanisms, notably the Cohesion Fund but also financial instruments such as LIFE, have contributed to some steps forward in the implementation process. Remarkably, around 28 percent of the total Cohesion Fund for the period 1993–99 funded environmental projects in Spain, with priority given to water supply and treatment and quality control projects (European Commission, 2001). Finally, constant EU compliance pressure on national government through infringement proceedings and ECJ judgments has contributed to improving effectiveness.

The emergence, however embryonic, of new modes of governance has largely influenced the ways in which environmental policies have been implemented over recent years. The following section examines the implementation of EU environmental directives on water management, industrial air pollution and nature protection, and explores both EU and domestic drivers of change in the modes in which environmental policies are processed.

Coping with the challenge of accession

Water management: mixed patterns of policymaking

The Spanish water sector has traditionally been a sensitive policy area because of historical problems of scarcity and the uneven geographical distribution of water across the territory. Water quality issues have traditionally been problematical but less noticeable in the political agenda. The combination of cyclical droughts with a rapid increase in the number and type of water uses over the past decades has led water policy to become a focal point of public intervention and an object of great social discontent and distributive conflict. The traditional approach to dealing with the water issue has consisted of the promotion of state-subsidized, large-scale infrastructure, namely dams and water diversions, in order to satisfy increasing demand for water. Yet, we can observe a recent trend towards a more integrated water regime. Although water management approach continues to regulate supply, it draws on alternative modes of intervention that appear to be more oriented to sustainability. While it is too early to assess whether those developments are constitutive of a regime change, it seems that the need to implement EU directives, and in particular the participatory requirements contained in the WFD, may open new avenues for change. In contrast, the implementation of the DWDs followed a more traditional and less problematic path.

Prior to accession, drinking water in Spain was regulated by the Technical Health Regulation of the Supply and Quality Control of Drinking Water, which was adopted in 1982. This defined drinking water for human consumption and fixed the technical and health standards for the supply, treatment, distribution and quality control of such water. The regulation absorbed most of the requirements contained in the first DWD, namely on the definition of drinking waters, the method of analysis and the list of parameters, although the directive was in some aspects more demanding (Börzel, 2003a). The directive was formally incorporated into Spanish legislation in 1990 through the Real Decreto [Royal Decree] (RD) 1138/1990, which merged previously separate pieces of legislation. Later, Directive 98/83/EC on the quality of water intended for human consumption, which included new parameters and health criteria, was transposed by RD 140/2003 establishing the sanitary criteria guaranteeing the quality of water for human consumption.

The implementation of the DWD posed capacity problems for state actors as it implied considerable adaptation costs, in particular with regard to investment in monitoring procedures. Various cases of incomplete and incorrect transposition were reported for the period 1993–95 and 1996–98. In particular, legislation contained less stringent values for some parameters than those of the first DWD and some waivers were in place for a number of parameters because of the nature and structure of the soil and because of drought (Kiwa, 2002). Beyond transposition, the practical application of the two DWDs presents mixed results. Effective implementation has involved a wide range of state and nonstate actors, which has led to the emergence of more encompassing modes of governance. The Ministry of Health and Consumption is responsible for the establishment of quality standards, the monitoring of water quality and coordination of water analysis and sanitary control. Regional health administrations are in charge of monitoring tasks and have the responsibility of informing the national administration in cases of failure to comply with quality standards. Municipal administrations are responsible for carrying out analysis at the point of delivery (the consumer's tap). Finally, suppliers of water for human consumption are in charge of water analysis and control tasks. As regards the provision of water services, delegation to private companies through public-private partnerships (PPPs) is increasingly common.

Insufficient monitoring capacities, especially at the municipal level, have traditionally made it difficult to assess Spain's compliance with the DWDs (Börzel, 2003a). The quality of drinking water is generally satisfactory, although some parameters may not yet be met. At the same time, however, monitoring capacities have been deficient, as a result of which it is unclear to what extent really Spain complies with the parameters of the DWDs (OECD, 2004). Most cases of non-compliance of the first directive during the 1993–98 period were caused by the nature and structure of the ground, including overexploitation of groundwater resources, climate and treatment (Kiwa, 2002). With regard the second directive, the application of RD 140/2003 has been deficient in terms of the adoption of sanitary criteria.

The EU has been active in seeking the correct implementation of the DWD by putting pressure on national authorities and, to a lesser extent, by improving technical capacities. On the one hand, the ECJ condemned Spain in 2003 for failing to adopt or to communicate to the Commission the laws, regulations and administrative provisions necessary to comply with the second directive (C-29/02). On the other hand, a DWD committee involving member states and the Commission has attempted to provide guidance on harmonized reporting methods and formats for the directive.[3]

New modes of governance have barely been set up in the adoption of and adaptation to the DWD as the participation of domestic nonstate actors has been limited. The Spanish Association of Water Suppliers has regularly provided information on the implementation of the DWD to the Ministry of the Environment.[4] Yet, given that most companies belong to the private sector and thus compete with each other, they do not have many incentives to cooperate with each other and with the national administration in order to find joint solutions.[5] Cooperation between municipal administrations and supply and treatment companies has improved over recent years, although environmental groups have normally been excluded from the policy process. Overall, there is little evidence that points to the emergence of new modes of governance that systematically involve nonstate actors, despite regular consultation. Overall, effectiveness in the implementation of the DWD has generally improved mainly through the combination of EU compliance pressure and capacity building, with domestic mobilization, in contrast to other water subsectors, not being significant.

A relatively different situation is observed in case of the WFD, the implementation of which has enhanced consultation between state and nonstate actors. In contrast to the DWD, which is processed in relatively impenetrable arenas and outside public scrutiny, the WFD affects one of the most sensitive policy issues in Spain. Prior to accession, water was regulated through Act 29/1985. Broadly, this saw water as a unitary source, extended the notion of public domain, formalized the idea of hydrological planning, introduced environmental and quality concerns and promoted public participation (Costejà et al., 2004). Since then, water legislation has been reformed several times in order to address recurring problems of water shortages. Significantly, Act 9/1996 adopted extraordinary, exceptional and urgent measures to cope with drought situations and Act 13/1996 modified fiscal and administrative measures relating to the construction and the exploitation of water works. Later, the 46/99 Act regulated the creation of water rights exchange schemes in order to improve efficiency by making the water concession regime more flexible. In spite of the bulk of legislation, it is far from compatible with the principles laid down in the WFD. RDL 1/2001 adopted the Consolidated Water Act, which introduced a series of provisions that had been absent in previous legislation: an integrated approach towards pollution and resource management, the principle of river basin and planning unity, a participatory approach to policy making and the recovery of environmental and economic costs. Thus, the implementation of the WFD required the adaptation of administrative arrangements regarding the designation of river basin districts and the elaboration of water plans for each of them, harmonization of inland and coastal water management and protection, expansion of the scope of public participation and, finally, revision of the traditional problem-solving approach on water policy based on intervention in the supply of water.

Given the high policy mismatch, the transposition of the WFD has been discontinuous and fragmented. The directive was formally incorporated into national legislation through Article 129 of Act 62/2003 on fiscal, administrative and social measures, which introduced changes to the 1/2001 Consolidated Water Act. Yet, complete transposition was delayed as Article 3 of the WFD on the designation of the competent authorities and delimitation of river basin districts was not incorporated into national legislation until 2007 through RD 125/2007 and RD 126/2007. In general terms, national legislation introduces integrated protection for inland surface waters, coastal waters, transitional waters and groundwater, while it also defines new management, planning and protection schemes based on river basin districts, the so-called *demarcaciones hidrográficas*. Further, as a result of integrating transitional and coastal waters, hitherto a competence of the autonomous communities, the practical application of the WFD requires reinforced cooperation between national and regional administrations within water basin authorities. Finally the polluter pays principle, the principle of aquatic ecosystem protection and the principle of sustainable water usage have been included among the main policy goals. Overall, significant political, economic and technical efforts, most of which still have to be made, are required to apply the WFD.

The practical application of the WFD has had mixed results. The communication to the European Commission of river basin district limits as well as the list of competent interregional water basin authorities was significantly delayed.[6] In addition, the development, monitoring, review and update of river basin management plans have hardly resulted in the creation of new administrative structures, although human resources have been increased since the late 1990s.[7] In order to guarantee a uniform application of the WFD across Spain, the Ministry of the Environment has taken a leading role in the writing up of the reports required by the direct by coordinating expert committees and modifying the Regulation on Hydrological Planning (Fundación Nueva Cultura del Agua, 2007). In addition, multilevel coordination has been enhanced through the creation in 2007 of a committee of competent authorities in the case of the interregional water basin authorities. However, such changes have hardly improved effectiveness. Preexisting water basin authorities, the so-called *confederaciones hidrográficas*, which were independent public legal organizations attached to the Ministry of the Environment, have taken on both their previously assigned tasks and those deriving from the WFD. In many cases, the management tasks required by the WFD have run parallel to the tasks already being carried out on a daily basis, and as such no new approach reorientating the established *modus operandi* has been developed, nor have additional human resources with a focus on natural sciences been provided (Fundación Nueva Cultura del Agua, 2007). In addition, delays in the transposition process and in the designation of interregional basin districts have hampered the internal reorganization necessary to comply with the WFD's goals (Fundación Nueva Cultura del Agua, 2007). Such delays are partially a result of a lack of coordination between national water authorities, which are responsible of cross-regional basins, and regional administrations, responsible for coastal waters.

The participatory requirements contained in the WFD have enhanced the emergence of timid modes of governance, mostly based on consultation, in water planning and management. To this end, district water councils have been created in order to offer information and promote active public participation in the planning and management of inter-regional river basin districts. Their members include representatives of the national administration, the relevant autonomous communities, local governments, business organizations and environmental organizations. Generally, public participation remains restricted compared to the potential levels of participation outlined in the WFD, particularly with regard to the involvement of the interested public in the planning process (Barreira, 2003). State actors have not lost the control over the policy process, as nonstate actors have no formal or informal say in the decision-making process.[8] However, the national administration has become increasingly willing to consult environmental groups, business organizations and users, since they provide technical expertise and political support.[9] From the societal side, willingness to participate has been uneven. Water users in Andalusia, for instance, have not always had an incentive to cooperate with state actors as they oppose the principle that water should be paid for at full cost recovery prices. In contrast, environmental groups have been widely involved in the implementation of the WFD: for instance, WWF-Spain has actively participated in the development of EU strategies on the WFD and is a member of the Common Strategy for Implementation of the Directive.[10] At the national level, WWF-Spain has advanced amendments and suggestions on the legal transposition of the WFD, published reports and launched initiatives involving the scientific community, environmental organizations and industry.[11]

In addition to internal mobilization, the EU has contributed to the strengthening of the governance capacities necessary to implement the requirements contained in the WFD by drawing up guidelines and promoting training activities. Significantly, the European Commission and the member states elaborated the Common Strategy for the Application of the WFD, which was adopted in 2001. The strategy placed emphasis on information exchange, public participation and involvement of all the interested parties, the integration of activities derived from the implementation of the directive, capacity building in member states and the creation of working groups and informal guidelines on specific issues contained in the WFD.[12] Unsurprisingly, the EU has combined this strategy with exerting pressure on national governments that fail to meet the objectives of the directive properly. In this respect, the Commission has launched infringement cases against Spain for noncommunication of the administrative arrangements pursuant to Article 3 of the WFD (A2004/2305) and for noncommunication of the environmental and economic analysis required by Article 5 (A2005/2316) (European Commission, 2007).

Overall, the study of the implementation of the DWD and the WFD reveals certain variations as regards the extent to which they rely on new modes of governance. On the one hand, the implementation of the DWD is deeply grounded in hierarchical regulatory schemes. State actors have been reluctant to adopt more inclusive styles of governance outside the traditional channels of consultation. Under such constraints, nonstate actors' involvement in policy making has remained limited. By contrast, the participatory requirements contained in the WFD as well as EU compliance pressure to adopt more participatory schemes have fostered the emergence of stable patterns of consultation in its implementation. The involvement of nonstate actors, including policy experts, environmental groups and user organizations in the policymaking process has contributed to the improvement of effective implementation by means of providing expertise, scientific knowledge and consensus. In sum, the EU has encouraged the emergence, however timid, of new modes of governance. Yet the involvement on nonstate actors in water management remains limited to consultation, not least because of a lack of full compliance with the participatory requirements of the WFD.

Industrial air pollution: the legacies of the past

The first laws regulating air quality and emission standards were adopted in the early 1970s with the 38/1972 Act on the Protection of the Atmospheric Environment. Regulation was further developed in 1975 by RD 833/1975, which was later modified by RD 1613/1985 in order to introduce new standards for air quality. In spite of the existence of air pollution regulations, there was a significant mismatch between EU air pollution regulations and Spanish law (Börzel, 2003a). When the EU adopted the LCPD, Spain was dependent on coalfired energy production and large combustion plants that used domestic coal with high sulfur content (Ramus, 1991). Thus, the implementation of the LCPD and its 'mother' directive, the IPD, required both the reduction of emissions and the reorientation of the system of energy production, including the use – thus the importation – of less polluting coal. In addition, national air pollution control legislation was not based on a precautionary and technology-based problemsolving approach. In particular, the application of the concept BAT was not in use in either the reduction or the monitoring of emissions (Börzel, 2003a).

Within this context, Spain transposed the 1988 LCPD into national legislation in 1991 through RD 646/1991. The EU regulation, which was incorporated more or less intact into domestic law, basically replaced all the provisions of previous legislation. In doing so, Spain came into formal compliance with the EU regulation in relation to emission limits, but in practice measurement technology did not correspond to BAT requirements (Börzel, 2003a).[13] Later, Act 646/1991 was modified by 1995 RD 1800/95 in order to comply with the 94/66/EC directive, which extended the SO_2 emission limits for new plants. The LCPD was modified in 2001 by 2001/80/EC in order to update emission standards according to new technologies and technical capacities. The new EU regulations were incorporated into national legislation in 2004 through RD 430/2004.

In spite of adequate transposition, practical application has been inefficient because of the high economic costs mostly falling on older industrial facilities. The compliance with the LCPD on emissions required huge economic investments in SO_2 and NOx emission reductions, especially after the five-year exemption from SO_2 emission reductions, and in meeting the BAT requirements (Börzel, 2003a). According to the directive, Spain had to reduce its SO_2 and NOx emissions by half up to 2003 and to incorporate the BAT standards in the measurement of air quality. For this purpose, ENDESA, which was the largest Spanish electricity producer, designed the installation of postcombustion desulfurization systems at the most polluting plants, namely Andorra-Teruel, and the replacement of national coal with foreign coal at the As Pontes-A Coruña plant. ENDESA, mostly owned by the state, relied heavily on state subsidies to reduce emissions. Yet, with the privatization of the electricity sector in the 1990s, electricity companies were no longer allowed to receive subsidies arising from environmental costs and found lower EU support for the use of national coal.[14] As a result, the national plan for emission reduction, which had exempted Andorra-Teruel, the third most polluting LCP in Europe at the time, was aborted. Moreover, the Spanish government was reluctant to exert pressure on industries and adopted a flexible position with regard to the necessary changes in existing industrial facilities, mainly because of employment and economic considerations (OECD, 1997).

The situation was substantially different with regards to the adoption of Directive 2001/80/EC on the limitation of emissions of certain pollutants into the air from large combustion plants, the negotiations for which saw the active involvement of both the national government and the main electricity companies. In contrast to the negotiations for the LCPD, which had been adopted shortly after Spanish accession, Spanish electricity companies intensively lobbied Brussels through the Union of the Electricity Industry and, in some cases, by establishing direct contacts with EU institutions against the adoption of stringent emission standards.[15] In the process of transposition, several drafts were discussed by the state administration and autonomous communities on the one hand, and by the state administration, electricity companies and the Spanish Business Confederation on the other.[16] The directive was transposed into national legislation by RD 430/2004, with a two-year delay. In 2005, the Ministry of Industry, Tourism and Trade drew up an exhaustive national emissions reduction plan, the final version of which was adopted in 2007 after the introduction of the observations and modifications proposed by the European Commission.[17] The National Plan for the Reduction of Emissions from Large Combustion Plants, covering the period 2008–15, affected 97 plants existing in 2000, mostly from the electricity sector. Its main objective is to reduce emissions of SO_2 by 81 percent with respect to 2001 levels; emissions of NOx by 15 percent and emissions of particles by 55 percent. The elaboration of the plan involved the autonomous communities and the industrial sector.

Effectiveness in the application of the LCPD has improved slightly over recent years. According to the data reported by the OECD in 2004, Spain, which is one of the main producers of SO_2 in Europe, had reduced emissions of this pollutant by the energy production sector by 33 percent since 1990. Two main factors account for the gradual improvement. On the one hand, Spain has gradually adapted its system of energy production: less dirty sources of energy have been increasingly introduced, as the economic gap between Spain and its EU counterparts has been closed. Coalfired power stations abandoned the use of high-sulfur coal and replaced it with imported low-sulfur coal and/or have introduced desulfurization processes. Electricity companies also started to diversify their sources of energy. For instance, Iberdrola – one of the main Spanish electricity companies – reduced its consumption of coal and oil by 8 percent between 2000 and 2004.[18] This gradual shift has been accompanied by an increasing degree of expertise in the understanding and use of BAT. In this respect, cooperation and mutual exchange of information between national and regional administrations and industry has gradually improved over the years. Such dialog normally consists of bilateral channels of consultation, from which environmental groups and other nonstate actors are excluded.[19] Moreover, both national and regional administrations have progressively developed funding programs in order to help industries to adapt their facilities to meet EU requirements. Initially, the costs of implementation fell exclusively on industry, but this has slowly changed as the administration has become increasingly aware of the need to invest in new forms of energy. For example, the government of Andalusia launched a program in 2005 to subsidize investment by the industry to reduce the emissions of SO_2 and particles.[20] In spite of dialog between government and industry, more encompassing governance styles in this field have not generally emerged.

Effectiveness of implementation continues to be low. Deficiencies are mainly the result of two factors (cf. OECD, 2004). On the one hand, investments have increased but financial resources are still insufficient, especially in the case of the oldest facilities that require modernization. Significantly enough, NOx emissions from the energy production sector have risen 31 percent since 1990. On the other hand, effective enforcement is also impaired by the fact that the Spanish regulation of the electricity industry gave incentives for the use of national coal (OECD, 2004). Additionally, the European Commission has been comparatively inactive in the supervision of the national emissions reduction. Only once, in 2004, did it refer Spain to the ECJ, for failing to comply with Directive 2001/80/EC (C-17/04).

While the LCPD has been largely in line with the regulatory tradition, the IPPCD represents a departure in the prevailing policy approach for at least three reasons. First, it has involved a shift from a fragmented approach towards a comprehensive one based on one single permit, the so-called Integrated Environmental Authorization. This holistic approach has required the integration of the four previous permit issuance systems into one common procedure and the improvement of interadministrative coordination. Second, the IPPCD involves adopting a preventive approach to pollution through the systematic employment of BAT. This requirement has encouraged the Spanish administration to introduce a BAT-based emission limitation system in environmental policy and to provide regional authorities with updated information, particularly since Spain had not implemented the IPD (Börzel, 2003a). Finally, effective implementation of the IPPCD has involved enhancing general public access to environmental data on major industrial activities, as national information on permit applications and emission data were not available in the form of a public register before its adoption.

The IPPCD was fully transposed into Spanish law in 2002 through Act 16/2002. Adaptation to this directive involved exchange and discussion of information between the national administration, the autonomous communities and stakeholders. According to the distribution of powers, the national administration is responsible for establishing the common principles and minimum criteria for legal implementation, while the autonomous communities have the competence of developing and complementing them, for instance, by adding specific regimes on sanctions or inspection systems. The regions have used this constitutional right in different ways: while Andalusia did not incorporate the IPPCD norms until 2005, Catalonia did it as early as 1998 through Act 3/1998, four years before the national government. Indeed, Catalonia served as a model for the transposition at the national level of the directive in 2002 (Bohne, 2006).

In terms of regulatory content, the implementation of the IPPCD has not brought about a fundamental change in the prevailing problem-solving approach. The main adaptation process has consisted of replacing the former water and waste permits by a single environmental license granted by the regional administration. In practice, permit procedures have been reduced from four to three and the number of regulatory decisions concerning the construction and operation of large industrial facilities has remained untouched. However, the 509/2007 implementing act allows regional governments to simplify the procedures for those industrial sectors that use externally certified systems of environmental management, for example, EMAS or ISO 14001, in order to speed up the administrative procedures. Some autonomous communities have developed inspection and control mechanisms either directly or through delegation to external bodies. In order to ensure enforcement of the IPPCD, the national government has also established its own sanction system.

The effectiveness of the IPPCD in Spain was at first deficient, although gradual progress has been observed. It was incorporated into Spanish law in July 2002, after a delay of nearly three years. As a result, between 1999 and 2002 the European Commission opened several proceedings against Spain for noncommunication of incorporation and failure to adopt the laws, regulations and administrative measures necessary to comply with the directive (European Commission, 2003). In addition, Spain has only partially adapted its regulations to the requirements and principles upon which the IPPCD is based. Basically, the integrated character of environmental protection is undermined, the distribution of competences is unclear and there is a source of potential conflict.

Indeed, a positive environmental assessment from the issuer of the environmental permit could be contradicted by a negative evaluation by a local authority in terms of local impact or overruled by the binding report from the water basin authorities (Bohne, 2006). Apart from that, Spain was also late in adaptating its emission values system to BAT guidelines, as a result of which industry has only in recent years had access to this information at the national level.[21]

Two main factors initially impaired the effective implementation of the IPPCD. On the one hand, the coexistence of different permits issued by three different levels of government represented a huge and complex administrative burden for industry. On the other hand, the lack of technical expertise hampered the drawing up of BAT guidelines.[22] In spite of initial difficulties, several factors have contributed to a slow improvement in effectiveness over time. In 2002, the government created the National Register on Emissions and Polluting Sources in order to comply with the principles of transparency and public participation. The register's main function consists of the collection and dissemination of data on industrial facilities, emissions and sources of pollution. It includes updated information concerning BREF and BAT guidelines and detailed information on permit requests, initial licenses and their revisions. Perhaps more importantly, an increasingly cooperative governance approach has contributed to making some progress in implementation in at least three ways: universities, research institutes, industrial organizations and individual companies have been consulted in the definition of BAT guidelines; some regional governments have sought to involve nonstate agencies in the systems of inspection and control, albeit under the supervision of the former (Bohne, 2006), and, finally, the Spanish government has fostered the signing of voluntary agreements with some industrial sectors in order to develop coresponsibility in the implementation of EU requirements on quality standards, monitoring systems and technical solutions (Bohne, 2006). In addition, the EU itself and, in particular, the compliance pressure exerted by the European Commission and the ECJ have contributed to improve effectiveness. The Commission has been active in issuing implementation reports and opening infringement proceedings, while the ECJ convicted Spain for not implementing the directive in time (C-29/01). Apart from EU compliance pressure, domestic mobilization has eventually had positive effects in this respect, such as when, on 26 August 2004, Greenpeace denounced Montecinca S.A. in Huesca for violating the IPPCD. A day later, the Ministry of the Environment and the regional governments of Aragon and Catalonia urged the company to comply with EU law. More recently, in 2007, Greenpeace asked the European Parliament to investigate chemical and radioactive pollution in Huelva.[23]

Air pollution control reproduces trends in governance that are similar to those in water management. Significantly, variations on governance schemes and effectiveness are mostly accounted for by both domestic and EU factors. As regards the LPC and its 'mother' directive, the IPD, a traditional top-down problem-solving approach has been prevalent, with most nonstate actors being excluded from the implementation process. In contrast, the government has delegated to industry and other nonstate actors certain technical tasks required for the implementation of the IPPCD. In this case, EU pressure, capacity building and, to a lesser extent, domestic mobilization have helped to improve effectiveness.

Nature protection: opening up the policy process

At the time of accession, Spain lacked a comprehensive policy on nature conservation. Legislation had been adopted in the early 1970s through the Hunting Act of 1970 and the Protected Natural Areas Act of 1975. Yet, they had a specific and sectoral character.[24] Following accession, the 4/1989 Act on Conservation of Natural Areas and Wildlife, which was adopted in 1989, expanded the scope of regulated nature conservation and formally transposed Wild Birds Directive. The process of adoption went very much in parallel to the implementation of the FFHD. For this reason, some of the issues contained in the FFHD were already included in the 4/1989 Act, although most of the former's requirements, typically those referring to Natura 2000, were not formally incorporated into national legislation until 1995 through RD 1997/1995. Later, RD 1993/1998 modified the 1995 RD by establishing additional measures to guarantee biodiversity through the conservation of natural habitats and wild fauna and flora.

Since the national problemsolving approach, policy instruments and standards failed to meet EU requirements, the implementation of the Natura 2000 directives implied huge adaptation costs. On the administrative front, rivalries and the lack of administrative coordination prior to 1996 hampered adaptation to the FFHD (Aguilar Fernández, 2003). In addition, according to the vertical distribution of tasks, autonomous communities are to draw up a list of potential SPAs, which are then sent to the national administration. Subsequently, the autonomous aommunities declare those areas as SPAs and define the conservation measures. The complex administrative structure involved in the implementation of the FFHD has required the reinforcement of coordination capacities. Additionally, the effective implementation of the nature conservation directives required the mobilization of cognitive and economic resources in order to elaborate inventories and technical studies, as well as to adopt specific measures to implement the conservation requirements. Technical and scientific expertise, in particular, has traditionally been dispersed among state and nonstate actors at different territorial levels.

The transposition of the nature conservation directives was partially effective. The 4/1989 Act did not specify the establishment of the aim of conservation or the definition of the legal status of the SPAs. Later, RD 1997/1995 did not correctly transpose the FFHD and was, therefore, further modified by RD 1193/1998.[25] Beyond transposition, the application in practice of the FFHD was initially insufficient, too. At the outset, only a small number of areas were protected, little information was available and the responsible administrative authorities were understaffed and uncoordinated.[26] After the mid-1990s, some improvements resulted in the development of a provisional Natura 2000 map. In short, in 1999 there were 170 designated SPAs (European Commission, 2002). By end of 2007, 1,381 Sites of Community Importance (SCIs) had been proposed and 512 SPAs had been designated.[27] The major task still to be implemented is the conversion of Natura 2000 into a genuine ecological network, since conservation is at present poorly integrated into territorial planning.[28]

The main factors leading to the emergence of new modes of governance include institutional leadership, EU capacity building and compliance pressure, as well as social actors' in-depth involvement in policy making. The specific mode of new governance as regards the implementation of the FFHD is commonly based on the provision of technical support and cognitive resources by environmental groups and the scientific community. Relying on EU funding, the Ministry of the Environment enlisted more than 30 research centers and several environmental groups in the tasks of data collection, mapping and inventorying in order to elaborate a List of Areas of Community Interest.[29] As well as the delegation of technical and scientific tasks, the development of the list required the coordination with and political consensus among all the autonomous communities (Luaces, 2002). In addition to the ministry's institutional leadership, the active role of the EU, both in terms of capacity building and compliance pressure, has encouraged the adoption of more cooperative schemes in at least two ways. On the one hand, the European Commission has cofinanced several cognitive-related tasks that were of crucial importance in the earlier stages of Natura 2000.[30] Also, it created two technical commit-tees, ORNIS and HABITAT, involving all member states and aimed at improving information exchange and coordination in the implemen-tation of the two nature conservation directives.[31] In addition, the Commission developed a guidance document in order to provide better clarification of the Wild Birds Directive in relation to hunting.[32] On the other hand, the European Commission has repeatedly taken action against Spain for infringement of the Wild Birds Directive and FFHD. In the early 1990s, the European Commission referred Spain to the ECJ for nonapplication of the Wild Birds Directive in relation to the Santoña wetlands. As a result, in 1993 the Court convicted Spain for failing to comply with the provisions of the Wild Birds Directive as the public authorities had not classified the marshes as an SPA and had failed to take the appropriate measures to protect them (C-355/90). Additionally, the ruling, which had its origins in a complaint filed by the Spanish Society of Ornithology (SEO/BirdLife), revealed nonstate actors' emerg-ing capacity to influence domestic environmental policies through litigation at the EU level. Subjected to EU pressure, the national govern-ment initiated the effective implementation of the Wild Birds Directive. Later, the Commission considered that the adoption of the directive was insufficient and in 2004 it referred Spain to the ECJ for insufficient designation of SPAs (C-235/04). In addition, it opened several infringe-ment cases against Spain for not meeting the requirements contained in the FFHD, while the ECJ has condemned Spain for not complying with it. In 2004, the Court argued that Spain had failed to fulfill its obliga-tions under the Wild Birds Directive by allowing hunting using limed twigs in the Community of Valencia (C-79/03) (European Commission, 2005). Similarly, in 2005, the ECJ condemned Spain for allowing the hunting of Wood-pigeons (*Columba palustris*) in Guipúzcoa during their return to their breeding grounds, in breach of the Wild Birds Directive (C-135/04).

In addition to continuous EU compliance pressure, the implementa-tion of the Wild Birds Directive and FFHD has also been improved due to domestic mobilization. Since the mid-1990s, the scientific commu-nity and a wide range of environmental groups have been increasingly involved in the policy process. A number of scientific networks funded by public administrations and involving the scientific community as well as a handful of environmental groups have worked on the identifi-cation and inventory of natural species and habitats (Luaces, 2002). In some cases, nonstate actors have also assumed management tasks. For instance, in 1998 the Catalan environmental organization Lliga per a la

Defensa del Patrimoni Natural [the League for the Defense of the Natural Heritage] launched the implementation of a sustainability plan at the Punta de la Mora coastal area in Tarragona, which is included in Natura 2000. The plan was financed by EU LIFE Programme, the Ministry of the Environment, the Catalan Departments of the Environment and Agriculture, the Tarragona municipal administration and the conservation group itself (Font, 2001b). However, a specific trend in environmental governance in the field of nature protection is that environmental groups' cooperative involvement does not rule out confrontational forms of participation in other areas. Significantly, SEO/BirdLife has published studies for the Ministry of the Environment on the implementation of the FFHD, while at the same time it has filed complaints to the European Commission denouncing the failure to designate SPAs in order to fulfill the objectives of the directive.[33] In a few but significant cases, complaints lodged with the EU by domestic groups have resulted in ECJ rulings against Spain (see above). Generally, state actors have resorted to domestic litigation by seeking the cooperation with NGOs to prevent further conflict in the application of EU environmental policies.[34]

Similar trends are observed as regards the factors facilitating the implementation of the EIAD, especially in those cases related to nature protection. When Spain entered the EC, there was no national legislation regulating EIA procedures. Legislation on the so-called classified activities, adopted in the 1960s, required the assessment of certain environmental impacts of projects during planning . However, national regulation did not meet the requirements of the EIAD in terms of the adoption of a preventive, cross-policy and participatory approach (Börzel, 2003a). For this reason, a great deal of complex adaptation was needed to meet the EIA requirements. First, since the administrative unit in charge of implementing the EIA was dependent on the Ministry of Public Works and Transport, the creation of a more 'independent' administration would have facilitated the inclusion of environmental issues into the policy-making processes. Second, the establishment of multidisciplinary teams was needed to deal with the evaluation of the cross-media consequences of a wide range of public and private projects. Third, the adoption of more integrated, preventive and participatory schemes of policymaking was needed in order to meet the directive's requirements. In addition to such adaptations, the implementation of the EIAD entailed huge economic costs derived from the development of environmental impact studies and, more importantly, the implementation of the necessary changes by public and private interests.

According to data from the early 1990s, the EIA process was expected to increase total economic costs by between 1 and 5 percent, and planning stage costs by between 5 and 20 percent (European Commission, 1993). Finally, technical expertise and interadministrative coordination capacities were lacking, while the directive's provisions for public participation and transparency in administrative procedures conflicted with preexisting administrative practice (Börzel, 2003a).

The EIAD was transposed into national legislation through RDL 1302/1986 and RD 1131/1988, which establishes the implementation procedure. In addition, Act 4/1989 on the conservation of natural areas and wildlife contained additional EIA provisions. Subsequently, Directive 97/11/CE modifying the first EIAD was transposed into national legislation through Act 6/2001. More recently, Act 9/2006 on Strategic Environmental Assessment of Plans and Programmes has been adopted. Most autonomous communities had enacted legal provisions on the EIAD by the early 1990s, some of which included additional provisions (European Commission, 1993).

The implementation of the EIAD takes place in a complex legal and administrative framework. National legislation is applied to those projects authorized by the national administration as well as those authorized by those autonomous communities that do not have specific regulation on EIA or who have lower levels of environmental protection. The responsibility for the execution of the EIA falls on the environmental administration at the same territorial level as the one granting permission for the project. At the national level, the environmental administration was part of the Ministry of Public Works, Transport and the Environment until the creation of the Ministry of the Environment in 1996. The former concentrated the functions of supervising unit, licensing authority and, in many instances, project promoter. Since 1996, it is the Ministry of the Environment, and in particular the General Directorate on Quality and Environmental Assessment, that is responsible for executing the EIA on projects whose competence falls on the national authorities, proposing the resolution of the Environmental Impact Statement and following up and controlling any corrective measures.[35] At the regional level, the EIA procedure is the responsibility of planning or environmental departments.

The effectiveness of the implementation of the EIAD during the postaccession period, both in terms of formal and practical implementation, can be described only as poor. On the one hand, formal compliance with the directive was incomplete, most notably as regards the interpretations about Annex II of the directive (European

Commission, 1993). On the other hand, the practical application of the directive also shows serious shortcomings. Significantly, the number of national Environmental Impact Statements (EIS) adopted during the period 1988–94 was only 150,[36] a far lower figure than the number of projects requiring an EIA. When conducted, the procedures often had important shortcomings: the EIS was incomplete and hardly met the minimum quality standards, mostly because of a lack of skill on the part of the evaluators and low levels of commitment by developers (European Commission, 1993); many projects disregarded the recommendations contained in the EIS or were required to incorporate them once work had already begun; and public and industrial projects were hardly ever rejected (Escobar Gómez, 1994). Public participation was also seriously limited, as the most contentious aspects of projects were not normally considered in the initial consultation process and the suggestions made were not often considered by the administration. In addition, some of the administrations consulted, namely those responsible for cultural heritage, tended to be overloaded and respond only after delays.[37]

Since the mid-1990s, effectiveness in the field of EIA has made significant progress. The number of EIA procedures has considerably increased and the quality of EIS has improved (Canelas et al., 2005). Public involvement and EU pressure have been crucial in facilitating this improvement. On the one hand, the EIAD has opened new avenues for citizen and social participation and consultation and has encouraged the emergence of a mixed type of governance. On the other hand, more cooperative schemes have been developed. National EIA legislation contains provisions allowing for public participation, and autonomous communities, hydrographical confederations, universities, environmental groups and other nonstate actors are consulted on a regular basis by the Ministry of the Environment. Environmental groups, often in coalition with local authorities, have increasingly made use of participatory channels provided by the EIAD to voice their opposition to certain projects (Börzel, 2003a). However, environmental organizations tend to be overwhelmed by the amount and technicality of the information provided by the ministry. According to a representative of an environmental movement, the Ministry of the Environment often delivers highly complex and technical dossiers so that only the largest environmental organizations can assume the cost of processing such information.[38] Moreover, beyond the participatory opportunities offered by EIA procedures, environmental groups have adopted a confrontational strategy by making use of the EU arena to denounce alleged infringements of the EIAD, especially when projects have been considered to affect protected areas. Significantly enough, the EIAD, together with the FFHD and Wild Birds Directive, accounts for the highest number of complaints from Spain lodged with the European Commission,[39] some of which have resulted in the opening of infringement proceedings. In many cases, environmental groups combine cases of infringements of the EIAD and FFHD. For instance, in 2002 WWF-Spain denounced the projected enlargement of the Baqueira-Beret ski resort towards the Vall d'Arreu. The project had obtained a negative EIA and affected an area included in the List of SCIs pursuant to the FFHD. The environmental organization claimed that the list had been modified in order to facilitate the implementation of the project.[40]

The Commission has been particularly sensitive to environmentalists' complaints, launching infringement proceedings and on a number of occasions referring Spain to the ECJ for failure to ensure the effective implementation of the EIAD. In 1990, it opened an infringement procedure against Spain for only including six of the Annex II projects of the directive and, in the face of further delay by the national authorities, referred the case to the ECJ in 1999 (Börzel, 2003a). In response, the 2001 6/2001 Act expanded the annexes and introduced new evaluation criteria. Similarly, the ECJ has strongly defended the EIAD and acknowledges the important role played by the public in the EIA process (Ryall, 2007). In this respect, Spain was condemned in 2006 for failing to transpose the directive correctly in relation the to a leisure complex in Valencia (C-332/04). The case had originated in a complaint by WWF-Spain to the European Commission five years before. It denounced the fact that the legislation transposing the directive had not stipulated that the final decisions concerning project permits had to be subject to public participation (Börzel, 2003a). In general, pressure from above and from below has led to a gradual adjustment of EIA procedures to fit the terms of the directive.[41]

Overall, both the FFHD and the EIAD present common features as well as variations with regards to the prevailing governance modalities. In both cases, EU pressure regarding the implementation of participatory schemes and domestic mobilization has been crucial in pushing Spain towards a more effective implementation. Public participation, however, has been greater in the implementation of the FFHD, where consultation with a wide range of nonstate actors and delegation of technical and scientific tasks to the scientific community and environmental groups have become regular practices.

Conclusion

During the early postaccession period, Spain faced serious capacity shortcomings that challenged the effective adoption of and adaptation to EU environmental directives. In spite of large capacity gaps, state actors had few incentives to tap into nonstate actors' resources in order to share the burden of implementation for at least three reasons. First, they were reluctant to abandon the traditional command-and-control approach that had long been embedded in the state-centered administrative culture. Second, they hardly felt any pressure to implement EU environmental policies effectively and were thus scarcely concerned with their environmental obligations. Finally, societal actors had little incentive or were too weak to cooperate. Within this context, the effectiveness of environmental directives was clearly deficient.

This situation was gradually transformed during the 1990s as a result of the combined push and pull factors emanating from both domestic and EU levels. At the domestic level, environmental groups have combined a cooperative and confrontational strategy. This dual approach has allowed them to gain access to, and influence, the policy process by means of providing technical cooperation without losing autonomy. At the EU level, the main drivers of governance change include the participatory requirements contained in some environmental directives, the distribution of both financial and technical resources to member states and the compliance pressure exerted by the European Commission and the ECJ on national governments. In this respect, the participatory requirements contained in the WFD, IPPCD, FFHD and EIAD have gradually pushed forward the creation of institutional arrangements involving state and nonstate actors. Those three directives prescribing far-reaching participatory schemes (the WFD, the IPPCD and the HFFD) and the one requesting ordinary consultation procedures (the EIAD) have facilitated the involvement of nonstate actors. In the four cases, both industry and environmental groups have been relatively willing to cooperate with state actors in transposition and practical application, giving rise to stable patterns of consultation and the delegation of technical and scientific tasks. This is in stark contrast to more conventional EU environmental directives, such as the LCPD, the DWD and the WBD, which do not stipulate any requirements for public participation. In both cases, more traditional styles of policy making have been the rule rather than the exception. In addition to the participatory requirements, the EU has provided material incentives for nonstate actors to become involved in the implementation of environmental policies and to build cooperative networks. The adoption of and adaptation to the FFHD clearly exemplifies this trend. At the same time, compliance pressure by the European Commission and the ECJ has increased state actors' willingness to engage in cooperation. Since the early 1990s, the European Commission has intensified pressure on Spain through the opening of infringement proceedings, a trend observed in all policies under study, with ECJ rulings in four out of the six cases. National authorities have responded to EU pressure by adopting adaptation measures, although not always promptly or in a fully satisfactory manner. EU pressure has exerted a constant push on the implementation of all the directives, increasing the general willingness of the Spanish government to cope with the compliance costs and to gradually build up implementation capacities. Moreover, by pushing Spain towards better implementation of EU directives, the EU compliance system broadened societal actors' opportunities to circumvent national authorities and litigate against state administrations. This trend is particularly dominant in the implementation of the FFHD, WFD, IPPCD and the EIAD, as state actors, facing increasing threats of litigation, have sought to prevent further conflict in the application of EU environmental policies by involving civil society organizations in the policy process.

Overall, more engaging modes of governance have gradually become a characteristic trend in the implementation of environmental policies. The comparison of the directives shows that both domestic mobilization of social actors and EU push and pull regarding the participatory requirements contained in some environmental directives have facilitated the emergence of more inclusive governance schemes. These trends have ultimately contributed to improving implementation. However, the move towards new modes of governance is still limited as state actors have been unwilling to give up autonomy by sharing the control of the policy process with other actors.

Notes

1. Interview, Ministry of the Environment, Madrid, 27 November 2006.
2. Ministerio de Obras Públicas, Transportes y Medio Ambiente, 1994, 1995.
3. http://ec.europa.eu/environment/water/water-drink/pdf/2007_05_09_guidance_doc_ reporting.pdf, (last access: 19 April 2008).
4. Interview, Ministry of Health and Consumption, Madrid, 27 November 2006.
5. Interview, water company, Barcelona, 4 April 2006.
6. Notwithstanding, the Catalan administration informed the European Commission in 2003 and 2004 about its proposed river basin districts and

the designation of the responsible administrative authority (Castañón, 2006).

7. Interview, Ministry of Health and Consumption, Madrid, 27 November 2006.
8. Interview Ministry of the Environment, Madrid, 28 November 2006.
9. Interview, Ministry of the Environment, Madrid, 28 November 2006.
10. http://www.wwf.es/aguas_continentales/directiva_marco_agua.php, (last access: 26 November 2007).
11. http://www.wwf.es/aguas_continentales/directiva_marco_agua.php, (last access: 26 November 2007).
12. http://ec.europa.eu/environment/water/water-framework/objectives/pdf/strategy.pdf (last access: 26 November 2007).
13. Spain was granted a temporary derogation for the full application of the SO_2 emission standards limits in order to allow the country to generate the considered necessary energy capacity for its economic development. This derogation expired in 1999.
14. http://www.acidrain.org/pages/publications/acidnews/2004/an2004_04.asp, (last access: 26 November 2007).
15. Interview, electricity company, Barcelona, 6 April 2006.
16. Interview, electricity company, Barcelona, 6 April 2006.
17. Interview, Ministry of Industry, Tourism and Commerce, National Emission Reduction Plan for Large Combustion Plants, 10 October 2007.
18. http://www.iberdrola.es, (last access: 6 May 2008).
19. Interview, Electricity Company, Barcelona, 6 April 2006.
20. Consejeria de Medio Ambiente, Boletin de la Junta de Andalucia, n. 34, 17 February 2005.
21. Interview, electricity company, Barcelona, 6 April 2006.
22. Interview, Ministry of the Environment, Madrid, 27 November 2006.
23. www.greenpeace.es, (last access: 6 December 2007).
24. Interview, Ministry of the Environment, Madrid, 1 December 2006.
25. http://www.mma.es/portal/secciones/biodiversidad/rednatura2000/normativa/estatal/ estatal.htm, (last access: 14 February 2008).
26. Interview, Ministry of the Environment, Madrid, 1 December 2006.
27. http://www.mma.es/portal/secciones/biodiversidad/rednatura2000/rednatura_espana/ index.htm, (last access: 6 December 2007).
28. Interview, Ministry of the Environment, Madrid, 1 December 2006.
29. Interview, Ministry of the Environment, Madrid, 1 December 2006.
30. Interview, Ministry of the Environment, Madrid, 1 December 2006.
31. http://ec.europa.eu/environment/nature/info/memberstates_en.htm, (last access: 19 April 2008).
32. http://ec.europa.eu/environment/nature/conservation/wildbirds/hunting/docs/ hunting_guide_en.pdf, (last access: 19 April 2008).
33. Interview, SEO/BirdLife, Madrid, 7 October 2005.
34. Interview, Ministry of the Environment, Madrid, 29 November 2006.
35. http://www.mma.es/portal/secciones/el_ministerio/estructura/organigrama/secg2_dgcalevamb_ sub_3.htm, (last access: 6 December 2007).
36. Ministerio de Obras Públicas, Transportes y Medio Ambiente, 1992, 1993, 1994 and, 1995.
37. Interview, Ministry of the Environment, Madrid, 26 November 2006.

38. Interview, environmental organization, Barcelona, 7 April 2006.
39. http://www.mma.es/secciones/info_estadistica_ambiental/estadisticas_info/ memorias/2006/pdf/mem0 6_6_2_quejasprocedimientos.pdf, (last access: 19 April 2008).
40. http://eurex.europa.eu/LexUriServ/LexUriServ.do?uri=OJ:C:2002:301E: 0224:0226: ES:PDF, (last access: 19 April 2008).
41. Interview, Ministry of the Environment, Madrid, 26 November 2006.

7
Hungary: The Tricky Path of Building Environmental Governance

Aron Buzogány

Introduction

Hungary's accession to the European Union (EU) has largely overlapped with the dual processes of democratization and marketization of the country. By applying for EU membership, Hungary has not only locked in its political and economic transition, it has also committed itself to harmonizing its domestic legislation with the *acquis communautaire*. The 'anticipatory and adaptive Europeanization' (Ágh, 1999) of public policies following from this commitment entailed institutional and financial challenges, which went far beyond what Spain, Portugal and Greece had had to cope with. The CEE states were confronted with a growing and ever more complex system of EU regulations. Moreover, the EU has been also much more demanding in its requirements for membership than was the case with the earlier accessions. In addition to the adoption of the *acquis*, the CEE accession countries were asked to build the institutional and administrative capacities necessary to make EU polices work on the ground.

While most institutions and laws were already in place when Hungary started the accession process, the comprehensive environmental regulatory system of the EU provided a unique opportunity to upgrade the legal framework and close institutional gaps (Greenspan Bell, 2004b: 62). At the same time, the top-down adoption process of EU environmental policies that were mainly designed by and for economically more developed EU member states carried with it the danger of running into serious problems of effective implementation if not adjusted properly into the domestic legal and institutional system or of undermining domestic innovations that developed during the past 20 years (Gille, 2004).

This chapter examines how Hungarian state and nonstate actors have coped with the challenges posed by accession in the field of environmental policy. Implementing the environmental *acquis* demanded state capacities that were often in short supply. At the same time, several EU environmental policies explicitly demand the involvement of nonstate actors in the policy process. This chapter explores to what extent the functional and legal imperatives of accession have led to a departure from hierarchical, top-down modes of governance in environmental policy towards more inclusive (new) modes of governance based on a systematic involvement of nonstate actors into the policy process. Analysis of EU environmental policies in water management, industrial air pollution and nature protection finds only scattered evidence for the emergence of new modes of governance. Ongoing institutional restructuring and the huge policy overload often did not allow for the establishment of consolidated relations between state and nonstate actors. In those cases where cooperation between state and nonstate actors has emerged, it has often reinforced existing networks rather than providing access to new (civil society or business) actors. At the same time, EU compliance pressure and capacity building channeled through preaccession funding programs have led to the development of an increasingly professionalized and diversified sector of environmental organizations, who are willing and able to use the opportunities provided by the EU in order to be *both* partners of and watchdogs over state administration in the implementation of EU environmental policy.

Environmental policy in Hungary

The basic tenets of Hungarian environmental policy emerged in the 1970s and 1980s when the predominant paradigm of policy was based on national quality standards and pollution permits (Kerekes and Bulla, 1994). First attempts made to create a more distinct body of environmental law resulted in the Hungarian Environmental Act on the Protection of the Human Environment, which was adopted in 1976. The predominant paradigm of policy was based on technological and end-of-pipe approaches and relied heavily on traditional command-and-control regulations accompanied by a highly inefficient system of fines for noncompliance that were levied by state authorities towards state-owned enterprises (Caddy and Vari, 2002).

By the early 1980s, environmental degradation caused by heavy industry became more than obvious and the state's inability to solve these problems emerged as a major societal grievance, leading to the emergence of a strong environmental movement. Effectively using the space provided for political mobilization by the legalization of associations and the rise of public concern on environmental damage, environmentalist groups became one of the main drivers of democratic transition in Hungary, while also providing a haven also for other opposition groups (Enyedi and Szirmai, 1998; Berg, 1999). After regime change, the importance of the environmental movement decreased but it is still the best organized segment of Hungarian civil society with a considerable number of professionalized groups actively engaging in both policymaking and protest (Rose-Ackermann, 2005: 175–90; Kerényi and Szabó, 2006). Contacts between the environmental movement and the ministry have become increasingly institutionalized and some of the leading personalities from the NGO sector have been appointed to high-ranking positions within environmental administration.

Business actors started becoming actively involved in the shaping of environmental policy during the mid-1990s, when some of the most polluting legacies of state socialist heavy industry had already been closed and a far-reaching and rapid privatization of most industry sectors had already taken place (Kerekes and Bulla, 1994). The opening of Hungarian industry towards Western markets and the massive influx of foreign investors had developed into a push factor towards the technological upgrade and embracement of environmental management practices (Kerekes, 2000; Kerekes and Kiss, 2003).

While the liberalization of the political and economic spheres has made the emergence of new ideas and a more participatory policymaking process possible, many of the old bureaucratic practices have prevailed (O'Toole 1997: 13). The conflicting coexistence of the 'old' and the 'new' administrative styles has become characteristic for environmental politics in Hungary and leads to a typically incremental policy process, a nature that is exacerbated by frequent restructuring of the national and regional environmental administration (Mocsári, 2004a). Up to nine ministries are in charge of some aspects of environmental policymaking, each of them overseeing various implementing bodies at the regional and national level, often having overlapping competencies as a result of frequent institutional reshufflings. The EU accession period was paralleled by a profound internal restructuring in order to rationalize the tasks within the administration. At the local level, 12 regional environmental inspectorates (REIs) and 12 water management authorities were established, which are coordinated by the National Environmental Inspectorate. The REIs perform the major functions related to production, monitoring and enforcement. However, most environmentally relevant public provision and supervision services like water, waste or sewage management are assigned to local governments, which are often overwhelmed by the administrative and financial tasks they are in charge of.

Environmental policy and the challenge of accession

The Environmental Framework Law (Act LIII/1995) – already incorporating many basic elements of EU environmental legislation – had already been drafted in 1995 after years of consultation with stakeholder organizations. Yet, the economic problems caused by transition decreased the importance given to environmental policy within government and parliament, as well as the population as a whole (O'Toole and Hanf, 1998: 101–02; Støle 2003: 64). With the environmental administration fighting an uphill battle against more influential departments, such as economy, transport or agriculture, EU accession emerged as a welcome opportunity both to integrate further and upgrade environmental policy and legislation and to secure finance for environmental projects (Greenspan Bell, 2004b).

For the state administration, institutional restructuring together with a huge policy overload resulted in a quasi-permanent state of emergency during the accession period, which absorbed most of the state capacities available. The perception of constant institutional flux was further aggravated by the changing composition of the environmental bureaucracy, which undertook a veritable odyssey through different parts of the state administration, becoming consecutively integrated with transport, water management, agriculture and regional development (Mocsári, 2004a). In addition to administrative fragmentation and conflict, high turnover rates within public administration (Meyer-Sahling, 2006) and uncompetitive salaries prevented stabilization both within the departments and with their external ties (O'Toole and Hanf, 1998). EU membership has not led to a consolidation of the civil service either, as postaccession administrative reform endorsing a 'lean state' has been accompanied by both budget cuts and dismissals of up to 30 percent of staff employed in the administration at the regional level and the national park directorates (Jávor and Németh, 2007).

In short, Hungary entered the accession process with an ambivalent heritage in the field of environmental policy. Unlike in the Southern European accession countries, a relatively integrated administrative structure was already in place with reasonable expertise and competence for the main requirements of the *acquis* (Greenspan Bell, 2004b).

At the same time, the Hungarian government faced a long list of short-comings. These concerned, among others, coordination deficits and overlapping competencies between different levels of administration (mainly on the national/regional level), deficient monitoring and sanc-tioning systems caused by the ineffective legal system, as well as short-comings in staffing and training, particularly at the local level. To solve just some of these shortcomings, the overall costs of the environmental accession of Hungary were expected to be over 10 billion euros in the 2000–10 period (ECOTEC, 2000). While large parts of these costs would have to be shouldered by the national budget and domestic business as a main target of EU environmental regulation, Hungary's membership also opened up the possibility of using EU Structural Funds to upgrade its environmental performance.

The remainder of this chapter will explore in more detail how the opportunities and constraints of EU accession have shaped the imple-mentation of EU environmental policies in water management, air pol-lution control and nature protection.

Coping with the challenge of accession

Water management: new standards and old networks

The Hungarian water management sector has been characterized by a long and internationally well-regarded professional tradition that has a strong standing within the state administration. The changes in regula-tory styles over the last century have closely followed societal and politi-cal trends in the country. The first water law entered into force in the second half of the nineteenth century, reflecting the needs of its time, which were mainly irrigation, flood prevention, transport and energy production. Regional water management associations were already established on a private basis in the nineteenth century (Somlyódy, 2000). Leading the process of technical modernization, the state admin-istration increasingly took on responsibility for water management and drinking water provision in the twentieth century. During the social-ist period, water was considered to be a basic public service, with the state in charge of securing water quantity, availability and affordabil-ity (Péter, 2007). Environmental problems caused by rapid industrial-ization and the needs of a growing economic liberalization triggered a shift towards increasing attention to criteria such as environmental soundness and economic cost-effectiveness in water management. From the 1980s on, the water management sector became confronted with growing criticism and public protest over the construction plans of the

Slovak-Hungarian Bős-Gabčikovo Dam (Harper, 2005). Mobilization against the centrally planned, environmentally dangerous and non-transparent policy making process in water management became a crystallization point for the emerging environmental movement and an important step towards regime change (Hajba, 1994; Láng-Pickvance, 1998). This process strengthened calls for more inclusive planning and public participation in water management policy. First experiments with more participatory policy instruments were already taking place in the late 1980s, when planning processes started using public hearings in order to settle environmental conflicts, although these were neverthe-less regarded as unsuccessful since they usually took place late in the planning cycle and were seen as window dressing in order to legitimize decisions already taken (Vari and Caddy, 1999; Ijjas and Botond, 2004). After regime change and in line with Western European examples, the National Water Authority put in a research consortium charge of developing a pilot river basin management plan and used this as a template across the country. The transition to a market economy triggered legal changes that were enacted with Act LVII on Water Management in 1995, which essentially provides for a central role for local governments in water provision and management as well as the gradual introduction of tariffs for water usage. This reflected growing requirements for regu-lation within the changed circumstances of privatized agriculture, the enhanced importance of the private sector in industrial production and the pressure for opening up to environmental groups wishing to participate in the water management process. The transition process also led to a gradual change in attitudes within the water management sector – which had traditionally been dominated by a strong elite of civil engineers – towards increasing accommodation of the views of local politicians and nature conservation experts (Fülöp, 2003). New policy instruments were introduced, including market-oriented regulations and strict environmental standards. Yet, collateral effects of political change, such as deep-seated political restructuring or institutional and regional fragmentation, produced a great variety of partially overlap-ping regulations.

The need to harmonize with EU water policy standards and policy instruments that was triggered by Hungary's accession to the EU has reinforced reorientation and reform within the water management sec-tor that started with political transition. As a result of the inclusion of Hungarian experts in transnational water policy networks during the socialist period, most of the policies that had to be implemented were not entirely new concepts in the country. However, their implementation often lacked coherence. Reforms associated with accession had already been predominantly regarded by Hungarian water management authorities as necessary steps before transition (Ijjas and Botond, 2004). These reforms could be achieved through accession conditionality and the financial resources made available through EU preaccession funds. The command-and-control approach underlying older EC environmental regulation, such as the DWD, was largely congruent with technology-based Hungarian legislation in this area, even if differences in standards existed (see below). In contrast, new policy instruments, which require complex cross-sectoral collaboration and include high participatory standards, such as the WFD, have been seriously at odds with the domestic regulatory regime.

The provisions of the EU DWD were introduced by amending the Water Management Law in 1998. Full legal transposition was achieved with governmental decree 201/2001 (X.25), which included monitoring requirements and new parameters. According to the legislation, full compliance is to be reached in two steps, by the end of 2006 and 2009, respectively.[1] In order to enforce sustainable water usage, EU water policy requires the cost-effective pricing of water by 2015. This is clearly not the case in Hungary, where subsidization and cross-subsidization between households and industrial users as well as between central and local governments is common (Boda et al., 2006, Péter, 2007). The highly fragmented and blurred ownership structure of water utilities in Hungary not only makes it difficult to reach cost-effectiveness but also affects the implementation of the DWD. Because of the wide-ranging decentralization and local government reforms that took place at the beginning of the 1990s, public utilities became the property of the 3,600 municipalities. This administrative restructuring left most communities short of funding and without the relevant administrative resources (O'Toole, 1994). Most of these municipalities did not raise the costs for water provision to cost-effective levels for political considerations and the existence of a very high number of independently run, money-losing water utilities became a central problem for the implementation of the requirements of the DWD, as a large part of the costs for compliance had to be carried by the municipalities.

One of the most serious and costly challenges that the state administration and local governments have been facing is the stricter drinking water quality standards of the EU. Because of geomorphologic characteristics, especially in Southern Hungary, the arsenic, ammonium and nitrate concentration of drinking water in some regions is far higher than is allowed by the parameters of the DWD, affecting 58 percent of the Hungarian population.[2] Raising drinking water quality standards to the EU level is made even more difficult by the poor quality of the sewage and pumping system and requires massive financial investments that makes the implementation of this directive one of the most expensive challenges of EU accession (Bod, 2007). Noncompliance with the requirements of the DWD became obvious by mid-2007 (Bod, 2007). There are several causes behind the ineffective application of the directive, largely related to weak financial capacities at state and local levels. First, the initial estimates of the National Drinking Water Quality Program for meeting the parameters of the directive effectively had grossly underestimated the costs, failing to take into account the deterioration in the quality of municipal sewage systems since the 1990s.[3]

Second, another problem emerged when it became clear that financing from EU Structural Funds would not reach the amount that the Hungarian government had planned. Originally, plans were for about 70–75 percent of the necessary costs to be covered by EU funding, with central government contributing 20–25 percent. In this case, municipalities would have had to bear the remaining 0–5 percent of the financial burden. However, as the EU financial provisions changed for the 2007–13 planning period, the share to be borne by the municipalities increased to 20–25 percent (Bod, 2007). According to the new guidelines, EU funding could not be used for general modernization of water utilities, so the attempt to tighten the parameters on drinking water was undermined by leaking water pipes. This adds to the fact that the costs are unequally distributed, with the regions most affected (the North and the South Great Plain) also being those lacking the financial resources to invest in their public utilities.

Third, the scientific evidence for the legitimacy of EU water parameters has remained controversial in Hungary. The Hungarian government contested the necessity of some of the parameters of the DWD using scientific arguments during the preaccession period, but could negotiate only a short derogation period until 2009 for implementing the directive. When the municipalities finally became aware of the full costs needed to reach the quality standards set by the directive, the mayors of the affected regions started to mobilize against its provisions, contesting them both scientifically (citing a lack of evidence for high arsenic levels in water causing health problems[4]) and politically, as the expected up to fivefold rise in local water tariffs might threatened their chances of being reelected (Péter, 2007; Bod, 2007).

Trying to cope with the new challenges in water management has given rise to reinforced patterns of collaboration between state and nonstate actors in Hungarian water management. Municipalities have typically sought to secure state subsidies for their water management sector. The aim of the complex state subsidy system is to reduce regional differences in water tariffs. However, the system is also open to abuse, as municipalities often raise water tariffs artificially in order to apply for state subsidies or use these funds for purposes other than subsidizing water prices. At the same time, the water infrastructure construction lobby has been successful in influencing policymakers to include the provision of mandatory water services into the Act on Local Government. The coalition formed by water infrastructure construction companies and local governments has allowed them to secure subsidies from the central government budget (Boda and Scheiring, 2006; Péter, 2007).

PPPs in the water management sector had emerged already well before the accession process as the result of municipal reform in the early 1990s. In search of revenue, several large municipalities, including Budapest, sold parts of their shares to international consortia of water multinationals (SUEZ and RWE) and transformed their water companies into PPPs that now provide 40 percent of the Hungarian water supply (Péter, 2004). However, the lack of a proper regulatory framework has largely led to less than optimal results with the PPPs, which could not be forced to invest in sector modernization, for two main reasons. First, PPPs only emerged in the central and metropolitan regions, which did not require heavy investment into infrastructure but were likely to provide revenues in a relatively short time. Second, improved economic efficiency of the PPPs has essentially been achieved through organizational restructuring, the job cuts and, sometimes, raised water tariffs (Boda and Scheiring, 2008). In sum, delegation in the form of PPPs had no direct effect on meeting the challenges of compliance with the EU directives.

While the implementation of the DWD has faced predominantly financial problems, the WFD primarily required a complex administrative restructuring. As the directive builds on cross-media integration of water management and environmental policy considerations, it caused a mismatch with the sectorally differentiated structure of the administration in Hungary. The two branches put in charge of the implementation of the directive, water management and environmental protection, tend to have opposing views on water policies with the former being responsible for planning and building infrastructure and issuing permits and the latter for environmental protection, two tasks that were already in conflict in the past (Fülöp, 2003). Adapting to EU requirements went hand in hand with a series of institutional reforms within the Hungarian water administration, which can, at least partially, be attributed to pressure from the EU and from below. Following the frequent institutional changes during the 1990s, institutional reform in 2002 moved tasks related to water management to the Ministry of Environment, thus unifying the national and regional levels of the two authorities and allowing them to function more coherently. The implementation of the WFD is coordinated and managed by the Water Director and the newly established WFD Department within the Ministry of Environment and Water, as well as the Interministerial Strategic Coordination Committee.[5]

The Hungarian government chose not to transpose the WFD in a single legal act, but instead to amend the existing Water Management Act and the Environmental Protection Act through several governmental and ministerial decrees[6] in order to bring them in line with the new requirements. Mirroring the incremental legislative development, Hungary opted for the so-called partial river basin approach (Vari and Kisgyorgy, 1998), which did not imply far-reaching changes in the institutional structure but merged the old system with the new one. Practical application of the WFD began in December 2006 and will last until late 2009 when the National River Management Plan has to be presented. During the 200 days reserved for public debate on the national conception of water management in 2007, more than 60 important stakeholders[7] provided written comments on the draft, representing several thousand stakeholders from the field.

Like its legal transposition, the practical application of the WFD has required first of all the mobilization of administrative and cognitive capacities. Different forms of formal and informal networks were established or empowered during the policy process. Being a relatively small and centralized country, the circle of water management professionals in Hungary consists of tightly knit networks with a high level of interaction among those involved directly with policymaking issues on the administrative, business and academic sides (Rozgonyi and Toarniczky, 2007). At the same time, strong links with foreign organizations working on water-related matters have been in place for a long time, with members of the Hungarian professional community holding important positions in different European or global-level professional associations and water management bodies. Members of NGOs, such as the Global Water Partnership or the Hungarian Hydrological Society, bring together water policy experts and overlap in membership with state administration and research institutions.

With accession, EU funding through PHARE twinning projects became available and was used extensively in various projects conducted with international partners. These projects have benefited from contacts forged through different professional networks such as ICPDR (International Commission for the Protection of the Danube River), the EU CIRCA information sharing network, and the Common Implementation Strategy of the WFD. The pan-European HarmoniCOP project, focusing on societal learning in water management, allowed the accumulation of expertise, which later became part of the official strategy on public participation of the WFD (Ijjas and Botond, 2004). The Regional Environmental Center based in Szentendre, Hungary, and funded by the EU and the US government became a central hub for bringing together and funding water policy expertise from the region in a number of conferences, workshops and publications. In addition, nonstate actors, such as WWF-Hungary, funded pilot projects dealing with the implementation of public participation principles in river basins (Bera, 2005). Close partnership with the state actor's position enabled WWF-Hungary to gain deeper insights into the policymaking process and, in some cases, also to influence it.[8] Yet collaboration with the state administration is not uncontroversial among NGOs. The Working Group on WFD of the environmental movement has, for instance, alleged that 'real' participation in WFD matters is still nonexistent and water management has remained in the hands of a few water professionals and their NGO allies, who do not understand local and environmental needs and merely simulate public participation.[9] Thus, the WWF also pursues more combative strategies, including the sponsoring of collective complaints to the European Commission about Hungary's definition of 'water services', which it perceives to be a violation of the directive.[10]

At the same time, the importance of highly professionalized consulting companies, which transcend the state versus nonstate or not-for-profit versus for-profit dichotomy, is growing. In line with this development, tasks related to implemention of the WFD were delegated to a specialized multistakeholder consortium that is mainly reliant on EU funding and brings together domestic and international consulting companies (Öko Zrt., VTK Innosystem Kft., ARCADIS Euroconsult BV), NGOs, such as WWF-Hungary, and academic institutions.[11] The consortium was put in charge of developing an economic analysis for the WFD implementation and pilot projects and of proposing guidelines for public participation in water-related issues. This contracting out can be seen as a departure from hierarchical steering in order to mobilize necessary expertise not available in the state sector. While the state administration could use its engagement capacity based on existing networks in the policy field, the scope of new modes of governance has remained restricted to providing specific expertise. As in the case of the DWD, the involvement of nonstate actors has not helped in sharing the costs and administrative burden of compliance with the provisions of the directive. These costs are related to the exceptionally high levels of investment in infrastructure that remain the main challenge for implementing both directives. In the case of the DWD, compatibility between the regulatory style of Hungarian legislation and the EU policy meant that mobilization of additional cognitive capacities was not required. The mismatch regarding regulatory standards, however, was significant and hindered the effective application of the DWD. Because of the lack of domestic financial capacities and limited external funding possibilities, the Commission refrained from exerting compliance pressure and agreed to extend the derogation period until 2013 (Bod, 2007). At the same time, the willingness of domestic consumer groups to mobilize has been limited, as the implementation of DWD will trigger significant increases in water tariffs for the population. Moreover, the beneficial effects of EU drinking water quality standards for public health are scientifically contested. While noncompliance with the DWD can be primarily related to the high costs imposed, it is too early to assess the effectiveness of the WFD. Implementation entails a longer time and the directive's provisions are less specific (e.g., as reaching 'good' water quality until 2015). In any case, the integrated approach of the directive and its participatory provisions provide possibilities for nonstate actors to mobilize and push for compliance.

In sum, the adoption of and adaptation to EU water regulations in Hungary has implied the use of financial, administrative and cognitive state resources. However, as a result of the fairly high level of professional expertise available in the water management sector, state capacities were not seriously challenged by EU demands. State administration has reached out to nonstate actors, consulting them for their expertise and information in the implementation of the WFD. At the same time, the weak financial capacities of the state have remained a major challenge for effective implementation of the DWD, where delegation failed to mobilize financial resources. With public authorities largely remaining in charge, Hungary has predominantly relied on derogations and EU funding to ease the pressure for adaptation.

Industrial air pollution: towards integrated permitting systems

Rapid industrialization was a clear priority for Hungarian governments during the last century, resulting in increasing levels of air pollution in several hot spot areas across the country. From the 1930s on, industrial pollution control was traditionally based on national quality standards, emission limits and strict fines to enforce compliance. Although some progress in reducing pollution was reported in the 1980s through the use of this system, it mostly resulted in a largely unrealistic scheme of administration imposing limits that were neither achievable nor adhered to by industrial polluters. Usually, the fines were too low to force installations to invest in new technologies and informal contacts between state administration and state-owned installations provided for leverage in pollution abatement. Altogether, this resulted in an overly complicated and overbureaucratized system of regulations (Caddy and Vari, 2002).

At the end of the 1980s, environmental problems caused by industrialization became more and more evident. Academic experts and the emerging environmental movement called for introducing complex integrated permitting procedures, such as EIA. This has widely been regarded not only as a central legislative requirement, but also as a symbol for a revolutionary move from hierarchical towards more open and democratic planning methods, giving citizens the possibility of becoming involved in the policy processes. Hungary was among the first of the CEE states to introduce EIA requirements in 1993. It used the existing horizontal legislation as a starting point towards fulfilling EU requirements, not only with regard to the EIAD, but also in the field of industrial pollution.

Except for the concept of BAT, the traditional regulatory approach of the LCPD did not seriously challenge the Hungarian regulatory framework. The command-and-control, technology based standards of this directive corresponded largely with domestic priorities, the regulatory tradition and the monitoring capacities available. The only serious mismatch has been of a financial nature, resulting from the costly investment in clean technologies necessary to meet the strict EU standards. Law 21/1986 (VI. 2) had provided the legal basis for regulating air pollution by industry. A ministerial decree 22/1998 (VI. 26) adapted the law to the LCPD by applying the limit values for large combustion plants but without transposing the national emission ceilings legislation because of the high investment costs the new technologies implied for the domestic energy sector. Ministerial Decree 10/2003 (VII. 11) fully harmonized the LCPD with domestic laws. The EU agreed to a short transition period until the end of the year 2004, by when all investment needed to reach the limits set by the directive had to be carried out. As all installations – the directive targets predominantly the energy sector, as well as the cement and sugar industries – successfully accomplished the installation of new abatement technologies, implementation of the directive can be considered as successful.[12] The public administration was able to motivate industry to take a long-term view of regulatory reform, consult the government early on and adapt to EU legislation well before the deadline. At the same time, private capital was available in the affected industrial sectors and technology transfer additionally enabled industry to invest in pollution control and clean technologies.[13]

In contrast, the introduction of the integrated environmental permitting systems as envisioned by the EIAD and IPPCD required a thorough restructuring of the procedure for issuing environmental permits and a departure from a dominant regulatory approach. The introduction of a precautionary problemsolving approach and the concept of BAT, which is at the core of the IPPCD, implied a change from the legalistic, prescriptive approach towards one based on coordination and communication between the regulators and the regulated that was alien to Hungarian administrative practice. Moreover, it involved a process of administrative decentralization, since regional authorities were to get more autonomy in setting the permit conditions.

Orienting itself towards EU legislation as early as the beginning of the 1990s, Hungary introduced a two-stage EIA process in 1993. The small expert community prepared the Hungarian EIA legislation and the EIA Unit of the Ministry of Environment and Water drafted the executive order in close collaboration with the NGO the Environmental Management and Law Association (EMLA) based on expertise gathered by Hungarian experts and activists in transnational Strategic Environmental Assessment (SEA)/EIA-related networks (Cherp and Antypas, 2003). Overall, the EIA decree, which became increasingly comprehensive as a result of its harmonization with EU law, has become a legal instrument that is frequently used by environmental groups.

The administrative challenge was to build institutions that could manage the new requirements, monitor their implementation and act as an interface for information on technical know-how. Second to establishing a new coordinating unit at the national level, the major workload of the EIAD and IPPCD has consisted of developing coordination capacity within the REI. As the IPPC permit integrates other permitting procedures, including EIA, the REIs' most important task has been to communicate and coordinate with a number of authorities that have to be included into the permitting procedure, such as the public health and medical officers, the national park directorates and the water authorities as well as the local authorities (Emmott, 1997).

At the same time, decentralization and restructuring within the local and environmental authorities have resulted in weakened administrative capacities and diminished the quality of environmental permitting. The ambiguous definition of the role to be played by the REIs has led to conflicts of interest, as often the inspectorate itself was both conducting and assessing the reviews (O'Toole and Hanf, 1998: 105). Major problems concerned the strong sectoral division of expertise within the environmental administration in handling EIA because of the multidisciplinary character of the permitting procedure. The REIs have been asked to cooperate closely with stakeholders by establishing active working relations with industry and civil society actors (Jávor and Németh, 2007). All these tasks require administrative and financial capacities that were scarcely available at the already heavily overburdened local and regional levels of environmental administration.

However, business actors have had to shoulder the major part of the cost of the directive. They have faced both high investment costs in order to reduce the pollution levels of their installations and have had to take into consideration an increasingly complex, time-consuming and expensive permitting procedure based on integrated permits. As the IPPC procedure relies heavily on the preexisting EIA system, it created overlapping regulations and was criticized by business actors for overburdening them (Mayer, 2002; Mayer and Dragos, 2005).[14] Giving in to the lobbying of employer organizations, Government Decree 314/2005 (XII. 25) introduced a new, coordinated EIA-IPPC permitting procedure that simplified the permitting requirements by establishing a 'one-window' (*egyablakos*) permitting system.

While it is too early to assess the effectiveness of the regulatory system, the implementation of the IPPCD can be regarded as a success as 96 percent of the installations that needed to obtain the certificates did so before the EU deadline in October 2007.[15] Hungary is considered a top performer in this regard within the EU, together with Luxemburg, Finland, the UK, Germany and the Czech Republic.[16] At the same time, the implementation of the IPPCD in Hungary differs between industrial sectors. These differences are related to the market orientation of each sector, the ownership structure and the prio existence of environmental management systems, such as EMAS or ISO 14001 (Kerekes, 2000). Whereas strongly export-oriented industries, mostly characterized by a high level of foreign ownership and significant transfer of capital and technical know-how, could afford to invest in environmental quality, small enterprises and farms are in general confronted with high costs compared to their financial possibilities (Mayer and Dragos, 2005).

During the implementation process, new forms of collaboration between state and nonstate actors started to emerge. State actors, most importantly the small IPPC Unit within the National Environmental Inspectorate, were able to mobilize business actors, using their profound knowledge of capacities and shortcomings in different industrial sectors, to connect national and EU initiatives and partners. At the national level, the IPPC Unit maintained close relationships with sectoral industry associations, which were tasked with the identification and formulation of national BAT guidance procedures. Suggestions for simplifying the permit procedure were based on a detailed survey carried out by the Hungarian Chamber of Industry and Trade (MKIK, 2004). In several cases the IPPC Unit kick-started such processes by targeting external assistance, such as PHARE projects, to enable the sectoral industrial associations starting their work.[17]

The implementation of the IPPCD was accompanied also by a 'pull' of domestic nonbusiness actors taking advantage of capacity building programs. Benefiting from both domestic and EU PHARE funding, the National Conservationist Society has run a program that included spreading information on IPPC, on-site visits and participation in IPPC permitting procedures as observers in five regions of the country (MVTSZ, 2003).[18] Consulting companies, having their roots in academia or the environmental movement, such as the Cleaner Production Center, the Association for Environmental Management and the Environmental Economics Center became part of the epistemic community working on IPPC related issues and received funding through PHARE or participated in the AC IMPEL (Accession Country EU Network for the Implementation and Enforcement of Environmental Law) 'Project on environmental enforcement practices' (PEEP) monitoring mission.[19] In addition to initiating and funding such networks in order to monitor the development of Hungarian legislation in this field during the preaccession period, the European Commission started to exert compliance pressure after accession. As one of the first legal actions initiated against Hungary, in October 2007 the Commission sent a letter of formal notice stating that Hungarian legislation omitted certain categories of projects mentioned in the EIAD and covered other categories inadequately so that environmentally significant projects might escape impact assessment procedures.[20]

Several structural shortcomings in the implementation process raise questions about the quality of the EIA and the IPPC permitting procedure. One of the main reasons for this lies in the weak administrative capacities of the environmental management system. REIs do not only handle integrated permits but also issue about 400 different types of other permits. During the accession period, the number of permitting procedures doubled, while the staff numbers of the REIs only increased slightly during this time and were even reduced after accession because of government austerity measures following accession (Jávor and Németh, 2007). There is also a shortage of expertise and technical resources needed to process different monitoring requirements, as well as of training for the complex integrated tasks the authorities have to perform at a local level.[21] While there is reasonable collaboration between state and nonstate actors in the implementation process, its whole potential remains scarcely exploited. In the absence of a tradition of cooperation, state and nonstate actors maintain little trust in their collaboration and expect defection (Greenspan Bell, 2004b). Added to this, legal concepts introduced by new EU directives do not fit easily with domestic regulatory traditions. The *de*scriptive rather than *pre*scriptive regulatory style of the IPPCD poses difficulties for both state and nonstate actors in interpreting its legal provisions. Guidance documents, such as BREFs, which play a large role in integrated permitting, are alien to Hungarian legal thinking and practice as they do not hold immediate direct legal effects and dilute the role played by the state as the main regulator.[22] In practice, the lack of trust on the part of both industry and public authorities has given rise to uncertainties surrounding the BREFs. As a result, state actors have tended to 'harden' initially soft instruments for everyday administrative use by applying stricter standards than EU legislation would require (Mayer and Dragos, 2005).[23] In a similar vein, business actors, such as the Federation of Hungarian Employers, do not trust the enforcement capacities of public authorities. They also prefer hard regulation since soft regulatory measures are more difficult for REIs to monitor and enforce effectively (Center for Environmental Studies, 2003). Whereas voluntary agreements are recognized as a possibility for improving implementation within the business community, the lack of transparency and enforcement capacities is seen as a major obstacle to the uniform application of the IPPCD across different regions and sectors (Center for Environmental Studies, 2003). While business shies away from new modes of governance to avoid their distorting effects on competition, public opinion is extremely skeptical of the involvement of business in the policy process, for fear of corruption. Saturated with news stories of abuses of public resources, different derogation periods or phasing in arrangements can easily become misinterpreted as corrupt practice and are therefore applied only cautiously by the state administration (Center for Environmental Studies, 2003).

Overall, the adoption of and adaptation to EU air pollution policies in Hungary can be regarded as a partial success. As the implementation of EU directives was preceded by and partially overlapped with the process of industrial modernization and restructuring, most business actors regarded investments into new and green technologies as necessary prerequisites for their competitiveness in the EU. Consultations between the state administration and business actors in determining sectoral BREFs, going in some cases as far as delegation to business actors, was further encouraged by twinning projects, where the state administration acted as a network broker. At the same time, the growing complexity of regulatory tasks attributed to local level authorities was not followed by an increase in administrative capacities. While environmental permitting procedures became more business friendly, mutual mistrust between state and nonstate actors prevails.

Nature protection: wild birds, watchdogs and sites of conflict

Hungary's geographical position at the crossroads of different climatic and biogeographical regions promises to enrich the EU with relatively high biological diversity and well preserved natural values. At the same time, similarly to Western Europe, the last century saw a sharp decline of biodiversity due to rapid industrialization and the intensification of agricultural production. To counter this trend, Hungarian nature conservation had already established a fairly developed institutional system under the socialist regime. While the economic crisis until the mid-1990s helped the regeneration of the biosphere, the new economic upswing led to urban sprawl, a rapid increase of greenfield investments and a boost in highway construction (Bulla and Tamás, 2003).

Hungarian nature conservation legislation has differed only in some minor points from the EU Wild Bird Directive and the FFHD; for example, with regard to the definition of protected natural areas or the lack of explicit targeting of the protection of wild birds. Relevant Natura 2000 legislation has been incorporated into Hungarian law on various levels. Nature Conservation Act No. 53 of 1996 introduced the basic notion of Natura 2000 areas and delegated legislative powers to the government and the Ministry of Environment and Water Management. The Natura 2000 decree contains comprehensive regulations regarding terminology, designation of areas, rules of compensation and detailed provisions with regard to Natura 2000 areas. Nevertheless, the implementation of the FFHD and the Wild Birds Directive was one of the most challenging tasks Hungary had to face during its harmonization with EU legislation. The process of site designation was been seriously delayed by five months, making Hungary to the only member state from the accession countries that entered the EU without having had the Natura 2000 Network in place.

The implementation problems that the Natura 2000 Network faced in Hungary can be traced back to several problems. Within the Nature Conservation Office at the Ministry of Environment and Water there was an obvious lack of staff, with initially only two, later three persons working on NATURA 2000 coordination. A department devoted to the complex tasks related to Natura 2000 was established only two years before accession. This seriously delayed the preparation for the designation process, as first contacts concerning this issue between the ministry and the national parks took place just one year before the designation deadline (Mocsári, 2004b: 23).

The Ministry of Environment and Water established a consortium, in which several national and international consultancies, research institutes of the Hungarian Academy of Sciences and nonstate organizations, such as MME/BirdLife Hungary and the RSPB, participated. All these major scientific institutions and their experts collaborated in small working groups to prepare the work on different species and resystematize the existing databases.[24] This consortium made an assessment of available sites and collected information and prepared a proposal for SPAs and SCIs in the framework of a PHARE project. Thanks to this outsourcing, the Natura 2000 designation process could build on extensive sets of data collected within a wide range of national and pan-European projects dealing with biodiversity monitoring. SPAs were mainly designated based on data available to the national park directorates and taking into account the database collected by the NGO MME/Birdlife Hungary as part of the Important Bird Area (IBA) project. For protected habitats, designation was based on the result of the CORINE (COoRdination of INformation on the Environment) pan-European program that Hungary carried out in the mid-1990s. This was supplemented with data from the National Biodiversity Monitoring Program that was cofunded by the PHARE project. There was no systematic participation of NGOs in the overall process of proposed SCIs' (pSCIs) designation, but local NGOs helped in the designation with advice and provided data for both SPAs and pSCIs.

Based on these preparations, as a second step, the ten national park directorates set up a detailed strategic designation plan including local information from researchers and NGOs. There were some misunderstandings during the consultation period, and some problems with data provision, but in the end these procedures provided a sufficiently well designed network covering 21 percent of the country's area (MTVSZ,

2003). The MME/BirdLife Hungary participated in the designation process of SPAs from the beginning, as it had the relevant capacities and was involved in the gathering of the IBA international data, on which the EU pSCI data is partly based. During the designation process, local communities were not involved and NGO participation was weak. Altogether, the designation process was rather chaotic and nontransparent; the list of proposed sites was treated as confidential and was not available for review, since the government feared that early publication might lead to a wave of unfounded complaints. Initially, the Ministry of Environment and Water planned to organize debates about the proposed sites, but refrained from this as the deadlines agreed with the European Commission needed to be met. Moreover, the Commission expected that site designation would only take into account strictly scientific criteria, thus effectively blocking public participation in determining NATURA 2000 sites.[25]

Local communities were systematically informed about the designation process and its implications only after the Nature Conservation Office of the ministry had signed a contract with the Natura 2000 Coalition, set up by the most important NGOs in the nature protection field, such as the Central and Eastern European Bankwatch, MME/BirdLife Hungary, the National Society of Conservationists and WWF-Hungary. The coalition was created in order to represent the interests of environmentalist groups that were only marginally included in the process during the designation phase. Based on the agreement with the Nature Conservation Office, the coalition started an awareness-raising campaign to increase societal acceptance of the NATURA 2000 designation and promote best practice for managing conflicts related to conservation. During 2004, the NGOs, with the support of the ministry, published leaflets for farmers and organized meetings with stakeholders. However, the inclusion in the process of ENGOs, which could have helped to increase its legitimacy, and the information campaign designed to spread information about the Natura 2000 Network came very late. While ENGOs finally agreed to participate in the process, other important stakeholders, such as landowners, land users, hunters or fishermen, were not involved at all (Mocsári, 2004b). The secrecy of the designation process, together with the lack of information about the implications of the site designation for the landowners, led to increasing animosity between the groups involved. Even though the Minister of Environment emphasized that designation did not mean a 'nationalization' or 'recollectivization' of the NATURA territories, the flawed communication strategy of the ministry did not mitigate the fears of the agricultural interest groups. After the designation process had taken place, some of the initial fears of the agricultural lobby and forest owners were calmed by the promise of compensation payments for protected areas included into the Natura 2000 Network. However, new controversies emerged when the government announced that compensation payments would be postponed until 2009 while agricultural activities had to be reduced on designated sites from 2006.[26]

The lack of coordination between different branches of government ultimately became the major stumbling block for finishing the designation process. The Ministry of Finance and the Ministry of Agriculture and Regional Development emerged as main veto players, and were supported in some cases by the Ministry of Defense having a veto right where NATURA 2000 sites impinged on areas of strategic relevance. The conflict with the Ministry of Agriculture went so far that it effectively blocked the designation process for almost a year and became the major impediment to implementation. Controversies between the two ministries particularly concerned access to the GPS-based land registry database of the Ministry of Agriculture, which was needed to identify the protected territories under NATURA 2000. This caused a serious delay in the official announcement of the land registration numbers of the designated sites and hindered the development of the institutional background for providing compensation payments for the farmers.

The delayed but ultimately successful designation process was made possible by several factors. The Commission closely followed the implementation of the NATURA 2000 Network in Hungary and intervened several times to help put the legal drafting and negotiations back on track. This happened both formally and informally, by ways of pointing to the shortcomings of the legislation or threatening to withhold funding from the Structural Funds after accession, if the list of designated territories was not completed on time. On several occasions, high level Commission officials were publicly pointing to Hungary's problematic Natura 2000 process (Mocsári, 2004a). The Commission found parts of the legislation to be insufficient to assure conservation, accountability and transparency and requested the Hungarian government to remedy these flaws. After accession, the Commission also brought legal action against Hungary concerning the quantity and quality of designated bird protection areas.[27] The active 'push' of the EU towards make nature protection legislation more comprehensive was paralleled by capacity building measures financed through different preaccession funds such as PHARE. The main initiative supporting implementation of the Natura 2000 network was the PHARE project 'Preparation for

Implementing the Habitats Directive in Hungary', where Finnish and Spanish preaccession advisors contributed to the development of the institutional setup for the Natura 2000 network in Hungary.

At the same time, the accession process has led to an empowerment of domestic civil society groups working on nature conservation issues. On the one hand, environmental groups have been able to benefit from their transnational and EU-level networks that supplied them with policy expertise and resources. On the other hand, the Commission emerged as a new actor readily supporting nonstate actors by both offering funding and emphasizing the need to include them into the policy process. Brussels provided civil society actors with a platform to highlight the shortcomings of the designation process and pushed the government towards giving NGOs a role to play in communicating the results of the site designation process the stakeholders and the general public. At the same time, the Natura 2000 Coalition developed into an efficient watchdog of the government that has been ready to use the new legal opportunities provided by harmonization. For instance, as the designation process was delayed through conflicts within different branches of the government, the Natura 2000 Coalition set a deadline of September 2004 for solving the problems around designation; otherwise they would initiate legal action against the government.

In sum, the Hungarian Natura designation process was delayed because of the lack of administrative capacities and the weak coordination between the different ministerial branches involved. The level of inclusion of nonstate actors in the process was inconsequential and nonsystematic during the designation process. When the delay in implementation, not least caused by the incapacity of the Hungarian authorities to raise the awareness of the Natura 2000 Network among stakeholders, became obvious, state actors gradually started to change their attitude towards consulting NGOs. Ultimately, a more effective implementation of the nature protection directives was reached by compliance pressure and the provision of much needed capacities to the Hungarian state, both by the EU and domestic NGOs. The strengthening of their capacities fostered a more cooperative approach on the part of state actors towards NGOs in the application of NATURA 2000 giving rise to patterns of consultation and delegation.

Conclusion

The adoption of and adaptation to the EU's environmental *acquis* has posed serious challenges to both state and nonstate actors in Hungary.

The transfer of European environmental policies came with significant costs, which have met weak state capacities. Moreover, the profound legal and administrative changes required by EU regulations were often contradictory to the regulatory tradition of the country. At the same time, the accession process opened up new funding possibilities and gave leverage over the state administration to nonstate actors allowing them to influence the policy process. Even if this influence has increased during the accession process, this chapter has shown that the state has remained the central actor in determining the (in)effectiveness of the policy process. We have found only weak forms of new modes of governance, including consultation and the delegation of technical and scientific tasks. Deficient coordination among different ministries and levels of government as well as a lack of financial and administrative capacities of state actors are the main causes for the ineffective implementation of EU environmental policies in Hungary. Against this background, traditional command-and-control approaches have prevailed or were even reinforced by the accession process. The time pressure and huge implementation load allowed only for weak and nonsystematic forms of nonstate actor involvement. In those cases in which nonstate actors did manage to participate, it often took the help of transnational actors, such as international environmental organizations, policy consultancies, companies or EU-level confederations to achieve this. Both the increasing effectiveness and the emergence of more inclusive modes of governance were fostered by EU compliance pressure and its capacity building channeled through preaccession funding programs. EU push and pull factors have not decreased since accession and, therefore, will further help to improve the conditions for the emergence of new modes of governance. This is all the more likely since EU membership has provided Hungarian nonstate actors with additional legal and political opportunities to make their voices heard in the policy process. Thus, we might see similar dynamics to those we have observed for the Southern European accession countries after they joined the EU in the 1980s.

Notes

1. In places where the arsenic concentration is higher than 30 µg/l, the deadline was set for December 2006, while in places where the concentration is above 10 µg/l the deadline was set for the end of the year 2009.
2. While the EU limits for arsenic concentration are 10 µg/l, in several Hungarian regions this can reach 50 µg/l.
3. Interview, Public Official, Ministry of Environment and Water Management, Budapest, 4 December 2006.

4. This higher standard meets the WHO's health requirements related to arsenic. Arsenic intake comes from two sources: water and food. It is argued that because the Hungarian diet means that the intake from food is much less than in the EU and this allows a higher intake from water.
5. One place is officially reserved to civil society.
6. Gov. Order 1189/2000. (XI.7.) established the Hungarian Strategic Plan on WFD harmonization. Gov. Order 221/2004 (VII. 21.) is one of the more important legal acts establishing the basis on principles of integrated water basin management, while 314/2004 (XII.22) outlines the system of competencies in dealing with water policy.
7. Including the Regional Water Management Councils, the Scientific Board on Water Management Research of the Hungarian Academy of Science, the Water Utilities Association, the Annual Meeting of Environmental Civil Society Groups and the Hungarian Hydrological Association.
8. Interview, ENGO, 5 September 2006.
9. See the communication issued by the NGO Working Group on WFD, A 'Víz Keretirányelv és társadalmi részvétel - van, de mégsincs?' c. szekció állásfoglalása, Környezet- és Természetvédő Társadalmi Szervezetek, XVI. Országos Találkozója 2006. március 10-12., Veszprém (on file) and the WFD Message Board of BITE Baja, http://forum.sg.hu/listazas.php3?azonosito=BITE&id=1109973788, (last access: 8 December 2007).
10. Complaint to the European Commission concerning failure of Austria, Belgium, Denmark, Estonia, Finland, Germany, Hungary, Ireland, Poland, Sweden and The Netherlands to comply with the provisions of the EU Water Framework Directive 2000/60/EC ('WFD') Article 5§1.
11. Víz Keretirányelv végrehajtásának elősegítése II. fázis [Helping to implement the WFD. 2 phase], http://www.vizeink.hu/, (last access: 15 March 2008).
12. Interview, Public Official; Ministry of Environment and Water Management, Budapest, 7 December 2006.
13. Interview, Public Official; Ministry of Environment and Water Management, Budapest, 7 December 2006. It should be mentioned, though, that one of the industries targeted by the LPCD, the sugar industry, had to close most of its production sites after enlargement, mostly as a result of the provisions of the EU's Common Agricultural Policy.
14. One of the better known cases also widely discussed in national press was the integrated permitting procedure for a factory with a long glass-making tradition in Tokod, which lasted almost 500 days and was one of the causes of the bankruptcy of the company Rajnai, A.2004. Tokodon a helyzet változatlan. *Élet és Irodalom,* http://www.es.hu/pd/display.asp?channel=RIPORT0430, Romhányi, T.2004. A bürokrácia ötszáz napja [The 500 days of bureaucracy]. *Népszabadság.*
15. No Hungarian companies to close for lack of special pollution certificate, 5 January 2007, bbj.hu (Accessed 13 February 2008).
16. EDS Europe News: Delays in IPPC implementation 'unacceptable', 30 October 2007.
17. Interview, Public Official, General Inspectorate of Environment Protection and Water, 7 December 2007.
18. http://www.mtvsz.hu/programok/vallalat, (last access: 8 December 2007).

19. Several externally financed projects were run in order to strengthen Hungarian IPPC capacities: IPPC Capacity Development and Strengthening of Regional Environmental Authorities - UK DFID Know-How Fund CNTR 01 2465/Hungary; IPPC - HU/IB/2004/EN/04 PHARE Twinning project; 'Implementation of the IPPC Directive and its Legal Enforcement in Hungary' financed by PHARE (HU 9513-03-01-L002); 'Capacity Building in Implementation of the Environmental Acquis at the Local and Regional Level' - EuropeAid/116215/CSV/PHA.
20. European Commission: Environmental impact assessment: Commission to take legal action to improve implementation in Hungary, Latvia, Lithuania and Slovenia, Reference: IP/06/1397, 13 Obtober 2006.
21. Interview, Public Official, Ministry of Environment and Water Management, Budapest, 5 December 2006.
22. Interview, Public Official, General Inspectorate of Environment Protection and Water, 3 December 2007.
23. Interview, Consultant, 29 November 2007.
24. Interview, ENGO, 27 November 2006.
25. Interview, ENGO, 28 November 2006.
26. Népszabadság Online: Natura 2000: késik a támogatás. [Natura 2000: Compensation delayed], http://nol.hu/cikk/420049/, (last access: 21 February 2007).
27. Nature protection: Commission takes legal action against 11 Member States over protected bird areas http://europa.eu/rapid/pressReleasesAction. do? reference=IP/07/938&format=HTM, (last access: 21 December 2007).

8

Poland: When Environmental Governance Meets Politics

Sonja Guttenbrunner

Introduction

Transition to democracy in Poland demanded a complete reorganization of the political system. Especially in the economic field, Poland chose a radical transformation known as the Balcerowicz Plan.[1] However, the economic 'shock therapy' did not completely sideline environmental issues (Zylicz and Holzinger, 2000). This is partly because democratization, marketization and Europeanization occurred simultaneously. Like the other CEE candidate countries, Poland had to implement the entire environmental *acquis* before accession to the EU. Moreover, the EU did not grant much flexibility in adapting domestic structures of environmental governance to its legislation. The implementation of EU environmental policies has required vast financial and administrative capacities from the Polish administration, whose resources were already tied up in managing the transition process. Establishing working relations between state and civil society actors posed even more of a challenge since structures of intermediation between interest groups were only just emerging in the new democracy. More cooperative and inclusive forms of governance were not only necessary to conform to the more participatory requirements of EU environmental directives, but could also help Polish authorities to acquire the resources of nonstate actors, which were desperately needed to make the EU policies work.

How has the EU accession process shaped environmental policy making in Poland? Which capacities were required to fulfill the conditions for accession and how were they built up? Most importantly, what new opportunities for the collaboration of state and nonstate actors did emerge and how were they used? This chapter examines whether environmental enlargement has led to more inclusive modes

148

of environmental governance or if the traditional command-and-control approach has prevailed in Polish environmental policymaking. The first section of this chapter deals with the traditional patterns of environmental policy making in Poland. Then, an overview of the challenges posed by accession is given. Finally, the emerging modes of governance are examined in the fields of water management, air pollution and nature protection.

The case studies will show that environmental policy making in Poland is still dominated by hierarchical modes of governance. EU legislation together with decentralization, capacity building by the European Commission and a more active role for private actors have partly led to a reluctant opening up of governance processes. However, old administrative traditions inherited from the socialist regime, weak financial and administrative capacities, mistrust and the fear of state capture, as well as the feeble organizational capacity of nonstate actors and low environmental awareness on the part of the public still shape the relations between state and nonstate actors.

Environmental policy in Poland

Unlike the Southern European countries, Poland was not an environmental latecomer when it entered accession negotiations; legislation on nature and water protection dates back to the early 1930s. In response to the deteriorating state of the environment in the 1970s, Poland sought to establish a comprehensive Environmental Act, which was passed in 1980. Its effectiveness, however, was limited. Under the socialist regime, environmental protection was mainly a sectoral task delegated to technical experts. Economic growth was the top priority and environmental legislation had little impact on the economic development of the country. As a consequence, interaction between environmental policymakers and the various sectors of the economy remained minimal (Andersson, 2002).

As in the other socialist countries, environmental protection played a minor role and this was mirrored in the environmental administration. Although ministries concerned with environmental protection existed, their position remained weak and they had a very small personal accoutrement (Andersson, 2002). This started to change only in the mid-1980s. As with other areas, environmental governance was dominated by the command-and-control approach adopted by the socialist regime. While nonstate actors were largely excluded from the policy process, the effectiveness of top-down regulation was seriously compromised by mismanagement and political patronage. These legacies of the past still haunt governance structures and processes in Poland today (Grosse, 2005).

As in Hungary, environmental protest played an important role in the opposition movement that carried the velvet revolution in Poland. Ecological activism was the only societal activity that was tolerated under the socialist regime in Poland (REC, 1997; Andersson, 2002). With environmental problems becoming ever more visible in the early 1980s, environmental organizations appeared on the political scene. An ecological 'subtable' was established at the round table talks between Solidarnosc (Solidarity) and the communist regime, which started in 1989. It was agreed that a draft for a new environmental law should be codified within two years. A commission was put in charge of the codification but failed to get a new law passed. Instead, the Environmental Protection Act of 1980 was amended, adapting it to the new conditions of a market economy and democracy (Jendroska and Bar, 2005). Even these changes were seriously delayed because of the instability of power, with frequent changes of government (Sommer and Rotko, 1999). Moreover, while environmental concerns ranged high on the political agenda after regime change, public interest in ecological issues soon faded during the economic reforms and gave way to more pressing social and economic issues (Żylicz, 2000). Only in 2001, was a comprehensive Environmental Protection Act[2] finally passed. This framework law provides the main basis of Polish environmental legislation and includes detailed provisions and prescriptions. While air pollution control is fully included in this general law, water protection is regulated by separate laws, as is nature protection.

The Ministry of the Environment (MOE) was created in its current form in 1990. There are several state environmental agencies, which operate outside the extensive departmental structures even though they report to the Minister of the Environment. These encompass:

- the State Forest Administration, a state-owned company responsible for managing state forests on a commercial basis, and for monitoring the compliance of nonstate-owned forest with applicable regulations;
- the National Park Authority, a small administrative unit established mainly to coordinate budgetary allocations among the 23 national parks;
- the Geological Concessions Office, responsible for granting concessions and negotiating fees;

- the National Fund for Environmental Protection and Water Resource Management, an institution responsible for financing environmental investments and other activities on a contractual basis;
- seven regional board of water resource administration, whose function is to maintain river courses, coordinate counterflood activities, and collect small river-transport fees (Zylicz and Holzinger, 2000);
- the environmental protection inspectorates, which since 1998 have been attached to the MOE (Zylicz and Holzinger, 2000; Andersson, 2002).

Certain aspects of environmental legislation are dealt with by other ministries, including the Ministry of Health and the Ministry of Agriculture (Zylicz and Holzinger, 2000), while a series of environmental management responsibilities were transferred to provincial or municipal authorities partly because of the EU's financial investment and assistance system, which encouraged accession countries to reform their administrative structures at the regional level in order to manage structural funds (Yoder, 2003).

While the environmental administration was taking shape, it could not rely on established forms of intermediation between interest groups to facilitate cooperation with nonstate actors. In general, state actors have mostly lacked the political will to give civil society a real say in decision making. Prospects for a strong environmental movement had been somewhat muted by the withdrawal of foreign aid when democracy began to consolidate in Poland (Carmin and Hicks, 2002). Nevertheless, the Polish environmental sector went through a process of consolidation and professionalization during the 1990s, featuring a large variety of organizations ranging from national umbrella groups (League of Nature Protection, Polish Ecological Club), national branches of international NGOs (WWF-Poland) to expert, think-tank type organizations (Polish Environmental Law Association and the Institute for Sustainable Development). Yet, as we will see below, the involvement of environmental organizations in environmental policymaking is limited. The organization of business interests, finally, has been weak overall and is highly differentiated. Several industrial sectors are still mainly state-owned and enjoy privileged access to decisionmaking arenas. Moreover, sectors subject to foreign investment are usually better organized than sectors that are still controlled by the state or are dominated by domestic private companies.

Environmental policy and the challenge of accession

Poland hosts some of the most valuable ecosystems in Europe, which suffered from decades of uncontrolled industrialization under a centrally planned economy. After the collapse of the communist regime, one of the main challenges was to set up an efficient governance system to restore and protect the environment. As all other candidate states, Poland had to implement the entire body of environmental legislation before accession. The institutional legacy of state socialism, on the one hand, and the weak capacities of the Polish administration, on the other, rendered the adoption of and adaptation to EU environmental law very difficult.

During the accession process, the overriding concern of the European Commission was to make sure that Poland fulfilled the formal requirements of the accession agreements to transpose and apply in practice the environmental *acquis*. The Commission largely ignored the existence of legal and administrative traditions that could delay or impair effective implementation and enforcement of new environmental policies. At the domestic level, the drafting of environmental legislation was dominated by small and closed groups of experts and was still seen as a technical issue that should not hinder economic development. The weak position of the environmental ministries, financial problems[3] and the inexperience of administrative staff often prevented the effective implementation of new and old laws alike (Homeyer et al., 2001). Finally, entrenched bureaucratic interests resisted administrative changes that would help to overcome the fragmentation of responsibilities and strengthen the capacities of environmental authorities.

The next sections will analyze how the Polish administration has coped with the challenge of accession in three different sectors and explore to what extent it has enlisted the help of nonstate actors to adopt and adapt to the environmental *acquis*.

Coping with the challenge of accession

Water management: going local

The reorganization of water resources management has been one of the most costly and most sensitive issues in the adoption of and adaptation to EU environmental legislation. In communist Poland, the development of heavy industries was more important than the protection of water resources, which are anyhow scarce. By the mid-1990s, 70 percent of the length of the main rivers Odra and Vistula did not meet the physical and chemical criteria for water use of any kind (Andersson, 1999; Fay, 2003;). Poland had laid down its first legal and organizational regulations concerning water management in 1919. Since the 1950s, several complex programs containing basic elements of water management had been developed (ENGREF, 2003), but enforcement was poor and regulations inadequate given the level of heavy pollution by industry. In 1991, seven regional water management authorities were established.[4] Their institutional design followed Western European water management models. They are responsible for the maintenance of state hydraulic structures, such as dams and reservoirs; are in charge of waterways and state rivers; collect and organize data about water resources and use and put forward opinions concerning projects of water use. The water management authorities also play a prominent role in water management, such as for hydroelectricity, river regulation and flood prevention, and carry out investment in hydraulic projects of national importance (ENGREF, 2003).

The legal setting of standards of drinking water goes back to a regulation of 1977.[5] The Water Statute of 1990 is based on this regulation.[6] It should be mentioned that the standards set in the 1990 statute were already very close to EU drinking water regulations. The MOE had to make only minor adjustments to European law through regulations issued in September 2000, the most important of which are the Act on Water Law of 2001,[7] and the Act on the collective water supply and waste water discharge systems, also of 2001.[8] However, some additional laws and amendments still had to be passed. For example, new laws concerning the quality of 'materials having contact with water' and the organization of a relevant supervisory system were necessary. The parts of the EU DWD that are clearly defined and provide specific standards were easily incorporated in national law. Where European regulations, however, have left room for national provisions, they have been seldom fully transposed, giving rise to competing interpretations among different stakeholders and public authorities.[9]

The main problem, especially with these amendments, is administrative fragmentation, which hinders the effective implementation of the DWD. There is no clear 'institutional leadership' and no clear distribution of competencies among relevant government agencies and ministries.[10] The main public administration body responsible for the implementation of the DWD is the Chief Sanitary Inspectorate, which acts under the auspices of the Ministry of Health. It is the supervisory body in charge of the quality of water pumped into the water system. The supervision of the quality of materials having contact with water (for water pipes) lies within the responsibility of the Ministry of Infrastructure. The Ministry of Agriculture is in charge of the extension of water and waste water networks into rural areas. Within the MOE itself, a new department for water resources was created in December 2000 with responsibility for water cultivation and adjustments to fit with European legislation in the water sector. In addition, the 'Bureau of Water Management' was established within the structures of the MoE. This bureau coordinates the regional board of water resource administration that have monitoring duties. No central regulatory body exists to unify the dispersed responsibilities for the water and waste water sectors. Horizontal fragmentation is exacerbated by the vertical dispersion of water competencies. During the administrative reform of 1999,[11] the main responsibilities for water supply and management were transferred to the municipal level.

When Poland entered accession negotiations about water quality, about 80 percent of the urban population and only 60 percent of the rural population were connected to water supply systems (Hughes and Bucknall, 2000). Moreover, the poor quality of the surface water abstracted for drinking water and the naturally high mineral content of the groundwater posed additional difficulties for maintaining the quality of drinking water.[12]

Compliance with EU Directive 98/83/EC requires greater efficiency in water purification and the modernization of the system for monitoring drinking water quality (there are over 18,000 water and sewage companies). In accordance with Polish regulations, water quality was monitored where it was fed into the supply network rather than at the users' end, as required by the EU directive. This means that high investment is needed in this sector to modernize the water supply infrastructure (e.g., new pipes) and their monitoring systems (e.g., additional staff, more and better equipped laboratories). In 2000, the World Bank estimated the costs to be US\$ 3–8 billion (Hughes and Bucknall, 2000). The municipalities (*gminas*), which are ultimately responsible for ensuring compliance with European drinking water standards, have to find most of these funds. The environmental administrations in the districts (*poviats*), in turn, have to mobilize technical expertise and adopt new management tools to decide about water resources and monitor the compliance of the *gminas*.

The shift of responsibility to the local level involves choosing the appropriate form of water management, approving investment projects and finding funding for them, as well as making decisions on prices and services. At present, water utilities are either companies under commercial law, budgetary units,[13] water associations or state-owned companies (Fay, 2003). Despite their weak financial capacities, municipalities have barely made any attempt to bring in private investors. Most of them have chosen to retain 100 percent ownership of the utilities operating on their territory, including those with the status of companies in commercial law (OECD/DANCEE, 2003). Minority shareholdings by private actors or jointly owned operating companies are the exception. Widespread skepticism and strong reservations against the privatization of local drinking water treatment plants on the part of the population and local governments alike have prevented the emergence of new modes of governance in the drinking water sector. So far, local politicians have largely resisted pressures to improve the infrastructure emanating from requirements to meet EU standards (Fay, 2003). Not surprisingly, the implementation of the DWD is still wanting in Poland. Of course, the EU provided ISPA (Instrument for Structural Policies for Pre-Accession) grants for towns and cities of more than 100,000 inhabitants to fund improvements in their water and waste water infrastructure in order to meet its requirements. However, to access these grants, municipalities need to contribute around 25 percent of the required investment themselves.[14] Given the poor financial capacities of most local governments, they would have to raise their share from private investors. As a result, and unlike in the other CEE accession countries, EU capacity building has largely been absent. Nor has Poland faced much compliance pressure from below, not least because of the low acceptance of the DWD among the broader public. Nevertheless, so far, the European Commission has not opened any infringement proceedings against Poland on this matter.

In case of the WFD, Poland has made greater efforts to meet EU requirements. The biggest challenge was to overcome the traditional approach to water management that considered water resources as a mere technical and economic issue, while paying little attention to ecological standards and integrated ecosystem-based approaches. The main aim of the WFD – to achieve 'good water status' – by the end of 2015 is only vaguely defined (Scott and Holder, 2006). Yet, determining 'good water status' calls for high levels of scientific expertise, improved technical know-how, public participation and, most of all, heavy investment in infrastructure.

With the main challenges lying with application in practice, the legal transposition of the WFD was relatively smooth. The Water Law of 2001[15] transposed all European water regulations. Other relevant reference documents are the Environmental Protection Act,[16] the Law on

Collective Water Supply and Collective Sewage Disposal[17] and the Law on Waste Disposal.[18]

In order to facilitate the administrative coordination necessary for the application in practice and enforcement of the WFD, the Polish government decided to create a new institution. The basics had been laid down in the Water Law of 2001, but in the end it took five years before the necessary money from the state budget was allocated.[19] In July 2006, the National Water Management Board was finally established. It is an agency which answers to the MoE, coordinates the actions of the regional water management authorities and is responsible for planning water use and flood prevention. New projects for water management have to obtain its agreement.

In order to meet the participatory requirements of the WFD, a water council for public participation was established in each of the seven water management authorities. These councils act as institutionalized advisory bodies and are composed of 30 different stakeholders (different water users, local authorities, NGOs, experts), who are appointed by the MoE. Responding to the criticism of NGOs that the councils were restricted to only 30 stakeholders, the Polish government created commissions of public participation. Unlike the water councils, these commissions lack a legal basis and work at a more informal level. They are subordinate to the water councils and composed of 20 different stakeholders, five of whom are also members of the corresponding regional water council. The decentralization of water management and the participatory requirements of the WFD have provided stakeholders with new access points to the policy-making process.

The regional water management authorities have also received funding to help them develop special public participation procedures.[20] They were first tested in a pilot river basin, covering the subbasin of the Vistula, and were conducted within a twinning project under French coordination.[21] In this first test, which was designed to provide best practices for the other river basins, public participation was realized at different stages. The first stage was executed during June and July 2005. It started with surveys among representatives of local government and inhabitants, as well as to elementary and secondary students. The surveys conducted among inhabitants aimed at obtaining information on perceptions of local environmental problems. Of particular interest were problems concerning water, the causes and sources of hazards and the influence of various types of users (households, agriculture, industry, tourism, and so on) on the quality and usage of river water. At the second stage, meetings with representatives of local authorities, as well as representatives of other interest groups, took place. The aim was to inform them and to get them involved in conducting and organizing public participation. The broader public was included in form of written consultations and a public hearing (Chammas and Bogdanska-Warmuz, 2006).

The outcome of the public participation procedure was assessed as being positive, notably by the regional water management authorities. Most interestingly, stakeholders pointed to different aspects of water management to those noted by public administrators. The procedure also revealed that environmental awareness among the public was low and that it was extremely difficult to gain funding for specific projects concerning water protection. A nationwide estimate of the tested participation procedure is not possible as the programs are not fully implemented in all regions yet. But given the success of the trial, the Polish government has allocated sufficient financial resources to the regional water management boards in order to organize public participation procedures, thereby responding to the issues raised by the stakeholders.[22]

Nevertheless, the national administration has been less open to the involvement of nonstate actors than the regional authorities have. The legacies of state socialism appear to prevail, rendering public administrators rather hostile to opening up the policy process (Grosse, 2005). Moreover, frequent power changes and low public support for environmental issues have largely impaired cooperation with environmental organizations. Thus, nonstate actors are largely left to exert pressure by using the leverage of the EU by informing the European Commission about issues of noncompliance with EU regulations.[23]

In sum, unlike in case of the DWD, where EU push and pull factors have largely been absent, the implementation of the WFD has seen the emergence of some timid forms of new modes of governance at the regional level. Consultations with the broader public (including different stakeholders) have been facilitated by EU participatory requirements and further advanced through various twinning projects that have helped to build the capacity of regional authorities to implement the EU water management policy. Moreover, both public and private actors have learned to acknowledge the mutual benefits of multi-stakeholder consultations. While public authorities receive access to local knowledge, stakeholder involvement fosters public acceptance of the decisions taken. In return, stakeholders are regularly involved in the policy process. At the national level, however, lack of political will and frequent government changes have greatly impaired the involvement of nonstate actors. It remains to be seen whether multi-stakeholder involvement at the regional level is sufficient to foster a more effective implementation of the WFD, particularly since EU push through compliance pressure has been limited. Public mobilization is not very high in this specialized field of water management. If civil society seeks to get involved in the implementation of the WFD, it is via cooperation rather than confrontation.

Industrial air pollution: the fear of state capture

Next to water pollution, air quality used to be one of the pressing environmental issues in Poland. The rapid transformation from a largely agrarian to an industrial society in the 1950s resulted in a high energy dependency on brown coal and hard coal. Under the socialist regime, air pollution control was based on command-and-control regulations and some economic instruments. However, they were barely enforced and, thus, were not complied with by industry (Andersson, 2002). In 1966, the Air Protection Law introduced the concept of 'permissible concentrations' and fines for air pollution. The system was based on the granting of individual permits. In the 1980s, the disposal of waste and activities causing air pollution were made subject to charges. Fees were to be paid by all economic entities for their use of natural resources. The combination of permits, charges and fines persisted into the 1990s (Andersson, 1999). However, there has been a substantial reduction in industrial emissions in Poland since 1988, because of the decline in economic activity, the shutting down of the most polluting plants and improvements in management operational practices and environmental controls (Hughes and Bucknall, 2000).

When Poland opened accession negotiations with the EU, its energy sector was dominated by combustion plants with inadequate pollution control technology. While a number of old installations had been closed down or were operating at lower capacity in the 1990s, the implementation of the EU requirements in this sector still entailed substantial investment in new technologies. The World Bank put the costs of fighting air pollution in Poland at US$ 4.8 billion (lowest scenario) to US$ 14.5 billion (highest scenario) (Hughes and Bucknall, 2000).

The LCPD affected practically all Polish power plants, most of which failed to meet the standards of the directive at the time of accession. The LCPD has been implemented through the Environmental Protection Act and several ministerial decrees on emission standards and the measurement of these emissions. For certain emission limit values (ELVs), transition periods were negotiated with the European Commission, some of them lasting until 2017.[24] These temporary derogations have helped to diffuse any adaptational pressure of the LCPD on Poland, giving both government and industry several years to face up to the significant compliance costs.

Whereas the LCPD follows a command-and-control approach, imposing strict ELVs, the implementation of the IPPCD was more complex since Poland had to change fundamentally all of its permitting procedures. From the 1970s, single medium permitting procedures were in use in Poland. ELVs were set individually for each plant, depending on the so-called background pollution (the current state of air pollution in a given area) and the real pollutant emission levels. No institution was in place to issue integrated permits, and environmental authorities issued individual permits regarding each different medium of the environment (Börzel, Buzogany and Guttenbrunner, 2006).

Preparations to implement the requirements of the IPPCD into the Polish arena started in March 2000 with a preliminary program; a more comprehensive implementation program followed in March 2001. The IPPCD was fully transposed into Polish law through various articles in the Environmental Protection Act.[25] Executive orders and ordinances play an important role in the specification of these articles, as the necessary standards gain legal force through such acts. The IPPCD distinguishes between 'existing' and 'new' installations. The Polish statute, adopted in anticipation of EU membership, uses the date of 30 June 2003 as the cutoff for 'existing installations'. Facilities constructed after that date must comply immediately. The IPPCD also directly applies to any existing installation 'substantially changed' prior to 30 October 2007.

While the transposition of the IPPCD went fairly smoothly, its application has required some profound administrative reforms. In Poland, the permitting authorities exist at two different administrative levels. The Voivodships (at regional level) are responsible for installations that have a significant impact on the environment (*circa* 60 percent of installations). These are mostly installations that also require an EIA. The Powiats (at county level) are responsible for all other installations. The duality of the permitting administration proved difficult to reconcile with the IPPCD, which requires a uniform management of the applications by the permitting institutions. Moreover, the application process and the necessary requirements for permissions can differ from region to region. Finally, because of their lack of capacity, permitting institutions have often not been able to handle the necessary permits within the time limits.[26] In the issuing authorities, there is often only one person to deal with the integrated permits and allocate their processing to other administrative units. This fosters administrative fragmentation, which is reinforced by the differential treatment of industrial sectors. The Polish Steel Association, for instance, successfully bargained for longer transition periods. In return, it offered the expertise and financial resources of its members to help authorities to establish the licensing procedures. Thus, steel companies have financed the training of public administrators and other projects to help strengthen the administrative and cognitive capacities of state actors needed to apply and enforce the directive. These PPPs helped to promote effective implementation. In the end, more than 85 percent of the IPPC installations in the steel sector were able to submit their applications for the integrated permit by January 2007.[27] The as yet state-controlled chemical industry, in contrast, could not negotiate a similar arrangement, mostly because of frequent changes in government that resulted in repeated reshufflings of the boards of directors.[28] As a result, compliance with the IPPCD has remained low in this sector.

To assist the licensing authorities and companies in defining BAT standards at the national level, the European Commission has initiated an exchange of information between experts from EU member states, industry and environmental organizations. This work is coordinated by the European IPPC Bureau of the Institute for Prospective Technology Studies at EU Joint Research Centre in Seville (Spain). The IPPC Bureau organizes the Information Exchange Forum, which is made up of representatives of the member states, large associations and the Commission; the definition of any particular BAT is delegated to sectoral technical working groups. In the end, a reference document is produced for each relevant BAT (BREF) (Koutalakis, 2005). At the national level, technical working groups, composed of representatives from business, consultancies and environmental organizations, are responsible for the translation and adaptation of the reference documents. The BREFs developed in Seville are not legally binding. The idea is to identify and disseminate best practices and techniques, taking into account local environmental, technical and economic conditions. In Poland, however, BREFs are very often literally translated and made legally binding rather than used as guidelines. While the technical working groups include representatives of industry, companies have not been able to push for more flexible standards. On the contrary, Polish standards tend to be even stricter than those defined at the EU level. Lacking the expertise to deal with the technical details of the BREFs, Polish authorities prefer to adopt regulations that leave no discretion in the application of the directive. Adjusting BAT requirements to local conditions carries the risk for public authorities to be captured by business actors with their superior expertise.[29] While public authorities need the technical expertise and financial support of industry, the latter get engaged in the process because national standards for BAT provide legal certainty in the granting of the integrated permit they need to keep their business running. The main actors interested in the effective implementation of the IPPCD are the industries that have benefited from foreign investment or rely on foreign markets. They are also the actors who push most for the implementation of the IPPC requirements. They have an incentive for offering their resources because they want to avoid legal uncertainty and competitive disadvantages.

NGOs, in turn, have shown little interest in getting involved in the implementation of the IPPCD. Environmental organizations are not so technically versed as to be able to deal with the specific requirements of the IPPCD, for example regarding the definition of BAT, and pursue a broader approach to environmental protection.

In sum, EU air pollution control policies have posed a serious challenge to state and industry in Poland. While the Polish government managed to obtain temporary derogations for the LCPD, postponing compliance for several years, it had to take on the IPPCD, including its integrated approach, which is entirely new to environmental policy-making in Poland. Since public authorities have lacked the necessary capacities to adopt and adapt EU requirements for granting integrated permits, they have sought to enlist the resources of business. While companies have offered their expertise and money to ensure legal certainty in the implementation of the IPPCD, their involvement has not given rise to new modes of governance. On the contrary, afraid of being captured by more resourceful business actors, Polish authorities have harked back to traditional command-and-control regulation methods. While subverting the procedural and flexible approach of the IPPCD, consultations between state and industry have nonetheless fostered the effective application of the new licensing procedure in industrial sectors that are well-organized and have access to the financial and technical resources to comply with the directive.

Nature protection: the pull of private actors

Poland has a rich and diverse fauna and flora, whose protection has had to be balanced with the country's strive for economic development. Nature conservation was not new to Polish environmental legislation. The first law came into force in 1934 and was replaced by the Statute on Nature Conservation in 1949. In 1991, a new nature conservation law was passed and remained in force for 13 years (Wasilewski, 2005). Although some ENGOs state that Polish legislation was even stricter than EU law, the Polish government has always prioritized economic development over nature conversation.[30] In any case, the harmonization of Polish law with EU nature protection policies required substantial revisions. The Nature Conservation Law of 16 April 2004 brought the necessary changes. But its implementation has proved to be very demanding, particularly with regard to the designation of protected sites.

As in the Southern European and other CEE accession countries, the designation of protected sites has been the biggest challenge in the implementation of the FFHD and Wild Birds Directive. The concept of inventory types underlying the two nature conservation directives was completely new to Poland. The establishment of the Natura 2000 network requires the designation of sites that include not only Special Areas of Conservation (SACs) but also areas SPAs designated according to the Wild Birds Directive. Poland had to identify SPAs under the Wild Birds Directive and to present a complete national list of proposed sites of EU importance under the FFHD by 1 May 2004. As a result of weak administrative capacities and a lack of political will, however, Poland submitted only an incomplete list that by no means satisfied the requirements of the EU directives.

The designation process developed in different stages. While the initial phases were marked by pilot projects and the first collection of relevant data, the first list was compiled in 2001. The MoE, the main institution responsible for nature conservation, had neither sufficient qualified personnel nor the data necessary to identify areas to be protected under EU legislation. As a result, it relied mainly on old data. The problem of weak administrative capacities was exacerbated by the unwillingness of the Polish government to allocate additional funds for the drawing up of the inventories.[31] In order to facilitate acceptance, local authorities and representatives of industry were consulted in the preparation process. Environmental organizations and other civil society actors, by contrast, were excluded. Their involvement was perceived as neither necessary nor legitimate.[32]

In 2003, Poland had to enhance the list, because of additional annexes of the Wild Birds Directive and FFHD. The modifications were discussed again among ministerial representatives, regional authorities, water management authorities and representatives of the state forest administration. The latter protested against the designation of large forest areas as Natura 2000 sites, foreseeing problems in forest management.

Likewise, the water management authorities lobbied against the designation of river valleys, arguing that flood control could not be reconciled with nature conservation (Makomaska-Juchiewicz, 2004). The MoE was also confronted with local resistance. Municipalities, often in coalition with politicians of the major parties, mobilized against the protection of particular sites as they feared a slowdown in economic development. Proponents of a comprehensive designation process remained excluded from the consultation process. Thus, domestic resistance by powerful veto players, the lacking or failed information strategy about management plans for the Natura 2000 sites and the unclear financing situation resulted in a first draft list prepared by the MoE that only contained some of the sites originally considered and that the European Commission considered as vastly incomplete.

A group of Polish NGOs prepared a so-called 'shadow list', including all of the sites that the MoE had withdrawn from the original list because of domestic opposition. The Commission used the shadow list to push Poland towards substantial revisions by December 2005.[33] Moreover, in October 2004, it froze about 1 billion euros earmarked for Poland under the Cohesion Fund because of the insufficient designation of protection areas under Natura 2000 as well as for not meeting EU regulations regarding EIA (Bar, 2006).

These financial sanctions triggered some hasty reactions on the part of the Polish government. With the new Nature Conservation Law of 2004, a special regulation on EIA for Natura 2000 sites was enacted. First attempts to introduce the principle of EIA into Polish law had already been made within the framework of the Environmental Protection Act of 1980. Projects with considerable effects on the environment required a construction permit on the basis of an EIA (Jessel and Mackowiak-Pandera, 2004). Further important legal regulations emerged in the 1990s. In 1993, a new construction program was passed for the development of 2,000 km of new motorways. For this program, a decree, issued in 1995, distinguished three categories of EIA and established a coherent basis for them (Jessel and Mackowiak-Pandera, 2004). In the course of the harmonization with EU environmental law, the regulations were adjusted to the EIAD in 2000. Nevertheless, the implementation of the EIAD did not proceed smoothly. It was quickly incorporated into national legislation to secure EU financial support. Yet, the EIAD required substantial changes in the administrative structure of Poland and additional, qualified staff. In order to supervise the application of the directive, the Commission on Environmental Impact Assessments was established as early as 1999 as an advisory body to the Minister of Environmental Protection. Moreover, both at the national and the regional level, some new administrative units were created and extended and put in charge of the practical execution of the EIAs (Jendroska and Bar, 2005). The increase in administrative capacities, however, has often proved insufficient. Licensing authorities tend to be overwhelmed by the integrative assessment of a complex variety of data. At the same time, they have been reluctant to make information on EIAs accessible to the public. Citizens' and environmental groups, in turn, have exerted little pressure towards a more effective application and enforcement of the EIAD. Initially, the public was quite supportive of the EIA procedure. However, in the second half of the 1990s, a series of corruption cases seriously undermined its credibility, with NGOs taking money from companies for issuing positive assessments.[34] Overall, the implementation of the EIAD has been rather deficient, casting doubts on whether its application in the Natura process will be more effective.

Under the pressure of EU financial sanctions, the MoE finally sought cooperation with the environmental groups that had prepared the 'shadow list', charging them with drawing up parts of the inventory based on their expertise.[35] Although delegation helped to improve the implementation of the FFHD, Poland has remained a compliance laggard after accession. The European Commission accepted the list of Polish Natura 2000 sites in 2005. However, NGOs keep denouncing infringements of the directive. They provide the European Commission with information at an informal level, but have also lodged several complaints.[36] The most spectacular case has been the infringement case concerning the 'Via Baltica' project. Parts of the Via Baltica expressway have been routed through the 'Augustów Forest', which includes the mires of the Rospuda Valley, a proposed site under the Natura 2000 Network. A coalition of national ENGOs, including the Polish Society for the Protection of Birds (OTOP), WWF-Poland and the Polish Green Network, began to petition against the plan and were supported by the residents of Augustów as well as the local, regional and national authorities. Moreover, Polish NGOs managed to build a wide national and international coalition against the plan by using their media contacts and assistance from Brussels-linked environmental networks in which they were participating (CEE Bankwatch, Friends of the Earth, WWF-Europe and BirdLife International). Finally, Polish NGOs launched a set of lower-level court cases against the construction plans that took advantage of Poland's obligation to comply with EU environmental directives, such as the FFHD and the EIAD. In parallel, the European Commission also started to investigate the case by hiring a Polish-speaking lawyer, trying to sort out the conflict informally with the Polish government. When mediation failed, the Commission opened legal proceedings against Poland in December 2006 about several cases of highway constructions, including the Augustów bypass case (C-547/07). A lower domestic court had already declared the project illegal because it violated the FFHD. The ECJ decided that Poland had to suspend construction work immediately, until a final court judgment could be delivered. And indeed, in September 2008, the Highest Administrative Court (NSA) in Poland ruled that the section of 'Via Baltica' express road through the Rospuda Valley constituted a violation of the FFHD and repealed the environmental license of the project. In response to the legal action taken by Polish ENGOs, the Polish Ombudsman and the regional prosecutor, the Polish Minister of the Environment of the newly elected – and more EU-friendly – government of Donald Tusk initiated round table meetings in mid-2008 to seek a compromise solution in a new EIA. Polish NGOs, representatives of ministries, the Highways Agency and local authorities have been participating in these meetings, which are expected to result in a route around rather through the Rospuda Valley.[37] The case of the 'Augustów Forest' provides a clear example of how the EU can empower civil society and how, under pressure from 'above' and from 'below', governments are willing to involve nonstate actors in the policy process.

In sum, the case of nonstate actor (non)involvement in nature protection is indicative of the implementation of many EU environmental directives in Poland. Despite serious capacity problems, public authorities have been reluctant to involve nonstate actors in order to benefit from their expertise. If at all, they consult with stakeholders who oppose rather than support effective implementation. In case of the FFHD, it was only the external pressure from the EU that made the Polish administration enlist the help of NGOs, giving rise to some rare forms of consultation and delegation of technical tasks, which helped to improve implementation.

Conclusion

Despite serious capacity shortcomings in the adoption of and adaptation to the environmental *acquis*, Polish environmental policymaking remains dominated by a command-and-control approach. There is little evidence of the development of nonhierarchical and more inclusive governance modes that could help overcome capacity problems and increase the effectiveness and legitimacy of EU environmental policies. The top-down approach of the accession process did not leave much scope for national authorities to negotiate with nonstate actors. The European Commission insisted on a complete transposition of legal and technical standards. Where procedural regulations allowed for some flexibility, time pressure and the lack of governance capacities have largely prevented any opening up of the implementation process.

Capacity problems have been exacerbated by decentralization. Many responsibilities were shifted to the local level during the 1990s, without providing local authorities with the necessary financial resources. At the same time, the implementation of the WFD shows that decentralization can also be an enabling factor for the emergence of new modes of governance. Since devolution of policy competencies was part of the transition process, local authorities have not necessarily been imbued with the administrative culture of the socialist regime. Moreover, they are better positioned to reach out to the relevant stakeholders. Consultations with nonstate actors have been fostered by EU funding and twinning projects, strengthening the governance capacities of both state and nonstate actors. The implementation of the IPPCD corroborates these findings. At the national level, by contrast, unstable power relations, an administrative culture hostile to public involvement and fears of state capture have largely impaired the emergence of new modes of governance. They have been mitigated only by EU compliance pressure leading to the selective delegation of policy tasks and round table consultations as in case of the FFHD. In the absence of participatory requirements, the Polish government has sought to diffuse compliance pressures by seeking temporary derogations rather than by sharing the costs with nonstate actors. The DWD and the LCPD are clear examples of such an avoidance strategy, maintained by relevant stakeholders and by public skepticism towards privatization.

While the central administration in Poland appears to be trapped in socialist legacies , clinging to the traditional command-and-control approach and hostile to public involvement, those public authorities that are willing to cooperate often lack 'reliable' partners in society. The governance capacities of Polish industry and civil society are generally weak. Only some industrial sectors and ENGOs have been able to secure foreign investments and external funding, respectively. They, in turn, find it difficult to find reliable partners in government. Frequent government changes impair the emergence of stable patterns of engagement and render public commitments to mutual agreements scarcely credible.

Notes

1. A plan for economic reform, named after its author, the Polish minister and economist Leszek Balcerowicz; the plan was adopted in Poland in 1989.
2. Dz.U.2001.62.627 (Dziennik Ustaw/Law Journal).
3. To comply with EU environmental legislation, public sector investments under a low-cost scenario will amount to US\$ 22 billion rising to US\$ 43 billion under a high-cost scenario (Hughes and Bucknall, 2000).
4. Four of them are in the catchment area of the Vistula River, with their seats in Katowice, Cracow, Warsaw and Gdañsk. The other three are based in the Oder river catchment area, with seats in Wroclaw, Poznañ and Szczecin.
5. Dz.U.1977.18.72.
6. Dz.U.1990.35.205.
7. Dz.U.2001.115.1229.
8. Dz.U.2001.72.747.
9. Telephone Interview, Chief Sanitary Inspectorate, Warsaw, 13 February 2008.
10. Telephone Interview, Chief Sanitary Inspectorate, Warsaw, 12 February 2008.
11. The institutional reform, which came into force on 1 January 1999, reduced the number of regions (Voivodship) from 49 to 16. Voivodship is the largest administrative subdivision of the territory. Poviat is the second level of subdivisions and Gmina is the third level of subdivisions.
12. 38 percent of drinking water in Poland comes from surface water and 62 percent from groundwater.
13. Budgetary units are integrated into the administrative structure of local governments, without any financial independence or their own budgets.
14. http://ec.europa.eu/regional_policy/funds/ispa/provisions_en.htm, (last access: 13 December 2008).
15. Dz.U.2001.115.1229.
16. Dz.U.2001.62.627.
17. DZ.U.2001.72.747.
18. DZ.U.2001.62.628.
19. Interview, Public Official, Ministry of Environment, Warsaw, 10 October 2006.
20. Interview, Official, Regional Water Management Board Krakow, Krakow, 24 October 2006.
21. In Poland, a pilot river basin, covering the subbasin of the Vistula, from its sources to the confluence with the Raba, was selected to test the process of developing the river basin management plan. The experience gained has been used for the production of river basin management plans for other river basin districts in Poland. Different analyses, determined by the choice of the program of measures and the river basin management plans, as well as various tools for and forms of public participation were tested within the frame of the Polish-French project.
22. Interview, Public Official, Regional Water Management Board Krakow; 24 October 2006.
23. Interview, WWF, Warsaw, 11 October 2006.

24. These was an eight-year transition period from 1 January 2008 until 31 December 2015 on the emission limit values of sulfur dioxide (SO_2); a five year transition period dating from 1 January 2016 until 31 December 2020 on emission limit values of nitrogen oxides. Finally a transition period of two years was granted; a ten year long transitional period dating from 1 January 2008 until 31 December 2017 on emission limit values for dust from municipal heat-generating plants. This request was granted for 29 municipal heat-generating plants enlisted in the Accession Treaty; a transition period was granted until 31 December 2010 for 77 installations in respect of SO2 and dust.
25. Chapter 4 of this law deals with the different aspects of permits: General Aspects Art. 180–83; Issuing of the Permits Art.184–93; Expiring, Withdrawal and Limitation of Permits Art. 193–200; Integrated permits Art. 201–19; Permits for Release of Gases and Dust to the Air Art. 220–29.
26. The responsible administrations should handle the permits within six months of the application (for integrated permits; in the other cases it is even one to two months), but this deadline is seldom met.
27. Interview, Polish Steel Association, Warsaw, 23 October 2006.
28. Interview, Chamber for Chemical Industry, Warsaw, 18 October 2006.
29. Interview, Consultant, Warsaw, 16 October 2006.
30. Interview, League of Nature Conservation (NGO), Warsaw, 16 October 2006.
31. Interview, Public Official, Warsaw, 12 October 2005.
32. Interview, WWF-Poland, Warsaw, 12 October 2005.
33. Interview, Public Official MoE, Warsaw, 12 October 2005.
34. Interview, University of Warsaw, 12 October 2005, Interview EIA Commission Poland, Warsaw, 17 October 2006.
35. Interview, WWF-Poland, Warsaw, 12 October 2005, Interview Institute for Sustainable Development, Warsaw, 18 October 2006.
36. Interview, WWF-Poland, Warsaw, 12 October 2005.
37. http://www.viabalticainfo.org/-en-, (last access: 11 December 2008).

9
Romania: Environmental Governance – Form without Substance

Aron Buzogány

Introduction

Environmental issues – together with problems related to the functioning of the judiciary and competition policy – were the third major stumbling block for the Romanian accession to the EU. Romania significantly lagged behind most of the other CEE states with regard to its democratic development (Pridham, 2007), economic restructuring (Cernat, 2006) and public administration reform (Nunberg, 1999; Noutcheva and Bechev, 2008). While those CEE candidate countries that joined the EU in 2004 had rapidly embraced Western environmental policies, Romania only started to work on its environmental governance structures when it entered accession negotiations in 1999. The EU legal harmonization process became a major opportunity for Romania to reform its environmental institutions and to implement and monitor more efficient policies. EU pre and postaccession programs also provided Romanian authorities with access to know-how and financial resources to compensate for their poor capacities. At the same time, however, EU accession also put another burden on the transition process, as it required additional resources to be assigned for adopting and adapting to EU environmental policy.

This chapter analyzes how Romania mastered the changes and challenges associated with the 'Europeanization' of environmental policy and how accession to the EU has affected governance structures in this field. For both state and nonstate actors, the accession process has provided new opportunities and constraints that might foster mutual cooperation. While several EU directives prescribe the involvement of civil society and business actors, public authorities could benefit from the resources they have to offer. An examination of policy making on water management, industrial air pollution and nature protection shows, however, that Romania has hardly witnessed the emergence of new, more cooperative and inclusive forms of governance. On the contrary, EU accession has in many cases reinforced traditional patterns of command-and-control regulation through state administration, even if it continued to provide suboptimal results. So far, nonstate actors have remained marginalized in environmental policy-making. However, this might change as environmental organizations and companies become increasingly aware of the possibilities of influencing the policy process that are offered by EU accession.

Environmental policy in Romania

Similar to the other CEE accession states, environmental issues were not a priority in Romania during its state socialist period and even though its environmental legislation closely followed international standards, such laws were scarcely enforced. Seeking to promote rapid industrialization and economic autarchy, the Romanian government took only sporadic measures to reduce the effects of highly polluting industrial sectors and the heavy use of fertilizers in agricultural production (Dragomirescu, Muica and Turnock, 1998; UNECE, 2001). When increasing pollution of rivers and groundwater started to negatively affect irrigation in the early 1970s, the National Waters Council acquired overall responsibilities for environmental issues under the Environmental Protection Law of 1973. The changes, however, remained a 'legal curiosity' (Zinnes 2004: 447), were hardly implemented and had no support from any central government institution (e.g., Ministry of the Environment).

The first centralized environmental administration in Romania was only established after the breakdown of communism, when the Ministry of the Environment was formed in October 1991 and renamed to Ministry of Waters Forests and Environmental Protection in November 1992. For the very first time, this institution brought together different branches working on issues related to the environment, formerly spread over several ministries and research institutions. In 1995, the ministry was charged with drafting a comprehensive Environmental Protection Law (137/1995), which included progressive legal instruments, such as EIA. However, the general approach of this law was incoherent and piecemeal (Novac and Auer, 2004) and the weakness of the 'moribund and dysfunctional' (Zinnes, 2004) environmental portfolio prevented its implementation (Krüger and Carius, 2001; UNECE, 2001). Furthermore, political considerations and new challenges in the

EU harmonization process triggered frequent reforms of the environmental administration. In addition to the dispersal and reshuffling of its competencies, the environmental administration used to be heavily understaffed and underfunded (UNECE, 2001, Zinnes, 2004). This changed, however, during the last years of the accession process, when meeting the capacity requirements demanded by the EU became crucial for the successful competition of the negotiations.

The EU accession process also led to structural changes in the national and regional division of the work of the institutions subordinated to the Ministry of Environment and Sustainable Development (*Ministerul mediului şi dezvoltării durabile* – MMDD). At the national level, the National Environmental Protection Agency (NEPA) was created and is now in charge of the development of secondary legislation for implementation and enforcement. The regional environmental protection agencies (REPAs) were established in 2004 within the boundaries of the newly established eight development regions and are responsible for coordinating the local environmental protection agencies (LEPAs).[1] The 41 LEPAs and the Danube Delta Biosphere Reserve administration are charged with implementing and enforcing environmental legislation at the county level. In addition, the Environmental Guard (*Garda de Mediu*) was set up in 2005 as a specialized enforcement body answering to the MMDD (European Commission, 2005a).

Unlike in several postsocialist states in the region, where environmental issues were central to the protest movements that helped to bring down socialism in 1989–90, the Ceausescu regime largely suppressed (environmental) civil society organizations (Turnock, 2002; Olearius, 2006). After transition, the environmental movement started to emerge, particularly in areas with a significant tradition of mountaineering and nature conservation, but its impact has remained weak (Botcheva, 1996; Dragomirescu, Muica and Turnock, 1998) and its activities are mostly oriented towards the local level (Burada and Berceanu, 2005).

The role of industry in environmental policy has been equally weak. Reluctant economic liberalization during the 1990s left many industrial sectors in state ownership and highly dependent on state subsidies, which were often allocated according to political criteria (Gallagher, 2005; Cernat, 2006; Pasti, 2006). Export-oriented industrial sectors that could afford modern, less polluting technologies did not exist here before the end of the 1990s, when EU accession started to exert legislative and administrative pressure and Romania engaged in an economic catchup process with other CEE countries attracting foreign direct investments.

Environmental policy and the challenge of accession

Romania was the last of the ten CEE candidate countries to open negotiations on Chapter 22 of the *acquis communitaire* and environmental
issues emerged as a major stumbling block on the country's road towards
accession. Romania started the accession race with extremely weak
capacities in the administrative sector (Krüger and Carius, 2001); coordination between national, regional and local levels was largely unconsol-
idated, monitoring and law enforcement were scattered and corruption
was widespread (Craciun, 2006). Public administration was often understaffed at all levels of government (ECOTEC, 2000), and, as a heritage of
socialist environmental policies, its training remained largely technical.
Moreover, low wages in the public sector caused permanent personnel
changes (DANCEE, 2003: 69–73). EU accession has forced the Romanian
environmental administration to start an open-ended and often ad-hoc
learning on the job process. As a result of the persistent lack of financial[2] and administrative resources, constant institutional and legal
reshuffling processes and the tight deadlines dictated by the EU, public administration has largely muddled through the accession process.
Being under constant pressure from stronger ministries and struggling
with high fragmentation, environmental policy making usually leant
back on the command-and-control regulation that resonates well with
the administrative tradition of the country (Hinoea and Balogh, 2004).

At the same time, one of the main challenges of environmental accession in Romania was to break with the country's traditionally weak law
enforcement capacities. While the legal and institutional structures were
often in place, these remained merely 'forms without substance' (*'forme
fără fond'*), lacking proper implementation. This has been the case with
the crucial piece of horizontal environmental legislation regarding EIA.
While the Romanian Environmental Law (137/1995) already contained
the main provisions of the EIAD as well as the steps of the EIA procedures, lack of political will hindered any effective implementation of
the directive (Krüger and Carius, 2001: 55f.). Only in 2002, and because
of massive EU pressure, were details of the procedure included into the
law. Three years later, the European Commission still assessed that the
implementation of the EIAD was incomplete and that further strengthening of administrative capacities was required for a successful implementation (European Commission, 2005c: 64). While the legal and
institutional adaptation of the EIA was cumbersome and involved only
state actors, it was raised to prominence as it has been used to effect by
NGOs (Baga and Buzogány, 2008).

Coping with the challenge of accession

Water management: channelling modernization

As a result of the strong emphasis on industrialization and extensive agricultural production, Romanian water management during the socialist period focused on issues of water quantity. Romania had created a complex and cost-heavy network of dams, canals and waterworks that were perceived as a major economic necessity for fulfilling the energy needs of industry and the irrigation demands of the agricultural sector (Turnock, 2007). The prioritization of water quantity resulted in a lack of investment and the neglect of problems related to water quality (Zinnes, 2004). Intensive fertilization, uncontrolled industrial activities and the absence of waste water treatment facilities and technology led to high levels of water pollution. After 1989, water demand decreased significantly because many industrial and agricultural plants had collapsed. While water quality improved in several hot spot areas, most rivers still suffer from heavy pollution.[3]

Water management responsibilities in Romania are divided between the Water Department of the MMDD, the National Administration for Romanian Waters (Administratia Nationala 'Apele Române' – ANAR) and the Ministry of Local Public Works, which is in charge of the municipal water utilities. With its top-heavy administration and a long tradition of professionalism, ANAR is the key player in the water sector, holding full competencies for the regulation of water supply and acting both as a water regulator and a provider of water as a resource (Zinnes, 2004).[4] Since 1996, Romanian water legislation has been based on the Water Law (107/1996), which keeps the main water assets in the public domain and separates water ownership from water management. The local water management sector went through a series of far-reaching changes during the 1990s. Many of these were related to the protracted public utilities reform, which opened possibilities for several coexisting ways of managing water resources by local administrations (Popa et al., 2001). Municipalities could choose between delegating or subcontracting water supply service provision to private providers or assuming the managerial responsibility themselves (Hegedüs, Somogyi and Tönko, 2003). The first wave of reform produced hundreds of public utilities (*regii autonome*) owned by local authorities as a single shareholder. Often, these were politically dependent on local administrations and lacked both financial and technical means for sustainable management, which made them heavily reliant on state subsidies. This system also inherited the tradition of cross-subsidies by industry through applying different water tariffs for different groups of users. The low tariff levels (and their nonpayment) generated losses in most parts of the country, failing to cover even the operational costs, let alone investment requirements (Zinnes, Tarhoaca and Popovici, 1999). These capacity problems triggered a second wave of reforms, reinforced by EU accession, that promoted the modernization of water infrastructure and rational water use through introducing the use of economic instruments in water management and additional funding.

The legal transposition of the DWD did not cause serious challenges in Romania as its command-and-control approach fitted in the existing national legislation well. In 2002, the Romanian Parliament passed law 458/2002 transposing the EU definition of clean water into the Romanian legislation and stipulating the establishment in 2003 of the Action Plan for Drinking Water, which defines the implementation steps (Government of Romania, 2004a). Water quality standards and monitoring procedures were harmonized by two governmental decisions in 2004 (GD 974/2004, GD 273/2004) and Romanian law thus became fully compliant with the EU Directive (European Commission, 2005c: 64).

While transposition went rather smoothly, implementation of the DWD has been by far the most serious financial challenge Romania has had to tackle in the environmental field, with estimated costs reaching 10 billion euros (DANCEE, 2001; DANCEE, 2003; OECD/DANCEE, 2003; Ciupagea et al., 2006). The policy mismatch with the directive results mainly from structural problems. Romania's water distribution is uneven and less than two-thirds of the population have access to piped water. Moreover, the old water infrastructure is highly deficient and huge amounts of water are lost. Finally, many of the chemical substances stipulated by the DWD had not been monitored regularly in Romania as a result of a lack of technical expertise and financial resources to build up monitoring capacities (European Commission, 1999: 7; Krüger and Carius 2001: 63). Extending and upgrading the water system has required heavy investments and has met, moreover, with financial problems in local administrations, particularly in rural areas. At the same time, incentives for investing in drinking water infrastructure have been low, as the price of (subsidized) drinking water is 50 percent below the price of water provided for industrial use (Stefan, 2007). Moreover, customers are reluctant to pay for drinking water, which has traditionally been available for free from individual wells that are not controlled by public health authorities (Zinnes, Tarhoaca and Popovici, 1999).

In order to cope with extraordinarily high investment costs in the water utility sector, three strategies emerged. First, Romania successfully negotiated an extended derogation period until 31 December 2015 for full implementation of the directive, thereby diminishing immediate adaptation pressures.[5] Second, to receive financial and technical assistance, Romanian authorities sought to secure the necessary funds from EU preaccession facilities, such as PHARE, and to acquire the managerial capacities to apply for Structural Funds from the Strategic Operational Programme for the Environment once they become available.[6] As the domestic banking system has not been ready to provide long term loans of this magnitude, public administrators lacking the necessary expertise had to be trained in how to apply for EU funding or loans by international development banks to carry out these investments (ARA, 2004). Third, some municipalities entered PPPs involving private water companies of international standing. The European Commission and the European Bank for Reconstruction and Development (EBRD) together with domestic actors, including the Romanian Water Association, started to seek foreign involvement in order to facilitate technology transfer and bring in new funds for reconstruction and development of municipal water utilities. For instance, four municipal water companies (Bucharest, Ploieşti, Falticeni and Timişoara), receiving financial support from the World Bank and the EBRD, have signed concession contracts with international water companies. In Bucharest, the French multinational Veolia established an agreement with the municipal administration in 2002. The PPP had to settle conflicts with the sectoral trade union and faced consumer complaints over increasing prices for services and the malfunctioning of the sewage system (Hegedüs, Somogyi and Tönko, 2003). Despite these difficulties, the PPP is regarded a success story that might serve as a model for the modernization of the water sector (Curtea de Conturi, 2004; Rotariu, 2007). Yet, prevailing legal uncertainties, lack of expertise in setting up PPPs and their mixed record of effectiveness has so far prevented its diffusion. Moreover, private companies have been more interested in 'cherrypicking' utilities with relatively well-functioning infrastructure, leaving local administrations with high investment costs to turn to Structural Funds as the only possibile way to shoulder the costs of the directive.[7] In Timişoara, the EBRD granted a loan to facilitate a bid of Suez-Lyonnaise des Eaux for a water concession, which it received without putting it to a public tender.[8] However, the city council withdrew from the deal when it learned that involvement of the transnational company would restrict its access to EU funds (Baga and Buzogany, 2006). In sum, with delegation (PPP and outsourcing) being the exception, the provision of drinking water has remained under public regulation. The relative effectiveness of the implementation of this directive can be attributed to domestic investment from the state budget (before accession) and the massive inflow of EU funds earmarked for the modernization of drinking water provision. At the same time, Romania could also buy time for complying with these directives by negotiating extensive derogation periods for reaching the EU's standards.

In contrast to the DWD, which set the stage for a complex modernization of the water sector, the implementation of the WFD implied a thorough reform of the underlying principles of water management. The WFD stipulates both the strengthening of management structures in the river basins and the development of horizontal and vertical coordination structures. While Romania had a centralized system that set fixed and unitary water prices for the whole country and redistributed the charges among different river basins (Arcadis Euroconsult, 2004), the WFD aims at cost-effectiveness in water supply, implying that different river basins will produce different prices for their services. Moreover, provisions regarding public participation in the basin committees of the country had to be changed, as NGOs were not represented in these bodies.

The implementation of the WFD has been facilitated by the organization of water management based on river catchments introduced in 1976 (Law No. 1/1976). River basin management committees (*comitete de bazin*) were established in Romania's 11 river basins in 2001.[9] These committees have 15 members delegated by water management, public health, industry and environmental protection bodies, as well as county level administration (*judeţ*), local mayors, representatives of water users from industry and agriculture as well as one representative from an ENGO. Full compliance with the WFD was achieved through Law 310/2004, which modified and completed the 1996 Water Law.[10] Over the following years, a management structure was established, which is coordinated by the Interministerial Water Council (*Consiliul Interministerial al Apelor*),[11] formed by representatives of different ministries and delegates of ANAR (MMGA/ANAR, 2007). Under the new structure, the basin departments are responsible for the river basin management plans, approve the classification of water quality and recommend financing priorities to the central and local public administration.

The requirement for public participation in river basin management committees (RBMCs) has opened opportunities for nonstate actors to get involved in determining water management policies. Nevertheless, civil society organizations became mostly involved in activities related to raising awareness and communication, rather than in policy making. The main reason for this is the limited number of professional environmental groups – such as Focus Eco Center (*Târgu Mureş*) and Eco Counseling Centre (*Galaţi*) – specializing in complex water management issues and having the relevant administrative and cognitive capacities necessary for the development of river management plans.[12] But the participatory approach of the directive has also suffered from other shortcomings related to the profile of the environmental civil sector. In contrast to countries such as Hungary, which used to have influential 'river NGOs' in the 1980s, this tradition has been absent in Romania. Added to this, weak coordination capacities and conflicts among NGOs also have had negative effects in establishing NGOs as a relevant factor in this field. Thus, it has remained unclear how the relevant stakeholders in the basin committees should be identified and how, in case of the NGO sector, their representatives should be elected.[13] Moreover, the decision-making competencies and financial resources of RBMCs have been badly defined, even for their members, with the committees being dominated by the state administration (REC Romania, 2007). Other barriers to participation include lack of access by private actors to information, limited administrative capacities of public authorities to process information and the low awareness of the public regarding the specific competencies of public authorities in water management (REC Romania, 2005).

As regards the upgrading of the water management system, poor coordination at the national level and insufficient data exchange between the responsible ministries dealing with different aspects of water management have proved to be substantial obstacles. However, after experimenting with different institutional arrangements, the Water Department of the MMDD outsourced the WFD implementation to ANAR, putting it in charge of all issues related to the WFD. ANAR, a centralized and self-sufficient public institution with a strong local background and financing based on water tariffs, took charge of water management, which contrasted with the rather weak standing of the regional environmental administration.[14] While the effectiveness of implementation improved, this institutional decision has also strengthened old networks within water policy (Neagu, 2006) and kept the regional water management institutions as a parallel structure, thus, staying at odds with the underlying philosophy of the WFD, which favors the integration of environmental institutions dealing with all media.

Very much as in case of the DWD, the technical and financial capacities necessary to the implementation of the WFD have been built up with EU assistance under the PHARE and LIFE programs. Twinning projects involved the country's river basin authorities developing an expertise in different fields of water management and then diffusing this knowledge to other units. Thus, EU-funded projects helped Romania to develop a water quality monitoring system at the river basin level in the Argeş River Basin and to prepare pilot river basin management plans in the Someş-Tisa River Basin (Arcadis Euroconsult, 2004). A dense web of international contacts through global, European and regional water management related networks, such as the International Commission for the Protection of the Danube River and the International Association of Waterworks in the Danube Catchment Area, have also promoted WFD-related activities in Romania.[15] Finally, the US Agency for International Development (USAID) financed several complex, multiyear consultancy projects to establish pricing polices in collaboration with the state administration and local think tanks which are becoming increasingly effective for the establishment of cost-recovery calculations at the local and regional levels (United Nations Environment Programme, 1999; Zinnes, 2004).

The implementation of the EU's water directives in Romania has followed a path that has been almost exclusively influenced by state actors. Romanian water management competencies have remained centralized in ANAR. Given the large amount of investment necessary and the limited capacities of state and nonstate actors from the environmental protection field, the water management sector has effectively used the implementation pressure of the EU to strengthen its position within the administration and to secure substantial financial resources for modernizing water infrastructure throughout the country. Even though it follows closely the letter of the WFD and is formally including nonstate actors in the river basin management committees, Romanian water management has succeeded in protecting its supply side traditions and only marginally opened itself towards the principles of integrated water resources management. In the case of the cost-heavy DWD, EU accession has triggered a far-reaching modernization of the infrastructure and is pushing forwards the cost-effective usage of water resources. At the same time, private water companies have mostly been interested in 'cherrypicking' water utilities with a good chance of profitability, leaving the bulk of the huge investment needed in water management to public authorities reliant on EU Structural Funds. In sum, state actors in water management successfully defended their dominant position during the accession period and secured the effectiveness of implementation concerning the administrative and financial regulation of the policy field. This has reinforced the old top-down steering of the sector, leaving little space for the new provisions of participation and integrated management that are associated with new modes of governance.

Industrial air pollution: smoke screens for hot air

Industrial pollution has been the Achilles' heel of Romanian environmental accession. Struggling to modernize its highly polluting and outdated industrial infrastructure, Romania received a warning 'red flag' in the regular Country Report of the European Commission in 2005, risking the postponement of accession because of a lack of progress in addressing air pollution activities (Capital, 2005; European Commission, 2005b). After a six-fold reduction in the level of air pollution caused by the downturn in industrial production after 1990, progress remained rather slow because of limited investment capacities. Compared to other countries in the region, industrial restructuring in Romania has proceeded at a much slower pace.

Most of Romania's air pollution stems from its outdated large combustion plants which are regulated by the LCPD. While the regulatory style of this command-and-control directive has not posed a major challenge to the national and regional administration to handle, fulfilling its requirements has carried high investment costs. Emission limits for large combustion plants were introduced into Romanian legislation from 1993 on and have shifted gradually towards the emission ceilings of the LCPD.[16] However, finding the financial means necessary for the technological upgrading of installations has been difficult. First of all, most plants still burn low-efficiency solid fuels with a high-sulfur content for power generation. Switching towards more efficient energy sources is impaired by the regional monopoly of Russian energy providers (Cruceru, Marius Voronca and Diaconu, 2005: 1372).

Second, restructuring the energy sector and heavy industry involves high social costs by directly affecting the population and economic competitiveness through rising production costs (Manoleli et al., 2002).[17] Therefore, as most Romanian large combustion plants are still owned by the state through the Ministries of Economy and the Interior, threats of closing down plants that fail to comply with the LCPD have never been entirely credible. Capacities at the management level of the affected installations to work out investment plans enabling them to meet the requirements of the directive have remained very low; most of the plants prefer to call on the state administration to find an adequate solution to their problems. Indeed, since Romania successfully negotiated extended derogation periods from the LCPD lasting up to 2017, immediate pressure for adaptation has been considerably reduced.

Third, state ownership and legal uncertainties over the privatization process have prevented private investment in the acquisition of high efficiency equipment (cf. Cruceru, 2005: 1365). To attract the financial resources necessary for the modernization of the energy sector, the Romanian government established the Special Energy Fund (*Fondul Special pentru Energie*), funded through electricity and heating prices paid by the population. This strategy failed, however, when Termoelectrica, the most important contributor to the Energy Fund, became the biggest debtor of the state. Therefore, the Romanian administration had to apply for foreign loans from development banks to finance the modernization of the energy sector. Together with increasing consumer prices and EU preaccession grants, these loans have helped to cover the necessary costs, which will be complemented by allocations from EU funds under the Sectoral Operational Programme for Environment when these become available (Government of Romania, 2008). Additionally, the EU Emission Trading Scheme for greenhouse gas emissions has created opportunities for cogeneration heat and power plant operators, allowing them to take advantage of the Kyoto Protocol's flexible mechanisms of Joint Implementation projects.[18] The Romanian government has also considered the privatization of the energy sector to obtain the financial resources necessary to comply with EU air pollution standards. However, the labor unions have so far successfully vetoed any reforms in the energy sector, fearing that privatization and the transfer of power plants from the jurisdiction of local authorities would make their members' jobs more vulnerable to layoffs.

While the LCPD mostly targets the energy sector and heavy industries, the IPPCD affects virtually every productive sector of the country. Its implementation has been a major challenge for Romania in the field of environmental policy, because of serious policy mismatches concerning the designation of the competent authority for issuing the permits or the establishment of technical databases of pollutants. Moreover, the application of the IPPCD requires an increase in qualified staff in the regional permitting and monitoring authorities as well as the provision of information to industrial stakeholders on BATs, as well as public access to information.

Given the integrative character of the IPPCD, Law 645/2002 (repealed through emergency ordinance 152/2005)[19] had to build domestic regulation from scratch. While environmental permitting procedures have existed in Romania since the 1960s, they were based on single-media approaches (Government of Romania, 2004b). This permitting tradition was restated by the country's 1995 Environmental Act, which allocated permitting competencies regarding activities of 'national importance' to the MMDD, while all other permits had to be issued by the county-level environmental administration on a case-by-case basis. The introduction of the integrated permitting procedure was subject to a significant delay but gathered pace and the necessary permits were issued before the deadline of October 2007. Nevertheless, the quality of the issued permits remains controversial,[20] mainly because of the lack of competent personnel at the regional level. In addition, the existing monitoring procedures for detecting infringements by installations were not consolidated as a result of the continuous restructuring of the administration.[21]

Although the IPPCD opened possibilities for enhanced cooperation between state and nonstate actors, a legalistic handling of the BAT principle has prevailed. Thus, the BREFs have been validated through Ministerial Orders rather than industry covenants or codes of conduct.[22] Since the heavy costs of the directive have to be borne by industrial actors, their financial constraints as regards modernizing their production technology pose the severest challenges to the effective implementation of the IPPCD (Chivu, 2002). In many cases, cooperation between state and business actors has been futile, as state authorities are simply not in the position to provide the necessary funding.[23] Rather than pooling resources to improve implementation, state and business actors negotiated with Brussels for longer derogation periods – hoping that necessary investments could be covered after accession by the Structural Funds or through external bank credits.[24] About one-fourth of relevant installations and the vast majority of the highly polluting large combustion plants successfully lobbied the authorities to negotiate with the European Commission for individual transition periods of up to ten years (Capital, 2005).

Only a few industrial sectors sought cooperation with the environmental administration to ensure the effective authorization of plants under the IPPCD. The focal point of coordinating IPPC-related activities has been the Pollution Department of the MMDD and its BAT Technical Advice Centre, which organizes the technical working groups set up by industry and the administration. These working groups exist, for example, in the cement, pulp and paper and the petrochemical industries. While these sectors have potentially negative impacts on the environment, firms in them show high growth rates and possess significant expertise with European policies since they are frequently owned by investors from the old member states.[25] Consultations have mostly been facilitated through the professional associations of industries and research institutions connected to those industrial sectors (European Commission, 2005a). However, due to the high time pressure involved, these consultations were focused mostly on sharing information about the forthcoming new regulations and translating BREFs to help the owners of installations. Civil society organizations had only a marginal role in the process. Even though the directive allowed for civil society organizations to become involved in the implementation of the policy, only a very few NGOs specializing in energy efficiency or climate change issues, such as Terra Mileniul III, have become active in the matter. They have, however, restricted themselves to following the legislative procedure and spreading information about the existence of the directive to the general public.

Implementation of the IPPCD slowly improved with the building of administrative and cognitive capacities related to pollution control. The European Commission repeatedly stressed shortcomings of the application of the directive linking them to the lack of qualified personnel (European Commission, 2004, 2005a, 2005b). As a result, the environmental authorities pooled their resources and in 2004 created more than 200 additional posts at the level of the national and local Environmental Protection Administration and the Environmental Guard to deal with the IPPCD. This allowed them to finish the permitting procedure for relevant installations just in time. Moreover, several PHARE projects, mainly in collaboration with German, French and Polish experts, sought to tackle problems of administrative capacity, relating to training and management activities linked to the IPPCD.[26] Nevertheless, most activities concerning air pollution control were carried out by individual industrial installations. This has been particularly cost intensive for industries without strong and internationally well connected sectoral associations (*patronate*). In contrast, domestic industry sectors have gained a comparative advantage in dealing with the requirements of the IPPCD if they have had close ties with EU-level sectoral associations, such as the chemical industry's FEPACHIM, or received relevant technology through new owners or partners holding relevant expertise with EU policies.[27]

In sum, EU industrial air pollution control policies have imposed heavy costs on both state and business actors. However, since the state still owns most large combustion plants, the involvement of nonstate actors has been virtually nonexistent, since investment necessary to fulfill EU requirements has had to rely on the state budget. Business and government joined forces in seeking to postpone rather than to promote compliance with EU legislation. While this strategy might be seen as effective since it prevented the closure of some of the country's biggest companies, greening Romania's industry remains a burden that has largely remained unaddressed.

Nature protection: stitching a safety net with holes

Located at the cross-roads of five biogeographic regions, Romania is the EU member state with the highest level of biodiversity.[28] During the socialist period, the national nature protection system relied on a network of protected areas, which increased more than ten-fold between 1954 and 1985 (Soran et al., 2000). On paper, these sites provided far-reaching protection levels and prohibited most human activities in these areas. However, in practice, protection remained scant and there were no management plans to coordinate activities because of the weakness of the Commission for the Protection of Nature Monuments of the Romanian Academy, which was in charge of the process. Although Romania introduced the Law on Environment in 1973, it failed to adopt a more specific piece of law that would regulate the management of protected sites. The lack of a coherent policy and clear institutional structure for biodiversity conservation and the poor enforcement of existing laws remained a major problem during the accession process. Furthermore, these problems were further aggravated by new challenges: recent economic modernization and growth gave rise to large infrastructural investment projects, partly financed by EU funds. Therefore, the European Commission stressed that protected areas should be designated before increased land values made effective protection even more difficult after accession. While the implementation of EU nature protection policies did not pose a major financial burden (Manoleli, 2002), the establishment of the Natura 2000 network increasingly developed into a conflict between the seemingly contradictory goals of economic versus sustainable development. In addition to hard-to-solve conflicts underlying the policy, the policy-style of the EU's nature protection directives did not fit with the domestic system. The emphasis on the inclusion of stakeholders, the setting up of new institutional arrangements on the national, regional and local level and the need for large amounts of complex scientific data created serious capacity problems for the Romanian government.

Based on its new Law on Environmental Protection (L137/1995), Romania transposed the EU requirements for integrated biodiversity protection and spatial planning early (L5/2000). Yet, the law left many issues unaddressed, including the protection of privately owned sites or the funding necessary for implementing and enforcing the new regulation (Penu, 2004).[29] Further problems in the designation and implementation of the Natura 2000 network resulted from weak coordination within the state administration, mainly at the national but also at the regional level, as well as from the absence of a visible national strategy that could have guided the process. Moreover, public authorities lacked the information and expertise to conduct the designation process effectively. Data on species and habitats were either nonexistent or unavailable and there was no consistent classification system. Thus, the proposal of protected sites, which happened under enormous time pressure, was not coordinated with the competent authorities at the local level and did not draw on sufficient data.[30]

The designation process proved equally cumbersome. In addition to a late start, the repeated shuffling of responsibilities severely impaired the implementation process. Initially, the MMDD and the Ministry of Agriculture, Food and Forests had assumed coordination at the national level (Manoleli, 2002: 12). During the accession process, in March 2004, a cabinet reshuffle merged the environmental and agricultural portfolios. The downgrading of the environmental administration, however, threatened the successful completion of the environmental chapter. In order not to risk the country's EU accession foreseen for 2007, the Romanian government reestablished the Ministry of the Environment in December 2004. The division of responsibilities between the two ministries, however, has remained a cause of intra-institutional conflicts. These were particularly obvious during site designation and the forest restitution process, which saw the formation of a politically well connected lobby group of private forest owners (Novac and Auer, 2004). Likewise, the list of protected birding areas became a matter of conflict between the Ministry of Agriculture and the MMDD as influential interests within forestry and agriculture tried to reduce the number of protected sites.[31] In finalizing the list of protected birds, interministerial consultations were also hindered by the eruption of a corruption scandal in the Ministry of Agriculture that forced the resignation of the minister. As a result, the decision making process was blocked for several months. With the accession deadline approaching, the Romanian government decided to create a new National Agency for Natural Protected Areas (NAPA) in 2006, which was to be put in charge of the management of all protected areas, including Natura 2000 sites. However, the distribution of competencies among the existing nature conservation

administrations and the NAPA remained unclear, resulting in conflicts between different institutions. Two years after its founding was
announced, NAPA still had not materialized as an institution, leaving
an institutional vacuum in the Romanian nature protection system.[32]
Adding to this, the implementation of Natura 2000 has not only suffered
from deficient coordination capacities in the public administration, but
the Directorate for Biodiversity and Biosafety of the MMDD, which was
in charge of the designation process, has lacked sufficient qualified
personnel. In response to warnings from the European Commission
and international NGOs, including the WWF, the Romanian government increased the number of staff working on designation and management of Natura 2000 sites in the MMDD as well as in the regional
and local environment protection agencies. The research institutions
of the Romanian Academy of Science became responsible for the identification and classification of the NATURA 2000 sites, but the government did not make any funding available for data collection for the
network.[33] Only in 2005, under combined pressure from the European
Commission and ENGOs, the MMDD urgently allocated funds for site
designation.[34] Financial resources mostly came from EU twinning projects under the LIFE and PHARE programs, which also involved several
stakeholders, such as research institutes, administration and NGOs.[35]
In order to speed up the site designation process, the MMDD signed a
partnership agreement with two birding organizations with previous
experience in a number of international projects under the coordination of BirdLife International. The Romanian Society of Ornitologists
(SOR) and the Milvus Group were put in charge of carrying out and
supervising the site designation process for IBAs. The funding they
received came mostly from the EU (Papp, 2006). While the participation
of NGOs during the designation process was restricted mostly to a small
number of semiprofessional organizations, the implementation process
does offer a number of possibilities for local groups to become custodi-
ans of the Natura 2000 sites. Thus, in 78 out of Romania's 375 protected
areas, responsibilities are undertaken by NGOs who assume management functions without receiving any funding from the state.[36]

Overall, the European Commission has significantly influenced the
development of nature protection policies in Romania, both before
and after accession. It has used both formal relations with the administration and informal contacts with environmental organizations to
acquire relevant information and exert pressure on the policy process.
Most importantly, the Commission declared the list of Natura 2000
sites provided by Romania insufficient in summer 2008, and gave the

country a one-year extension to amend and hand in an extended list of species and habitats.[37] The Commission also issued a first warning letter in October 2007, as no Special Protection Areas had been designated at that time. Romania has subsequently designated 108 SPAs, but 21 areas identified as IBAs have not been designated. In addition, the area of the SPAs was smaller than the corresponding IBAs, with more than 1 million hectares identified as IBAs being excluded. Therefore, in 2008, the Commission sent a final letter of warning threatening legal action against Romania for the infringement of biodiversity legislation.[38]

In addition to compliance pressure, EU capacity building through financial and technical assistance (PHARE, LIFE) has significantly helped to improve the implementation of the EU nature protection policies in the country. EU twinning projects have brought together Western and domestic experts, ENGOs and business actors at all tiers of the environmental administration. For instance, three multiple-year twinning projects, both at the national and the regional level, were involved in optimizing the organizational structure of the national and regional levels of the Environmental Protection Agency. They also helped to develop guidance documents for the designation process in two 'pilot' REPAs in order to improve the knowledge and implementation of the Natura 2000 network (Dumeige et al., 2007). This capacity building has led to the establishment of cross-cutting clusters of professionals working on similar issues both within the REPAs and LEPAs and between NGOs working on nature protection, fostering cooperation at the regional level in the designation process and the future management of the Natura 2000 sites.[39]

External assistance has also empowered ENGOs to participate in nature conservation policy and to become a pull factor, facilitating implementation and enforcement of environmental legislation. Capacity building in the Natura 2000 site designation process has developed around influential NGOs that could build on their experience, financing and external ties. For instance, the WWF's Danube-Carpathian Programme (WWF DCP) emerged as a central network actor by initiating and coordinating the work of the 'NGO Natura 2000 Coalition'. Since 2003, the coalition, which includes 36 member organizations, has become increasingly involved with the designation process, awareness-raising activities and lobbying both in Bucharest and in Brussels.[40] The influence of the coalition has increased because it can bring together environmental groups that act locally and secure financing through EU programs such as PHARE ACCESS or bi- or multilateral aid schemes directed towards the strengthening of civil society organizations. While the NGOs have sought to become more actively involved in the policy process and to develop closer ties with the public administration (TERRA Mileniul III and ALMA-RO, 2008), public authorities have been reluctant to open up. Apart from an administrative culture hostile to public participation, tight implementation deadlines as well as frequent institutional changes have made the involvement of NGOs and other stakeholders difficult.[41]

At times, more adversarial strategies have appeared to be more promising in giving influence on the implementation process during the accession period. A coalition of NGOs was particularly engaged in monitoring government action in response to the policy shortcomings outlined in the Commission's annual reports (WWF, 2003). In addition, during 2007, the WWF DCP successfully lobbied for the removal of the Head of the Biodiversity and Biosafety Directorate at the MMDD.[42] And at the end of 2007, the General Assembly of the NGO Natura 2000 Coalition decided to lodge a complaint to the European Commission presenting a 'shadow list' of designated sites as well as denouncing 'alarming developments' in Romanian protected areas, mostly linked to illegal logging and road construction in Natura 2000 sites.[43] Finally, protest actions, for example against the planned 'Dracula' amusement park in an area in Transylvania protected under NATURA 2000 and against a joint Canadian-Romanian gold mine project in Roşia Montană, have not only fostered the effective implementation of EU policies but also have helped to raise the profile of the environmental movement (Baga and Buzogány, 2009). At the same time, domestic opposition has been seeking to water down the strict rules of the NATURA 2000 site designation process (Krónika, 2008).

In sum, the effectiveness of the implementation of the NATURA 2000 network has only slowly been improving and can be mainly attributed to strong pressure from the EU and domestic NGOs. Implementation has suffered from a severe lack of state capacities to work out the classification system required by the EU directives. With the inadequate financial and technical capacities of the environmental administration, Romania has come under increasing pressure from the European Commission, both before and after accession. At the same time, the EU has engaged Romania in substantial resource-transfer projects, which have regularly involved NGOs and policy experts. EU pressure and capacity building have empowered nonstate actors in the implementation process, inducing Romanian authorities to consult with NGOs and delegate certain tasks to them. However, administrative fragmentation and institutional reorganization, together with the time pressure of the accession process, have largely prevented the emergence of stable patterns of cooperation between state and nonstate actors.

Conclusion

The Europeanization of environmental policies in Romania has triggered profound changes in all three policy subsectors – water management, air pollution control and nature protection. At the same time, Romania was able to negotiate extended transition periods up to ten years for most of the cost-intensive directives, at least partially mitigating the pressure for adaptation. The continuous institutional and legal reshuffling, administrative fragmentation and lack of qualified personnel at all levels of government combined with the tight deadlines dictated by the EU has fostered a 'muddling through' approach in the public administration, which has largely relied on traditional command-and-control regulation to implement EU policies. As in Poland and Hungary, the involvement of nonstate actors has barely gone beyond consultation and outsourcing. Anything else has been considered by public authorities to be time-consuming and unrewarding, not least because environmental organizations have often had little to offer. NGOs still have only limited funding and largely depend on external donors. Moreover, environmental groups lack broad-based support and public visibility. The Romanian public has remained skeptical towards the civil sector in Romania partly because of the proliferation in the 1990s of 'parasitic' NGOs that were merely seeking to be tax loopholes for various business activities (IMAS, 2000; Pralong, 2004). While a certain level of rent-seeking behavior among environmental NGOs will prevail and could even become reinforced by funding made available from state or international donors (Cristorian, 2008), there are also signs pointing towards professionalization and organizational consolidation. Thus, NGOs have become increasingly aware of the possibilities to influence environmental policymaking that accession has offered them. Well orchestrated protest action against economic activities in areas protected under NATURA 2000, for instance, has helped to raise public awareness and has contributed to the fostering of the environmental movement.

Notes

1. Romania is subdivided into eight regions and in 42 counties (*judeţe*). Before this structural change took place in 2004 there were no institutions at the regional level; the regions were set up in 1998 as a result of the requirements of the European Regional Funds.

2. The costs of Romania's 'environmental' accession were estimated to be around 29.3 billion euros (DANCEE, 2003).
3. 'Apa potabilă va atinge standarde europene în 15 ani' (Drinking Water quality will reach European standards in 15 years), http://www.ngo.ro/site_item_full.shtml?x=444, (last access: 17 November 2008).
4. Zinnes, 2004 reports ANAR as having a staff of 15,000. After the most recent reorganization in 2002, it was converted into a joint stock company with the government holding all shares. The national administration includes central offices in Bucharest, 11 river basin (regional) offices, 42 county level offices and 57 hydrological offices.
5. The transition period is justified by the current state of the waste water treatment units and especially of the drinking water distribution systems, which require huge costs for repair and reconstruction.
6. This was also the case during the preaccession period: for the years 2005–06 about 50 percent of related costs was provided through EU funds, 20–25 percent was funded through loans and the state budget contributed less than 10 percent.
7. According to MMDD data, local administrations engaged in 264 contracts using PHARE funds, while only 23 regarded private businesses as a possible way to fund investment. The total amount of money invested with PHARE projects is 115 million euros. See *Act Media Energy and Environmental Bulletin*: 'One third of Romania's population not connected to water supply and sewerage networks', 28 February 2008.
8. 'EBRD supports first public-private partnership in Romania's municipal sector', EBRD press release, 22 December 1999, http://www.ebrd.com/new/pressrel/1999/ 88dec22.htm, (last access: 17 November 2008).
9. MAFWEP Decision No. 114/2001.
10. PHARE Report: 'Report on the Romanian Legislation harmonized to the EU Directives, Implementation of the New Water Framework Directive on Pilot Basins' (WAFDIP), EuropeAid/114902/D/SV/RO RO.0107.15.02.01 TR-1.
11. Published in the Official Gazette, nr. 234 4 April 2007.
12. Interview, Public Official, Bucharest, 14 January 2007.
13. For instance, at the Water Directorate in Cluj this led to controversies about the participation of the NGO representative, who was contested by other NGOs as not being their representative and being nominated by the administration.
14. E-mail communication with PHARE Project Leader, 5 January 2007.
15. E-mail communication with PHARE Project Leader, 5 January 2007.
16. The directive was transposed through governmental decision 541/2003, This government decision was modified two years later by GDs 322/2005 and 1502/2006 in order to meet the recently changed European requirements. The decisions stipulate that each existing LCP has to comply with the emission ceilings for sulfur dioxide, nitrogen oxides and dust by the end of the derogation period, which is set individually and lies between 31 December 2013 and 1 January 2016–31 December 2017.
17. Manoleli *et al.* have calculated that this would increase electricity prices by 6 percent and steel prices by 20 percent, see Manoleli *et al.* 2002.
18. As the Romanian economy was growing at a high rate, the Romanian government considered a lowering of its emission quotas as an obstacle to its economic development. Thus, in January 2007, together with all other

Eastern member states, except Slovenia, Romania sued the Commission for reducing its greenhouse gases emission cap by 20 percent (Ellison, 2008).
19. Published in the Official Gazette no. 1078, 30 November 2005. Other legal articles were Order no. 249/2005 by the Minister of Environment and Water Management establishing the national IPPC Center within the ministry to be in charge of coordinating IPPC related activities in Romania, including work on the BAT guidelines and communication with other European-level institutions.
20. Ecomagazin: 'Ministerul Mediului Attila Korodi a inchis cinci firme din care patru au disparut singure', (Environmental Minister Attila Korodi has closed five companies of which four have disappeared by themselves), http://www.ecomagazin.ro/ministrul-mediului-attila-korodi-a-inchis-cinci-firme-din-care-patru-au-disparut-singure/, (last access: 17 November 2008).
21. Originally, EPAs had their own monitoring departments, which were disbanded at the setting up of the National Environmental Guard, which was then moved from the control of the Ministry of the Environment to the National Authority of Control after the general elections in 2004, and back again two years later. See: Cotidianul: 'Miliarde de euro pentru intrarea aerului romanesc in UE' (Billions of euros for entering Romanian air into the EU), 22 June 2005.
22. Interview, Public Official, Bucharest, 12 January 2007; interview Consultant, Bucharest, 11 January 2007.
23. Interview, Public Official, Bucharest, 8 December 2005.
24. Interview Ministry of Environment and Water Management (now MMDD), Bucharest, 23 November 2005; Interview Consultant, Bucharest, 12 January 2007.
25. Interview, Public Official, Bucharest, 12 January 2007; interview Consultant, Bucharest, 11 January 2007.
26. Some of these projects include: PHARE 1999 'Pre-accession impact studies' and 'Impact of EU environmental Acquis on selected industrial sectors in Romania'; PHARE 2000; EPTISA 'Technical assistance for strengthening capacities of regional environmental management inspectorates'; PHARE 2000 ERM/PM EUROPAID/112525/D/S V/RO Technical assistance on integrated permitting; PHARE 2000, 'Implementation of the Environmental Acquis' 'Romanian French Twinning to develop an environmental strategy with particular reference to financial mechanisms'; RO 0107.15.04.02 'Technical supply for the implementation of the IPPC Directive'; RO 0107.15.04.01 'Technical Assistance for the implementation of the IPPC Directive'; EUROPAID/116215/C/SV/PHA 'Capacity Building in Implementation of the Environmental Acquis at the Local and Regional level'.
27. Interview, Public Official, Bucharest, 11 January 2007.
28. Romania has five of the 11 biogeographical regions of Europe – alpine, continental, pannonic, steppe and pontic – on its territory; the last two regions are not represented in any other EU country.
29. Legal gaps also continued after accession: Government Emergency Ordinance 57/2007 on Protected Areas fails to provide clear provisions on the implementation stages of the directive and the compensation provided for the owners of the designated sites. It also omits guidance on the responsible

administrative bodies able to execute these tasks, which will probably lead to conflicts regarding large investment projects for infrastructure and economic development coming up in Romania in the near future.

30. Interview, ENGO, Bucharest, 11 July 2008.
31. Interview, PHARE project coordinator, Sibiu, 16 June 2008; interview, ENGO representative, Oxford, 10 September 2007.
32. Interview, ENGO, Bucharest, 11 July 2008.
33. Gathering and completing data from several databases was done with the collaboration of research institutes such as the Danube Delta National Research Institute, the National Institute of Marine Research and the Antipa Museum. Proposals for the establishment of protected areas could be lodged by universities, research institutions or NGOs as well as the presidents of county councils.
34. Interview with Minister Sulfina Barbu in Romania Libera, 8 November 2005.
35. Projects such as the LIFE – Nature project FOREST ALP NATURA 2000, including a broad coalition of actors such as the University of Transylvania, Faculty of Silviculture and Forest Engineering (UTFF) together with WWF Danube Carpathian Programme (WWF DCP) and the National Forest Administration Romsilva (NFA Romsilva) submitted 50 sites hosting priority habitats that became designated as pSCIs, and is presently preparing the management guidelines and monitoring plans for priority forest, subalpine and alpine habitats. The NGO Coalition Natura 2000, coordinated by WWF DCP and ECOTUR Sibiu, has handed in proposals for 27 pSCIs. Other larger PHARE-financed projects included twinning partnership at two REPAs that have dealt with capacity building in REPAs and technical issues of site designation. One PHARE ACCESS project entitled 'The role of NGOs in Natura 2000' was directed towards capacity building and communication especially for NGOs.
36. E-mail communication, Natura 2000 Coalition representative, 10 September 2008.
37. E-mail communication, Natura 2000 Coalition representative, 10 September 2008.
38. 'European Commission issues final warning to Romania over nature protection shortcomings. European Commission', 18 September, 2008 http://europa.eu/rapid/pressReleasesAction.do?reference=IP/08/1347&format=PDF&aged=0&language=EN&guiLanguage=en, (last access: 17 November 2008).
39. Interview, PHARE project coordinator, Sibiu, 16 June 2008.
40. Coalitia ONG Natura 2000 Romănia: Raport de activate perioda 2005-06 (on file).
41. Interview, Scientist, Antipa Museum, Bucharest, 10/09/2005; interview, ENGO, Bucharest, 11 September 2008.
42. Interview, ENGO representative, Oxford, 10 September 2007.
43. Green Report: ONG-urile reclama la CE ilegalitatile din ariile protejate, 2007. 23.12.

10
After Accession: Escaping the Low Capacity Trap?

Tanja A. Börzel

New modes of governance have traveled South and East in Europe. Candidate countries in Southern, Central and Eastern Europe have made use of nonhierarchical forms of policy making to cope with the challenge of accession. However, nonstate actors have played a far less prominent role in the implementation of the *acquis* than the literature would lead us to expect. We have only found weak and scattered forms of new modes of governance, which operate under a strong shadow of hierarchy. Paradoxically, it is precisely the lack of governance capacities that has impaired the emergence of more inclusive and cooperative relations between state and nonstate actors.

Our comparative studies confirm that the implementation and application of the EU environmental *acquis* has imposed significant costs on the accession countries. In addition to the financial burden, the application of technical sophisticated policies, such as Natura 2000, the IPPCD and WFD, require significant personnel with the necessary legal, scientific and technical expertise. Such resources, however, were lacking in accession countries, whose scarce capacities were already stretched thin by managing the transition of their political and economic systems.

Thus, state actors had an incentive to seek the cooperation of companies, scientific experts and environmental groups, who could offer resources such as technical know-how and scientific expertise. Likewise, nonstate actors had an interest in exchanging these resources for influence on the legal and administrative application of the directives since their transposition into domestic law did not leave much leeway. While companies sought to reduce compliance costs by increasing flexibility and receiving derogations, environmental organizations wanted to secure the strict application of EU requirements.

Although state and nonstate actors have often had incentives to cooperate, nonstate actors have barely been involved in public policy making, especially in the CEE states. Nonstate actors are most actively involved where EU directives explicitly require their participation and the EU strengthens the capacities of both state and nonstate actors towards engagement with each other. But even where new modes of governance have emerged, they have not gone beyond more or less regular consultations and the delegation of technical tasks. These forms of nonstate actor involvement in public policy making may seem quite old-fashioned. Indeed, they barely satisfy our definition of new modes of governance. Voluntary agreements with business, the delegation of regulatory tasks to associations, the formal participation of stakeholders in the application of state regulations or private self-regulation, which are typical new modes of governance in Western countries (Marin and Mayntz, 1991; Kooiman, 1993), are extremely scarce in the Southern European member states and practically absent in the three CEE countries examined. We argue that this is mostly as a result of low governance capacities, i.e., the overall weakness of both state and nonstate actors in the six countries. Civil society actors often do not have sufficient organizational capacities to serve as reliable partners in cooperation with state actors. Moreover, civil society emerged in the accession countries in opposition to fascist and socialist repression. Many NGOs still see their role as independent 'watchdogs' rather than interdependent partners of the state. Companies, in turn, shy away from cooperation because they doubt that state actors are capable of translating mutual agreements into policy outcomes, given unstable majorities in parliament and frequent changes of government. To avoid legal uncertainty, business prefers rigid command-and-control regulation. Political instability also weakens the credibility of state actors to adopt and impose costly policies unilaterally. State actors themselves see their weakness as a major obstacle for cooperation with nonstate actors. Not only has industry little incentive to offer its resources for making policies that incur significant costs upon them, but state actors are also afraid of being captured by business, if it has superior resources. As well as their fear of 'state capture', policy makers and administrators are often faced with public skepticism about new modes of governance, which are seen as part of the socialist legacy or a Mediterranean culture (clientelistic networks) and in contradiction to democratic institutions. This perception is reinforced by the attempts of politicians to shift political decisions into multistakeholder forums in order to circumvent opposition or deadlock in parliamentary or party arenas. Finally, the privatization or delegation of public tasks to private actors, particularly in the area of public services (drinking water), meets strong opposition at the local level.

Our findings do not vary much across the six countries which differ significantly with regard to their political, social, economic and cultural institutions (Figure 10.1). They are also corroborated by the few other comparative studies on the Europeanization of environmental and regional governance in Southern European and CEE countries (Baker and Jehlicka, 1998; Paraskevopoulos, Panagiotis and Rees, 2006). While new modes of governance appear to be slightly more prevalent in Spain and Hungary, their governance capacities are also somewhat stronger than in the other four countries. We found the least evidence for new modes of governance in Greece and Romania,. Romania is among the European countries with the lowest governance capacities. Moreover, the effects of EU compliance pressure and capacity building in practice have been delayed because Romania joined two years later than Hungary and Poland. Greece also suffers from low state capacities and has not always been able to absorb the funds provided by the EU. While statistical data suggests that civil society is considerably stronger than in the other five countries, case studies maintain that civil society is weak (see Chapter 2). In any case, environmental activism has been much more 'grass-roots' and confrontational than in other European countries (Kousis, 1999; Kousis, Della Porta and Jiménez, 2008). The adoption of a more cooperative approach is hampered by low trust in public institutions and the suspicion, shared among both civil society organizations and the public in general, of new modes of governance, particularly when state actors appear to involve certain actors selectively (business and scientists) while excluding others (civil society organizations). The cases of Spain and Portugal, finally, confirm the positive effect of EU push and pull factors on the emergence of new modes of governance. While these were as hard to find as they would later be in the CEE countries when the two joined in the mid-1980s, Spanish and Portuguese state actors started to resort to consultation and delegation of technical tasks when they felt increasing compliance pressure from the European Commission and technical and financial assistance from the Structural Funds had shown some success in strengthening the capacities of both state and nonstate actors.

However, the findings on our three CEE countries and Greece demonstrate that (EU) capacity building and EU compliance pressure may be necessary but not sufficient to foster the emergence of new modes of governance. On the one hand, state actors have to be capable of

	Greece	Portugal	Spain	Hungary	Poland	Romania
Drinking Water	public regulation	Public regulation technical delegation	public regulation technical delegation	public regulation technical delegation	public regulation technical delegation	public regulation
Water Framework	public regulation consultation	Public regulation consultation	public regulation consultation	public regulation consultation technical delegation	public regulation consultation	public regulation
Large Combustion Plant	public regulation	Public regulation	public regulation	public regulation	public regulation	public regulation
Integrated Pollution Prevention and Control	public regulation consultation	Public regulation consultation technical delegation	public regulation consultation technical delegation	public regulation consultation technical delegation	public regulation consultation technical delegation	public regulation consultation
Fauna, Flora, Habitats Wild Birds	public regulation consultation	Public regulation consultation technical delegation	public regulation consultation technical delegation	public regulation consultation technical delegation	public regulation consultation technical delegation	public regulation consultation technical delegation
Environmental Impact Assessment	public regulation consultation (weak)	Public regulation consultation	public regulation consultation	public regulation consultation	public regulation	public regulation
Overall	public regulation consultation	Public regulation consultation technical delegation	Public regulation consultation technical delegation	Public regulation consultation technical delegation	Public regulation technical delegation	Public regulation

Figure 10.1   New modes of governance in accession countries.

absorbing EU resources and nonstate actors have to have the capacity to make use of the new opportunities offered by the EU. On the other hand, both have to generate trust in new modes of governance as effective means to implement EU policies. State actors often perceive the involvement of nonstate actors as time consuming and a further obstacle in taking decisions that are not geared towards particularistic interests. Even if new modes of governance may help in effective implementation, they are not always seen as a legitimate way of policy making because of their often informal character and the selective inclusion of nonstate actors.

Stuck in the low capacity trap?

Our findings support the assumptions on which the paradox of double weakness rests. The weak governance capacities of accession countries require new modes of governance but are unfavorable for their emergence and effectiveness.

First, the top-down nature of the accession process, in which the candidate countries have to download a vast number of EU policies in a fairly short period has most of the time not allowed for the involvement of nonstate actors. On the contrary, accession conditionality and the focus of the Commission on the absorption capacities of the candidate countries has strengthened the autonomy of central government actors in hierarchically imposing policy outcomes. This is even the case for social, regional and agriculture policy, in which the Commission and EU policies explicitly require and encourage the involvement of subnational and private actors (Grosse, 2006, 2007b; Bruszt, 2008).

Second, accession countries not only have to cope with the challenge of adopting and adapting to the comprehensive *acquis communautaire*. Their governments also have to manage the still ongoing transition to democracy and a market economy. Both accession and transition require immense resources, a demand that is scarcely met by the weak governance capacities of the candidate countries. On the one hand, state actors often lack sufficient financial (money), administrative (staff) and cognitive (expertise) resources and the capacity to mobilize existing resources (e.g., as a result of administrative fragmentation), respectively, to adopt and enforce public policies effectively. Moreover, given their political instability and frequently changing governments, they may not appear to be reliable negotiation partners. In the absence of a credible shadow of hierarchy, nonstate actors hardly have an incentive to cooperate with state actors by exchanging their resources for political influence. At the same time, state actors often shy away from cooperating with nonstate actors, too, because they are afraid of being captured by powerful private interests. Finally, the capacity of state actors for engagement has been severely limited since institutionalized arenas for interacting with nonstate actors have been largely absent. On the other hand, nonstate actors are often equally weak. They do not have sufficient organizational capacities to offer themselves as reliable partners to state actors. Or they lack any resources for exchange to begin with.

These findings are in line with an argument of the governance literature that new modes of governance require both a strong state and a strong society. In our six countries, weak governance capacities are complemented by a state tradition which is hostile to the involvement of nonstate actors in public policy making. Not only are new modes of governance incompatible with the legacy of authoritarianism and socialism, but new modes of governance do not necessarily correspond to the newly established institutions of representative democracies either. Nonelected interest groups and civil society organizations are not always accepted as legitimate representatives of societal interests. Moreover, their involvement in the policy process outside majoritarian institutions is often considered as a continuation of traditional clientelistic networks. As a result, new modes of governance may be seen as a source of legal uncertainty and arbitrary decision making. Even nonstate actors that will benefit from new modes of governance therefore tend to prefer rigid and hierarchical 'rules of the game'.

While the weak capacities of transition countries may render new modes of governance an important way of coping with the challenge of accession by pooling resources and sharing costs with nonstate actors, the conditions for the emergence of new modes of governance have been highly unfavorable in all six accession countries. As a result, there was and still is a clear dominance of traditional command-and-control regulation. If embryonic forms of more inclusive and cooperative patterns of policy making have emerged, they operate in a strong shadow of hierarchy.

At the same time, our Southern case studies, in particular, have allowed us to identify some factors that foster the emergence of new modes of governance and may help accession countries to escape the low capacity trap.

First, EU pressure is a prominent factor in inducing state actors to resort to new modes of governance. On the one hand, the EU may legally require the involvement of private actors (e.g., the principle of partnership or participatory policy instruments in environmental directives).

Thus, it may be rational for state actors to apply new modes of governance in order to avoid punishment and to receive rewards from the Commission, (accession conditionality and postaccession infringement proceedings). On the other hand, there is a normative logic that may drive the emergence of new modes of governance – it is the 'EU way of doing business'. In the Eastern enlargement, the Commission has actively promoted the idea of new modes of governance as a means of helping countries cope with the challenge of accession (Tulmets, 2005). In Southern Europe, the EU has supported new modes of governance under the Structural Funds (Kohler-Koch, 1996b).

Second, the EU not only provides incentives and governance paradigms that may foster the emergence of new modes of governance, but also helps to strengthen the governance capacities of accession countries. The transfer of money and expertise through Community programs and twinning processes provides state as well as nonstate actors with additional resources that they can exchange (Dimitrova, 2002; Sissenich, 2007). These processes also facilitate policy learning and trust building. Moreover, the monitoring and sanctioning system of the EU (accession conditionality and infringement proceedings) has empowered nonstate actors by opening new opportunities for them to pursue their interests, for example by taking their governments to court (Börzel, 2006). State actors may resort to new modes of governance in order to accommodate the interests of nonstate actors and avoid complaints to the Commission or legal proceedings.

The findings on environmental policy (see also Paraskevopoulos, Panagiotis and Rees, 2006) are corroborated by research on other policy fields (cf. Héritier and Rhodes, 2010). In social policy, accession countries introduced tripartite negotiations between representatives of employers, employees and the government in order to concur with the EU principle of social partnership. Yet, attempts to institutionalize social dialogs have had limited success. While the accession countries have transposed EU provisions on the involvement of social partners, the application and enforcement of these have been hampered by the weak capacities of both state actors and social partners (Falkner et al., 2005; Falkner, Treib and Holzleitner, 2008). In Poland, for instance, the work of the Tripartite Commission has been repeatedly stalled by political conflict and was circumvented by *ad hoc* consultations the Polish government launched. In Estonia, there has never been a permanent tripartite institution. Only in Lithuania does the Tripartite Council appear to produce some policy outcomes. The inclusion of social partners in the management of implementing agencies, for example in the distribution of EU agricultural subsidies, has been equally disappointing (Grosse, 2007b, 2008b). Southern European and CEE countries still lack sufficiently autonomous social partners with the capacity to negotiate collective agreements (Ghellab and Vaughan-Whitehead, 2003; Paraskevopoulos, Panagiotis and Rees, 2006; Kohl and Platzer, 2007a). Their industrial relations are dominated by the state. But unlike the 'Latin' system, the 'CEE transition model of industrial relations' is less marked by conflict and ideological differences (Kohl and Platzer, 2007b: 617–618).

In regional policy, new modes of governance appear to play a more prominent role – although they are still weak and remain firmly embedded in a hierarchical mode of governance. While central governments have been reluctant to share power with regional actors, the EU's insistence on the principle of partnership, combined with diverse preaccession assistance programs empowering diverse subnational non-state actors, spurred the emergence of more or less stable partnerships among various subnational authorities, firms, and civil society organizations in the design and implementation of regional development programs. Such development partnerships take different forms and do not conform to a particular national model. What they have in common, though, is their 'layering' – they all form part of a predominantly hierarchical and centralized governance regime that is characteristic of regional development policy in Southern European and CEE countries (Paraskevopoulos, Panagiotis and Rees, 2006; Bruszt, 2008).

Through normative and material pressure and capacity building, the EU has sought to foster the emergence of new modes of governance in accession countries. European push and pull factors have helped Southern European and CEE accession countries to escape the 'low equilibrium trap' (Bruszt, 2008), in which they were initially caught due to the weakness of state and nonstate actors.

However, the impact of EU push and pull factors is mitigated by the capacity of domestic actors to absorb financial and technical assistance of the EU and make use of its opportunity structure. Moreover, state and nonstate actors have to learn to trust each other, which takes time. Finally, the building of governance capacities has been unequal, favoring state over nonstate actors. Not only has the downloading of a vast number of EU policies in a rather short period of time not allowed for the involvement of private actors, but accession conditionality and the focus of the Commission on the absorption capacity of the candidate countries have strengthened the autonomy and the resources of central government actors in hierarchically imposing policy outcomes (Bruszt,

2002; Grabbe, 2006). This corroborates our findings on the dominance of state actors and the shadow of hierarchy they cast on any forms of more inclusive and cooperative forms of governance.

New modes of governance – hierarchy in disguise?

New modes of governance are usually embedded in old modes. EU policies do not just prescribe more participatory forms of policymaking, which can be hierarchically enforced by the European Commission and the European Court of Justice. Procedural regulation on public and stakeholder involvement mostly serves to help implement rather than substitute for legally binding standards adopted and enforced in the governmental arena. The result is often a 'layering' (cf. Jordan, Wurzel and Zito, 2005; Bruszt, 2008), in which new modes of governance are introduced without basically challenging or altering the dominant features of the traditional structures and processes. Thus, regional developmental programming in Southern European and CEE countries proceeds primarily through government-controlled sectoral programs, in which regional actors are not involved. Design and implementation, in contrast, allows for some regional input through a separate 'regional program' (cf. Paraskevopoulos, Panagiotis and Rees, 2006; Bruszt, 2008).

New modes of governance and soft instruments in accession countries are not just scarce: as in the old member states, they usually combine with old modes of hierarchical regulation by public actors. But since nonstate actors are still weak, the shadow of hierarchy looms much larger and gives rise to asymmetrical relationships between state and nonstate actors, or 'hierarchy in disguise' (Bruszt, 2008). As the cases of Spain and Portugal show, with increasing governance capacities, we may expect new modes of governance to play a more prominent role in accession countries. Yet, they are unlikely to replace old forms. Rather, they will increase the effectiveness and legitimacy of old modes. But even in this limited regard, the record to date is mixed.

Handle with care: The effectiveness of new modes of governance

To make policies work, state actors become increasingly dependent upon the cooperation and joint resource mobilization of nonstate actors, which are outside their hierarchical control. New modes of governance allow state actors to tap into the resources of nonstate actors and facilitate their implementation. The more the actors affected by a policy have a say in decision making, the more likely they are to accept the policy outcome to be implemented, even if their interests may not have been fully accommodated. In short, new modes of governance can significantly strengthen the capacity of state actors in public policy-making. If they emerge, we may expect them to improve the effective adoption of and adaptation to the *acquis* in accession countries.

There are, however, reasons to doubt that there is necessarily a positive impact of new modes of governance on effectiveness. Nonstate actors can certainly provide public actors with important resources in order to make public policies work. However, it is unclear whether the mutual resource dependency of state and nonstate actors actually leads to a net increase in the problem-solving capacity that is achieved by new modes of governance. If states are so weak that they have to share authority with nonstate actors, this can easily result in problem-shifting or agency capture. In some cases, new modes of governance simply amount to privatization and deregulation of formerly public services rather than the adoption of effective public policies. This explains at least partly why the attempts of accession countries to involve private companies in the provision of drinking water have met with fierce resistance at the local level. While private capital is badly needed, particularly by smaller municipalities, to meet the quality standards of the EU DWD, public pressure has prevented comprehensive privatization.

Moreover, states with weak regulatory capacities may not have the ability to resume responsibility for delegated tasks in cases of private failures as the functions involved were delegated because they were not capable of delivering them in the first place. Likewise, weak state actors may not be able to resist the pressure of nonstate actors to adopt policies that serve the public interest or, worse, are not able to judge what policies may be in the public interest since they lack the necessary information and expertise. Finally, the inclusion of nonstate actors as the primary targets in the process of rulemaking can certainly increase the problem-solving capacity by ensuring compliance. Yet, including those nonstate actors that ultimately have to comply with the rules to be made might simply lead to 'lowest common denominator' solutions or even result in deadlock. If those who have to bear the costs of compliance are involved in the negotiating process, they may attempt to weaken rules and regulations or prevent them altogether.

Empirical findings on the effect of new modes of governance on bringing accession countries closer to the *acquis* are as mixed as the arguments found in the governance literature. New modes of governance may indeed promote the timely, complete and correct adoption of and adaptation to EU policies in accession countries. Thus, the implementation of such complex regulations as the WFD, the IPPCD or the FFHD greatly benefited from the expertise provided by environmental organizations, scientific experts and business. They helped state actors to reduce compliance costs and to resolve conflicts among the actors involved. Likewise, the delegation of preaccession preparations to the Pan-European Regulatory Forum proved more effective in 'smoothing' the harmonization of pharmaceutical regulations in CEE accession countries with EU requirements than the traditional mode of bilateral negotiations between the Commission and central governments. The participatory regulatory network has significantly reduced the demand of CEE accession countries for derogations in the pharmaceutical area and has contributed to a smooth transition to the new regulatory regime. This is in sharp contrast to the environmental *acquis*, where no such new modes of governance have emerged (Koutalakis and Prange, 2006; Borrás, Koutalakis and Wendler, 2007).

In regional policy, development partnerships at the subnational level have helped improve the absorption capacity of CEE countries by mobilizing information and resources otherwise not available, discovering new options and improving local acceptance of governance policies. The cross-sectoral cooperation of state and nonstate actors at subnational level has encouraged the creation of encompassing and inclusive development programs by institutionalizing multistakeholder deliberations on the goals of development and the best ways to achieve them. Typical examples are local developmental associations among municipalities, firms and NGOs in Hungary that have helped microregions with weak and fragmented local administrations to mobilize resources for integrated developmental programs (Keller, 2008). Likewise, the inclusion of social partners in the distribution of EU agricultural subsidies was instrumental in improving the absorption capacity of EU funding in Poland by disseminating information and raising social acceptance of EU policies (Grosse, 2007b).

All in all, new modes of governance do contribute to the effective adoption of and adaptation to the EU *acquis* – if they emerge in the first place. However, they can also have the opposite effect, for example by delaying the implementation and application of EU policies. CEE governments have often circumvented social dialog because the long-lasting debates in the tripartite commissions threatened the timely adoption of EU social policies (Grosse, 2006). In a similar vein, the requirements for the introduction of new modes of governance, such as public involvement in water management, nature conservation or pollution prevention and control, are often not easy to handle for state actors in accession countries, who lack both the administrative capacities and the experience to cooperate with multiple stakeholders and accommodate their conflicting interests. While helping to foster the effective adoption of and adaptation to EU environmental policies, new modes of governance have at times created additional problems. For instance, the selective inclusion of environmental organizations and consulting companies into the NATURA 2000 processes in Hungary left other affected stakeholders, such as farmers and private forest owners, outside the policy cycle and diminished the overall legitimacy of the state's nature conservation efforts.

The effectiveness of new modes of governance may depend on certain scope conditions at least partly related to the governance capacities of state and nonstate actors. The shadow of hierarchy provides important incentives to nonstate actors, such as mitigating compliance costs and enforcing agreements. The threat of state regulation thus helps to get nonstate actors involved in regulatory networks and make them comply with their outcomes. In stark contrast to the Polish case, Hungarian state actors were far more successful in mobilizing private cognitive resources towards pharmaceutical harmonization through the institutionalization of credible, independent drug licensing authorities that facilitated close contacts and continuous interaction with the industry (Koutalakis, 2008b). At the same time, nonstate actors require sufficient capacities to make use of the opportunities offered by new modes of governance. Social partners in Estonia and Poland are too weak and divided to negotiate agreements (Grosse, 2006, 2007a). In particular local NGOs suffer from similar problems in sustaining their participation in the management of nature protection areas and subnational actors lack the capacities to make effective demands on the central state for a broader participation in regional development programs (Bruszt, 2002, 2008).

Finally, new modes of governance might improve effectiveness, but this might come at some costs with regard to legitimacy. While the involvement of affected parties and the mediation of conflicts of interest may increase the acceptance of a policy, they can also generate opposition and resentment. Because of their nonmajoritarian character, new modes of governance are often seen as clientelistic, nontransparent, exclusive and, thus, undemocratic. Social dialog, for instance, has given some social partners the opportunity to establish informal relations with decision makers and influence public policy in accordance with particularistic social interests (Grosse, 2006; Grosse, 2007a). But even business actors with privileged access to the policy process may prefer rigid command-and-control regulation over soft law to avoid risks of legal uncertainty.

Strengthening or transforming the State? The impact of new modes of governance on state-society relations

As a result of their inclusiveness, we might expect new modes of governance to strengthen civil society and the participation of a greater number and variety of state and nonstate actors more generally speaking. Yet, there is little evidence that new modes of governance have changed the societal structures in accession countries (cf. Börzel, forthcoming-a). Part of the reason certainly lies with their sparse emergence. But even where they have emerged, the impact of new modes of governance on (domestic) power relations is at best differential. They may empower nonstate actors and local authorities *vis-à-vis* their central governments by legally prescribing public involvement in the policy process and opening new legal and political venues to push their interests, for example by taking their case to court and lodging complaints with the European Commission. But nonstate actors have often been too weak to exploit these new opportunities. Thus, accession to the EU has provided environmental actors with opportunities to put pressure on their national governments by lodging complaints with the European Commission in cases of noncompliance with EU environmental law (mostly in Southern Europe) or EU institutional requirements during the accession period (in the CEE countries). Yet, in all six countries, nonstate actors have initially been too weak to exert pressure systematically on their governments and to engage in stable and sustainable cooperation in order to make EU policies work on the ground. Spanish and Hungarian environmental groups, often supported by transnational organizations, have been more successful in using the participatory prescriptions of EU environmental policies than their Greek and Romanian counterparts, partly because environmental mobilization in Greece and Romania is much more localized. The latter were often not willing to exploit the new opportunities offered by EU accession either (see emergence).

The role of civil society in CEE accession countries resembles the situation in the three Southern European countries during the pre- and early postaccession period in the 1980s. In addition to their capacity constraints, environmental groups have yet to find their final place in public policy making. Pooling resources with the state requires a cooperative attitude, which conflicts with the role of civil society as a major opposition against socialist repression. As in Southern Europe, many NGOs see themselves as independent watchdogs rather than partners of government (Koutalakis, 2004; Obradovic and Alonso Vizcaino, 2007).

In the field of regional policy, the partnership principle and EU conditionality have empowered subnational actors and NGOs in accession countries to make effective demands for their inclusion in the preparation and implementation of regional development programs. Yet, their structural impact has been limited since they are embedded in predominantly hierarchical governance structures as a result of which they do not offer sufficient incentives and resources to foster horizontal cooperation and powersharing in the distribution of structural funds. Rather, the shadow of hierarchy induces regional actors to build up vertical relations. The 'layering' of new modes of governance has induced only slow change on the margins and mostly contributes to the reinforcement of hierarchical modes of governance (Paraskevopoulos, Panagiotis and Rees, 2006; Bruszt, 2008). Likewise, the introduction of social dialog institutions in Poland, Estonia and Lithuania has done little to transform the socialist legacy of the administrative state towards a more 'Western-type' network model (cf. Sissenich, 2007). On the contrary indeed, new modes of governance have reinforced some of the pathologies of these states by undermining 'classical' modes of democratic legitimating, allowing state actors to circumvent majoritarian institutions by resorting to civil or social dialog (cf. Vaughan-Whitehead, 2003; Grosse, 2006, 2007a). These findings resonate with arguments in the literature that soft modes of governance are too soft to be effective in countries with weak governance capacities, impairing the setting of stricter market-correcting regulations since state actors and civil society organizations are not strong enough to overcome the resistance of business (O'Hagan, 2004; Woolfson, 2006; Bohle and Greskovits, 2008).

Overall, new modes of governance have reinforced rather than changed existing domestic structures, particularly with regard to the dominance of state actors at the national and EU levels. While new modes of governance may have helped to get accession countries out of the 'low capacity trap' characterized by weak states and weak societies (Sissenich, 2007), they have moved toward a situation of 'stronger societies but much stronger states' (Bruszt, 2008). The EU may have strengthened the governance capacities of both state and nonstate actors; but the former have been much more empowered than the latter. These asymmetrical power constellations are hardly conducive to the fully fledged evolution of new modes of governance.

The structural impact of new modes of governance has not only been limited by weak governance capacities, particularly of nonstate actors, and the low harmony between the administrative and civic culture in the accession countries. The EU often does not exert sufficient pressure for adaptation, since either its own institutions are too weak, as in case of social dialog or the introduction of social and local partnership in executive agencies administering EU agricultural funds (Grosse, 2006, 2007b) or its policies inconsistently oscillate between encouraging the sharing and the concentration of central state powers as they have done in structural policy (Bruszt, 2008). The EU has also started to turn away from attempts to interfere directly in the domestic institutions of its member states, emphasizing competition and subsidiary (Grosse, 2008a: chapter 5).

Finally, since new and old modes usually work in combination, new modes complement old modes and (partly) compensate for their weaknesses. By increasing both the effectiveness and the legitimacy of hierarchical modes, they sustain rather than change traditional governance regimes, which severely limits the structural impact of new modes. So far, new modes of governance have done little to transform the state. On the contrary, they may have reinforced some of the pathologies of accession countries, particularly in Central and Eastern Europe.

New modes in old member states

While old modes prevail in new member states, new modes appear to play a more prominent role in old member states. The systematic involvement of nonstate actors in public policy making is, of course, not necessarily new in the EU 15 states, particularly not in those with neocorporatist or pluralist structures of interest intermediation, which includes virtually all Northern and Western European countries, with the possible exception of France (cf. Richardson, 1982; Schmidt, 2006). While the country is often treated as the ideal type of a statist polity, however, French authorities tend to open up the policy process informally in the implementation stage to accommodate stakeholder interests largely excluded from decision making (Mény, 1988; Schmidt, 1996). Public interest organizations and, in particular, pressure groups and companies, enjoy a variety of formal and informal access points at various levels of government, which grant them a say in the formulation and implementation of public policies (Saurugger, 2007). Finally, the 'negotiating state' (Scharpf, 1991), which emerged in Northern and Western Europe in the past century, gives social and economic actors a real stake in policy making by making them equal partners, for example in collective agreements in social and employment policy, or by delegating regulatory tasks to private or public-private bodies as in the case of professional and technical standards setting.

Since EU policy making has become an integral part of the domestic policy process, nonstate actors in Western and Northern EU 15 states enjoy broad opportunities to become involved, particularly in the implementation of EU Law (Héritier et al., 2001; Knill, 2001; Börzel, 2002; Schmidt, 2006). This is not to say that those member states have always endorsed the participatory requirements of EU policies. The EIAD and the FFHD met with similar resistance from the German, British and French authorities as in the Southern and the CEE accession countries (Börzel, 2003a; Börzel and Sprungk, in preparation). However, nonstate actors have 'pushed' and 'pulled' public authorities towards compliance, making ample use of the legal opportunities that the EU offers (Börzel, 2006). Overall, the increasing use of so called 'new policy instruments' in the EU 15 states, which employ nonhierarchical modes of coordination and encourage public participation in order to improve the effectiveness and legitimacy of public policies, has given nongovernmental organizations, interests groups, companies and citizens a prominent role, particularly in the implementation of (EU) environmental and social policy (Knill and Lenschow, 2000; Jordan, Wurzel and Zito, 2005; Falkner et al., 2005).

Interestingly, these findings do not seem to hold for the Open Method of Coordination (OMC), the archetype of a new mode of governance (Hodson and Maher, 2001). OMC has been applied in whole range of policy areas (see Chapter 2). While it encourages the participation of nonstate actors, it has largely taken the form of inter and transgovernmental negotiations with hardly any involvement of business and civil society, either in the formulation of joint goals at the EU level or in their implementation at the national level. Since policy making in the various areas is usually not sealed off to public involvement, the resistance of member state governments may well be explained by their general unwillingness to give the EU even a 'soft' role on sensitive issues.

While the effectiveness of OMC has been limited in the EU 15, too (cf. De la Porte, 2008), new modes of governance defined as the nonhierarchical involvement of nonstate actors in policy making are more prevalent in the old member states and show a greater variety covering the whole spectrum – even though they may not necessarily be new and tend to be embedded in old modes of command-and-control regulation (Jordan, Wurzel and Zito, 2005). These findings also hold for

Austria, Finland and Sweden, which joined the EU in 1995. As accession countries, they were fundamentally different from both their Southern and their Central and Eastern European counterparts. Not only were they not transition countries, but the three also had the necessary governance capacities to cope with the, admittedly much smaller, challenge of accession (Luif, 1995).

A more systematic comparison between old and new member states is beyond the scope of this volume. One of the few studies that has systematically compared the impact of EU (social) policy on old and new member states has been done by Gerda Falkner and her team. Their findings show that the involvement of social partners in the making and implementation of EU social policy is weaker in Southern European and CEE member states than in the Northern and Western member states (Falkner et al., 2005; Falkner, cf. Sissenich, 2007; Treib and Holzleitner, 2008).

The existing literature seems to confirm that nonhierarchical modes of governance require both a strong state and a strong society to emerge and be effective. This finding results in a serious dilemma or even paradox: the lower the capacity of a state, the greater the need for new modes of governance to compensate for state weakness or state failure but the less likely they are to emerge. This is particularly true if there is indeed a dialectical relationship between the evolution of a strong state and a strong society, as is assumed by the governance literature (Tilly, 1975; Mayntz, 1993). Whether this is merely a fallacy of modernization theory or simply the result of a selection bias towards the OECD world in governance research remains to be seen (cf. Börzel, 2007; Börzel forthcoming-c). We need more empirical research on countries that lack the prerequisites of a modern state to find out to what extent the governance paradox exists and how it can be eventually overcome (see Risse and Lehmkuhl, forthcoming). The few empirical studies that systematically explore the relationship between state and society, seem to support the mutual constituency of state and society (Katzenstein, 1984; Hooghe and Stolle, 2003; Sissenich, 2010).

Building strong states and strong societies?

The findings of the book bear some important implications for practical policy making regarding (new modes of) governance in Europe and beyond. Our analysis shows that while new modes of governance can increase the effectiveness of the implementation and enforcement of the *acquis,* they do so only under certain conditions. Relevant state and nonstate actor capacities, mutual trust among the stakeholders involved and constant and credible external pressure by the EU appear to be indispensible. These conditions are barely met outside the OECD world of industrialized democracies. Future accession countries in the South East of Europe have even weaker governance capacities than their CEE counterparts. This is also true for the EU's near neighbors, where the EU has relied even less on nonstate actors to draw states closer to the *acquis* (Lavenex, 2008; Börzel, Pamuk and Stahn, 2008). Thus, researchers and policy makers alike should tone down the high-flying expectations set into new modes of governance in the EU's internal policy making and its external relations. Our findings underscore the importance of other means to increase the effectiveness of European legislation in new member states, acceding and neighborhood countries, including capacity building oriented towards both state and non-state actors.

Yet, resource transfer as such will not necessarily do the trick. State actors have to be able to absorb financial assistance, which is still a major problem in Greece, even nearly 30 years after accession. Moreover, strengthening the capacities of the state may result in asymmetrical power relations with society. If anything, Europeanization has increased government autonomy in old and new member states, raising questions about the EU undermining rather than entrenching democracy. This is all the more problematic in semiauthoritarian states or countries where democratic institutions are still weak, which is the case for most of the EU's neighbors. Statebuilding needs to be balanced by empowering civil society.

The EU has developed a sophisticated tool box to strengthen the capacities of nongovernmental actors; but it is largely geared towards making EU policies more effective (Börzel, Pamuk and Stahn, 2008). EU strategies and programs reflect a rather functional understanding of civil society, which is shared by other international donors (Fagan, 2006b) and which Beate Kohler-Koch has aptly characterized as 'participatory engineering' (quoted in Trenz, 2008: 60). The EU 'instrumentalizes' civil society actors as 'coproducers of efficient and effective policy regulations' by providing information and expertise 'on demand' to EU policy makers, which need them to improve governance performance (Trenz, 2008: 60).[1] Legitimacy is not only neglected; it may be seriously compromised by EU capacity building (Sardamov, 2005). In order to receive external funding, many NGOs in accession countries have turned into service providers for the EU or their national governments. While becoming more professionalized, their membership base is low, and they have become detached from their root constituencies.

Moreover, the agenda of NGOs has been usurped by the funding priorities of the EU. Unlike other external donors, which left the regions when the EU started to increase its funding, EU grants come with significant strings attached and require relatively high matching funds (between 20 and 80 percent) as well as larger bureaucratic management capacities. Moreover, the EU's emphasis on funding projects with participants from several, old and new member states or on exchange of expertise in PHARE-financed 'twinning' projects have often forced participants from the new member states into the position of the junior partner. Accordingly, overwhelming percentages of EU funds have in fact been used for paying the foreign experts and consultants involved in capacity building. At the same time, EU funding channeled through large Western consultancies has significantly contributed to the development of a domestic consultancy-oriented professional sector. Training of NGOs by outside experts has focused on management, conflict resolution and decision making rather than campaigning, contestating and protesting skills. Overall, many NGOs have developed into elite organizations (Baker and Jehlicka, 1998; Fagan and Jehlicka, 2001; Fagan, 2006b; Lane, forthcoming). External funding has strengthened the more resourceful civil society actors that already had some skills in fundraising and lobbying (Raik, 2004). Local grassroots organizations, by contrast, have hardly benefited from EU capacity building. Their activities have been limited to their immediate community (Eder and Kousis, 2001; Carmin, forthcoming). To what extent the rift between 'haves and have-nots' of international assistance (Petrova and Tarrow, 2007) contributes to the emergence of a vigorous civil society where nonstate actors have sufficient autonomous action capacity to advance societal demands and hold state actors accountable remains to be seen. First insights into the effects of EU capacity building in the Western Balkans accession countries and its Eastern neighborhood are hardly encouraging (Fagan, 2006a, 2008; Börzel, Pamuk and Stahn, 2008).

Note

1. Some have criticized this 'partnership interpretation' of civil society as neoliberal ideology aiming at the 'rolling back of the state in areas such as policy development, regulation and implementation (Fagan, 2005: 531; Fagan, 2006b; Lane, 2007).

Bibliography

Ágh, A. (1999) 'Europeanization of Policy Making in East-Central Europe: the Hungarian approach to EU Accession', *Journal of European Public Policy*, 6, 5, 839–854.

Aguilar Fernández, S. (1994) 'Spanish Pollution Control Policy and the Challenge of the European Union', *Regional Politics and Policy*, 4, 1, special issue, 102–117.

Aguilar Fernández, S. (2003) 'Spanish Coordination in the European Union. The Case of the Habitats Directive', *Administration & Society*, 34, 6, 678–699.

Aguilera, R. (2001) 'La Relativa Europeización de la Política de Empleo' in C. Closa (ed.) *La Europeización del Sistema Político Español*. (Madrid: Istmo), 351–379.

Alberola, E. (2001) 'La Europeización de la Política Macroeconómica' in C. Closa (ed.) *La Europeización del Sistema Político Español*. (Madrid: Istmo), 330–350.

Alesina, A. and Rosenthal, H. (1995) *Partisan Politics. Divided Government, and the Economy*. (Cambridge: Cambridge University Press).

Amsden, A. H. (1989) *Asia's Next Giant*. (Oxford: Oxford University Press).

Andersson, M. (1999) *Change and Continuity in Poland's Environmental Policy*. (Berlin: Springer-Verlag).

Andersson, M. (2002) 'Environmental Policy in Poland' in H. Weidner and M. Jänicke (eds.) *Capacity Building in National Environmental Policy*. (Berlin: Springer-Verlag).

Andonova, L. B. (2003) *Transnational Politics of the Environment. The European Union and Environmental Policy in Central and Eastern Europe*. (Cambridge: MIT Press).

Andreou, G. (2004) 'Implementing the Habitats Directive in Greece', *OEUE Occasional Paper*, 4.3–08.04.

Ansell, C. (2000) 'The Networked Polity. Regional Development in Western Europe', *Governance*, 13, 3, 303–333.

Ansell, C., Parsons, C. and Darden, K. (1997) 'Dual Networks in European Regional Development Policy', *Journal of Common Market Studies*, 35, 3, 347–375.

ARA (2004) *Strategia de dezvoltare durabilă a serviciilor publice de alimentare cu apă și canalizare " România 2025* (Bucuresti).

Arcadis Euroconsult (2004) *Implementation of the new Water Framework Directive on Pilot Basins. Inception Report. Europeaid/114912/D/SV/RO*).

Archibald, S., Banu, L. and Bochniarz, Z. (2004) 'Market Liberalisation and Sustainability in Transition: Turning Points and Trends in Central and Eastern Europe', *Environmental Politics*, 13, 266–288.

Armstrong, K. A. (2003) 'Tackling Social Exclusion Through OMC: Reshaping the Boundaries of EU Governance' in T. A. Börzel and R. Cichowski (eds.) *The State of the European Union*. (Oxford: Oxford University Press), 170–194.

Armstrong, K., Begg, I. and Zeitlin, J. (2008) 'JCMS Symposium: EU Governance After Lisbon', *Journal of Common Market Studies*, 46, 2, 413–450.

Arriscado Nunes, J. (2004) 'Introduction: Democracy, Participation and Grassroots Movements in Contemporary Portugal', *South European Society & Politics*, 9, 2, 46–76.

Auer, M. (2004) *Restoring Cursed Earth: Appraising Environmental Policy Reforms in Central and Eastern Europe and Russia.* (Lanham, MD: Rowman & Littlefield).

Bache, I. (1998) *The Politics of EU Regional Policy: Multilevel Governance or Flexible Gatekeeping?* (Sheffield: Sheffield Academic Press).

Baga, E. and Buzogany, A. (2006) 'Europäisierung subnationaler Politik und die Rolle lokaler Akteure in Mittel- und Osteuropa' in D. Schmidt (ed.) *Osteuropaforschung – 15 Jahre "danach". Beiträge für die 14. Tagung junger Osteuropa-Experten* (Berlin: Deutsche Gesellschaft für Osteuropakunde), 131–135.

Baga, E. and Buzogány, A. (2008) 'Europa und das Gold der Karpaten. Lokale, nationale und transnationale Dimensionen des Bergbaukonfliktes in Roşia Montană' in G. Welz (ed.) *Projekte der Europäisierung.* (Frankfurt am Main: Kulturanthropologie Notizen).

Baga, E. and Buzogány, A. (2009) 'Europa und das Gold der Karpaten. Lokale, nationale und transnationale Dimensionen des Bergbaukonfliktes in Rosia Montană 'in G. Welz (ed.) *Projekte der Europäisierung.* (Frankfurt am Main: Kulturanthropologie Notizen).

Bailey, D. and Propris, L. d. (2004) 'A Bridge to Phare? EU Pre-Accession Aid and Capacity-Building in the Candidate Countries', *Journal of Common Market Studies*, 42, 1, 77–98.

Baker, S. and Jehlicka, P. (eds.) (1998) *Dilemmas of Transition: The Environment, Democracy and Economic Reform in East Central Europe.* (Ilford: Frank Cass).

Banfield, E. C. (1958) *The Moral Basis of a Backward Society.* (Glencoe: Free Press).

Bar, M. (2006) 'Umsetzung der Europäischen Umweltgesetzgebung in Polen', *EU Rundschreiben, Sonderheft*, 15, 11–12.

Barreira, A. (2003) 'La participación pública en la Directiva Marco del Agua y sus implicaciones para la Península Ibérica' in P. Arrojo and L. d. Moral (eds.) *La Directiva Marco del Agua: realidades y futuros.* (Zaragoza: Fundación Nueva Cultura del Agua), 153–172.

Bera, M. (2005) *A nyílt tervezés tapasztalatai a Rába folyógazdálkodási program-ban* WWF füzetek, http://www.wwf.hu/fletoltes.php?szam=79&tipus=1) last accessed 15.06.2009.

Berg, M. M. (1999) 'Environmental Protection and the Hungarian Transition', *The Social Science Journal*, 36, 2, 227–250.

Blaug, R. (1997) 'Between Fear and Disappointment: Critical, Empirical and Political Uses of Habermas', *Political Studies*, 45, 1, 100–117.

Bod, T. (2007) *Ivóvízprojektek: Árhullám.* Magyar Narancs.

Boda, Z. and Scheiring, G. (2006) 'Water Privatisation in the Context of Transition' in D. Chavez (ed.) *Beyond the Market: The Future of Public Services*: TNI / Public Services International Research Unit (PSIRU).

Boda, Z. and Scheiring, G. (2008) 'A vízprivatizáció politikai gazdaságtanáról' in Z. Boda and G. Scheiring (eds.) *Gazdálkodj Okosan! - A privatizáció és a közszol-gáltatások politikája* (Budapest: Új Mandátum).

Boda, Z., Scheiring, G., Hall, D. and Lobina, E. (2006) *Social Policy, Regulation and Private Sector Water Supply: the Case of Hungary*: UNRISD Working Paper.

Bohle, D. and Greskovits, B. (2001) 'Development Paths on Europe's Periphery: Hungary's and Poland's Return to Europe Compared', *Polish Sociological Review*, 33, 1, 3–27.

Bohle, D. and Greskovits, B. (2008) 'Neoliberalism, Embedded Neoliberalism and Neocorporatism: Towards Transnational Capitalism in Central-Eastern Europe', *West European Politics*, 30, 3, 443–446.

Bohne, E. (2006) 'Spain' in E. Bohne (ed.) *The Quest for Environmental Regulatory Integration in the European Union. Integrated Pollution Prevention and Control, Environmental Impact Assessment and Major Accident Prevention.* (Alphen: Kluwer), 333–382.

Boix, C. (1998) *Political Parties, Growth and Equality.* (Cambridge: Cambridge University Press).

Borrás, S. and Jacobsson, K. (2004) 'The Open Method of Co-ordination and New Governance Patterns in the EU', *Journal of European Public Policy*, 11, 2, 185–208.

Borrás, S., Koutalakis, C. and Wendler, F. (2007) 'European Agencies and Input Legitimacy: EFSA, EMeA and EPO in the Post-Delegation Phase', *Journal of European Integration*, 29, 5, 583–600.

Börzel, T. A. (1998) 'Organising Babylon. On the Different Conceptions of Policy Networks', *Public Administration*, 76, 2, 253–273.

Börzel, T. A. (1999) 'Towards Convergence in Europe? Institutional Adaptation to Europeanisation in Germany and Spain', *Journal of Common Market Studies*, 37, 4, 573–596.

Börzel, T. A. (2002) *States and Regions in the European Union. Institutional Adaptation in Germany and Spain.* (Cambridge: Cambridge University Press).

Börzel, T. A. (2003a) *Environmental Leaders and Laggards in the European Union. Why There is (Not) a Southern Problem.* (London: Ashgate).

Börzel, T. A. (2003b) 'Guarding the Treaty: The Compliance Strategies of the European Commission' in T. A. Börzel and R. Cichowski (eds.) *The State of the European Union VI: Law, Politics, and Society.* (Oxford: Oxford University Press), 197–220.

Börzel, T. A. (2006) 'Participation Through Law Enforcement: The Case of the European Union', *Comparative Political Studies*, 39, 1, 128–152.

Börzel, T. A. (2007) 'Regieren ohne den Schatten der Hierarchie. Ein modernisierungstheoretischer Fehlschluss?' in T. Risse and U. Lehmkuhl (eds.) *Regieren ohne Staat? Governance in den Räumen begrenzter Staatlichkeit.* (Baden-Baden: Nomos), 41–63.

Börzel, T. A. (ed.) (2010a) *Civil Society on the Rise? EU Enlargement and Societal Mobilization in Central and Eastern Europe. Special Issue of Acta Politica.*

Börzel, T. A. (2010b) 'Drawing Closer to Europe: New Modes of Governance and Accession' in A. Héritier and M. Rhodes (eds.) *New Modes of Governance in Europe.* Governing in the Shadow of Hierarchy.

Börzel, T. A. (2010c) 'Governance with(out) Government – False Promises or Flawed Premises', SFB-Governance Working Paper Series, Sonderforschungsbereich (SFB) 700, Berlin.

Börzel, T.A. (2011) 'EU Governance: Negotiation and Competition in the Shadow of Hierarchy', *Journal of Common Market Studies*.

Börzel, T. A. and Risse, T. (2005) 'Public-Private Partnerships: Effective and Legitimate Tools of Transnational Governance?' in E. Grande and L. W. Pauly (eds.) *Complex Sovereignty: On the Reconstitution of Political Authority in the 21st. Century.* (Toronto: University of Toronto Press), 195–216.

Börzel, T. A. and Sedelmeier, U. (2006) 'The EU Dimension in European Politics' in P. M. a. J. Heywood, Erik and Rhodes, Martin and Sedelmeier, Ulrich (ed.) *Developments in European Politics* (Houndmills, Basingstoke; New York: Palgrave Macmillan), 54–70.

Börzel, T. A. and Sprungk, C. (2011) *Obstinate or Inefficient? Why Member States Do Not Comply with European Law.* (Manuscript, Berlin, May 2009).

Börzel, T. A., Buzogany, A. and Guttenbrunner, S. (2006) 'Mapping the application of NMG to facilitate the implementation of environmental policy in Poland, Hungary, and Romania', *NewGov Contract Deliverable, Berlin*, 12/D03.

Börzel, T. A., Dudziak, M., Hofmann, T., Panke, D. and Sprungk, C. (2007) 'Recalcitrance, Inefficiency and Support for European Integration. Why Member States Do (Not) Comply with European Law', *CES Working Paper, Harvard University*, 151.

Börzel, T. A., Pamuk, Y. and Stahn, A. (2008) 'One Size Fits All? How the European Union Promotes Good Governance in Its Near Abroad', *SFB 700 Working Paper 18*, Sonderforschungsbereich (SFB) 700, Berlin.

Botcheva, L. (1996) 'Focus and Effectiveness of Environmental Activism in Eastern Europe:A Comparative Study of Environmental Movements in Bulgaria, Hungary, Slovakia, and Romania', *Journal of Environment & Development*, 5, 3, 292–212.

Bruneau, T. and Macleod, A. (1986) *Politics in Contemporary Portugal: Parties and the Consolidation of Democracy.* (Boulder, Colorado: Lynne Rienner Publishers).

Bruszt, L. (2002) 'Making Markets and Eastern Enlargement: Diverging Convergence', *West European Politics*, 25, 2, 121–140.

Bruszt, L. (2008) 'Multi-Level Governance – The Eastern Versions: Emerging Patterns of Regional Development Governance in the New Member States', *Regional and Federal Studies*, 18, 5, 607–627.

Bruszt, L. and Vedres, B. (2008) 'Preliminary Report on the Effects and Effectiveness of the Mode of Governing Regional Development Based on the Surveys', *NewGov Deliverable*, Project 15, D09.

Büchs, M. (2008) 'How Legitimate is the Open Method of Co-ordination?', *Journal of Common Market Studies*, 46, 4, 765–786.

Bulla, M. and Tamás, P. (2003) *Magyarország környezeti jövőképe.* (Budapest: Országos Környezetvédelmi Tanács).

Burada, V. and Berceanu, D. (2005) *Dialogue for Civil Society. Report on the state of civil society in Romania 2005 – CIVICUS Civil Society Index Report for Romania.* (Bucharest Civil Society Development Foundation (CSDF)).

Cabugueira, M. F. M. (2004) 'Portuguese Experience of Voluntary Approaches in Environmental Policy', *Management of Environmental Quality: An International Journal*, 15, 2, 174–186.

Caddy, J. (2000) 'Implementation of EU Environmental Policy in Future Member States: The Case of EIA' in C. Knill and A. Lenschow (eds.) *Implementing EU Environmental Policy: New directions and old problems.* (Manchester: Manchester University Press), 197–222.

Caddy, J. and Vari, A. (2002) 'Hungary' in H. Weidner, Jaenicke, M. (ed.) *Capacity Building in National Environmental Policy: A Comparative Study of 17 Countries.* (Berlin: Springer).

Calder, C. (1996) *Le Portugal et l'Europe: l'impact de l'intégration communautaire dans les domaines de l'agriculture et de l'environnement.* (Paris: IEP), 55–58.

Canelas, L., Almansa, P., Merchan, M. and Cifuentes, P. (2005) 'Quality of environmental impact statements in Portugal and Spain', *Environmental Impact Assessment Review*, 25, 3, 217–225.

Capital (2005) 'Fabricile romanesti polueaza dosarul integrarii [Romanian factories pollute the folder of the integration]'.

Carmin, J. (in preparation) 'NGO Capacity and Environmental Governance in Central and Eastern Europe', *Acta Politica*.

Carmin, J. A. and Hicks, B. (2002) 'International Triggering Events, Transnational Networks, And The Development of Czech And Polish Environmental Movements', *Mobilization: An International Quarterly*, 7, 3, 305–324.

Carmin, J. and Vandeveer, S. D. (2004) 'Enlarging the EU Environments: Central and Eastern Europe from Transition to Accession', *Environmental Politics*, 13, 1, 3–24.

Carter, N., Nunes da Silva, F. and Magalhaes, F. (2000) 'Local Agenda 21: Progress in Portugal', *European Urban and Regional Studies*, 7, 2, 181–186.

Castañón, O. (2006) 'Aspectes jurídics de la Directiva Marc de l'Aigua, en Generalitat de Catalunya' in *La Directiva Marc de l'Aigua a Catalunya*. (Barcelona: Generalitat de Catalunya).

Caviedes, A. (2004) 'The Open Method of Co-ordination in Immigration Policy: A Tool for Prying Open Fortress Europe?', *Journal of European Public Policy*, 11, 2, 289–310.

Cazes, G., Domingo, J. and Gauthier, A. (1985) *L'Espagne et le Portugal aux portes du Marché Commun*. (Montreuil: Bréal).

Center for Environmental Studies (2003) *Az önkéntes környezetvédelmi megállapodások bevezetése Magyarországon, http://www.ktk-ces.hu/onkentes_rep.pdf* KTK-CES (Budapest).

Cernat, L. (2006) *Europeanization, Varieties of Capitalism and Economic Performance in Central and Eastern Europe*. (Basingstoke, England; New York: Palgrave Macmillan).

Chammas, B. and Bogdanska-Warmuz, R. (2006) *Public Participation in Implementation of the Framework Water Directive - Experiences in the Upper Vistula Pilot Catchment Area*, Cracow: Global Water Partnership Central and Eastern Europe Task Force Working Paper.

Chayes, A. and Chayes, A. H. (1995) *The New Sovereignty. Compliance with International Regulatory Agreements*. (Cambridge: Harvard University Press).

Cherp, A. and Antypas, A. (2003) 'Dealing With Continuous Reform: Towards Adaptive EA Policy Systems in Countries in Transition', *Journal of Environmental Assessment Policy and Management*, 5, 4, 455–476.

Chilcote, R. H., Hadjiyannis, S., López, F. A. I., Nataf, D. and Sammis, E. (eds.) (1990) *Transitions from Dictatorship to Democracy. Comparative Studies on Spain, Portugal and Greece*. (London, New York: Taylor & Francis).

Chivu, L. (2002) 'Evaluari ale costurilor institutional -administrative generate de implementarea Directivei 96/61/CE privind controlul si prevenirea poluarii industriale (IPPC). (The Evaluation of the institutional and administration costs arising from the implementation of the Directive 96/61/CE (IPPC)'.

Christiansen, A. and Tangen, K. (2002) 'The Shadow of the Past: Environmental Issues and Institutional Learning in EU Enlargement Processes', *Journal of Environmental Policy & Planning*, 4, 67–86.

Christiansen, T. and Piattoni, S. (eds.) (2003) *Informal Governance in the European Union*. (Cheltenham: Edward Elgar).

Ciupagea, C., Manoleli, D., Niţă, V., Papatulică, M. and Stănculescu, M. (2006) *Direcţii strategice ale dezvoltării durabile în România*. (Bucuresti Institutul European din România).

Coen, D. (2008) *Lobbying in the European Union. Institutions, Actors and Policy*. (Oxford: Oxford University Press).

Coen, D. and Héritier, A. (eds.) (2006) *Refining Regulatory Regimes in Europe: The Creation and Correction of Markets*. (Cheltenham: Edward Elgar).

Coen, D. and Thatcher, M. (2008) 'Network Governance and Multi-level Delegation: European Networks of Regulatory Agencies', *Journal of Public Policy*, 28, 1, 49–71.

Colton, T. J. and Holmes, S. (eds.) (2006) *The State after Communism. Governance in the New Russia*. (Lanham, MD: Rowman & Littlefield).

Costejà, M., Font, N., Rigol, A. and Subirats, J. (2004) 'The Evolution of Water Regime in Spain' in I. Kissling-Näf and S. Kuks (eds.) *The Evolution of National Water Regimes in Europe – Transitions in Water Rights and Water Policies.* (Dordrecht: Kluever Academic Publishers).

Craciun, C. (2006) *The Learning Government: Assessing Policy Making Reform in Romania*. (Budapest Central European University – Open Society Institute).

Cristorian, A. (2008) *Misterele Ministerului Mediului: proiecte virtuale pe bani reali (The mysteries of the Environmental Ministry: virtual projects on real money)* http://www.catavencu.ro/misterele_ministerului_mediului_proiecte_virtuale_pe_bani_reali-2905.html (Homepage), 02 February 2009.

Cruceru, M., Marius Voronca, M. and Diaconu, B. (2005) 'Implementation of the EU Legislation on Romanian Power Industry. Romanian Legislation: Achievements and Shortcomings', *Energy*, 30, 8, 1365–1376.

Curtea de Conturi (2004) *The Performance of Concessioning Public Utilities in Water Distribution and Sewage. (in Romanian)* (Bucharest: Curtea de Conturi).

Curzon Price, V. (1999) 'Reintegrating Europe: Economic Aspects' in V. Curzon Price, Landau, Alice, and Whitman, Richard G. (eds.) *The Enlargement of the European Union: Issues and Strategies.* (London and New York: Routledge), 25–55.

Czada, R. and Schmidt, M. G. (eds.) (1993), *Verhandlungsdemokratie, Interessenvermittlung, Regierbarkeit. Festschrift für Gerhard Lehmbruch.* (Opladen: Westdeutscher Verlag).

D'Oliveira Martins, G. (1991) *Portugal. Institutions et faits.* (Lisbon: Imprensa Nacional).

DANCEE (2001) *The Environmental Challenge of EU Enlargement in Central and Eastern Europe* (Copenhagen: Danish Cooperation for Environment in Eastern Europe).

DANCEE (2003) *Romania's Road to the Accession: The Need for an Environmental Focus.* (Copenhagen).

De la Porte, C. (2008) *The European Level Development and National Influence of the Open method of Coordination: The Cases of Employment and Social Inclusion. Dissertation. Social and Political Science Department.* (Florence: European University Institute).

De la Porte, C. and Nanz, P. (2004) 'The OMC – a Deliverative-Democratic Mode of Governance? The Case of Employment and Pension', *Journal of European Public Policy*, 11, 2, 267–288.

DEMSTAR (2002) *Conceptualizing State Capacity. Research Report No. 6.* (Aarhus).

Dimitrova, A. (2002) 'Enlargement, Institution-Building and the EU's Administrative Capacity Requirement', *West European Politics*, 25, 4, 171–190.

Dimitrova, A. (2005) 'Europeanization and Civil Service Reform in Central and Eastern Europe' in F. Schimmelfennig and U. Sedelmeier (eds.) *The Europeanization of Central and Eastern Europe.* (Ithaca, NY: Cornell University Press).

Dragomirescu, S., Muica, C. and Turnock, D. (1998) 'Environmental Action during Romania's Eearly Ttransition Years', *Environmental Politics*, 7, 1, 162–182.

Drain, M. (1994) *L'économie du Portugal* (Paris: Presses Universitaires de France).

Duina, F. G. (1997) 'Explaining Legal Implementation in the European Union', *International Journal of the Sociology of Law*, 25, 2, 155–179.

Dumeige, B., Rungette, D., Terraz, L. and Thiry, E. (2007) *Descrierea responsabilitatilor si relatiilor in implementarea retelei Natura 2000 (Description of responsibilities and relations in implementing the Natura 2000 network)*. (Timisoara).

ECOTEC (2000) *Administrative Capacity for Implementation and Enforcement of EU Environmental Policy in the 13 Candidate Countries. A Final Report to DG Environment. Service Contract B7-8110 / 2000 / 159960 / MAR / H1* (Brussels).

Eder, K. and Kousis, M. (eds.) (2001) *Environmental Politics in Southern Europe*. (Dordrecht/Boston/London: Kluwer Academic Publishers).

EEB/WWF (2006) European Environmental Bureau.

Ellison, D. (2008) *On the Politics of Climate Change: is there an East-West Divide?* I. f. W. Economics (ed.), Working Papers (Budapest: Institute for World Economics Hungarian Academy of Sciences).

Emmott, N. (1997) 'The Theory and Practice of IPPC: Case Studies from the UK and Hungary and the implications for future EU environmental policy', *European Environment*, 7, 1, 1–6.

ENGREF (2003) *Water Management in Upper Silesia: an overview*.

Enyedi, D. and Szirmai, V. (1998) 'Environmental Movements and Civil Society in Hungary' in A. Tickle and I. Welsh (eds.) *Environment and society in Eastern Europe* (Harlow: Longman).

Epstein, R. A. and Sedelmeier, U. (eds.) (2009) *Beyond Conditionality: International Institutions in Postcommunist Europe after Enlargement*. (London: Routledge).

Escobar Gómez, G. (1994) 'Evaluación de Impacto Ambiental en España: resultados prácticos', *Ciudad y Territorio*, 2, 102, 585–595.

European Commission (1992) *Control de la Aplicación del Derecho Comunitario, 1991*. COM (1992).

European Commission (1993) *Report on the Implementation of the Directive 85/337/ EEC on the Impact of Public and Private Projects on the Environment'* COM (1993) 28 final.

European Commission (1999) *Romania, Screening Results:* Chapter 22 Environment, 6 October.

European Commission (2001) *Annual Report of the Cohesion Fund 1999*. COM (2000) 882 final.

European Commission (2002) *Report by the Commission on the application of Directive 79/409/EEC on the conservation of birds*. COM (2002) 146 final.

European Commission (2003) *Fourth Annual Survey on the implementation and enforcement of Community environmental law, 2002*. SEC (2003) 804.

European Commission (2004a) *Analysis of Member States' first implementation reports on the IPPC Directive (EU-15)*. Final Report June 2004.

European Commission (2004b) *European Union Programmes for Romania: Environment* (Bucharest Delegation of the European Commission in Romania).

European Commission (2005a) *Developing Capacity in Implementation and Enforcement through the AC IMPEL Network. Institutional Review - Romania* (Brussels: DG Environment).

European Commission (2005b) *Regular Report from the Commission on Romania's Progress Towards Accession:* (Commission of the European Communities).

European Commission (2005c) *Romania – 2005 Comprehensive Monitoring Report*: COM (2005) 534 Final.

European Commission (2005d) *Sixth Annual Survey on the Implementation and Enforcement of Community Environmental Law, 2004*. SEC (2005) 1055.

European Commission (2006) *7th Annual Survey on the Implementation and Enforcement of Community Environmental Law 2005*. SEC (2006).

European Commission (2007) *Communication from the Commission to the European Parliament and the Council Towards Sustainable Water Management in the European Union. First Stage in the Implementation of the Water Framework Directive 2000/60/EC*. COM (2007) 128 final.

Evans, P. B. (1995) *Embedded Autonomy: States and Industrial Transformation*. (Princeton: Princeton University Press).

Evans, P. B., Rueschemeyer, D. and Skocpol, T. (eds.) (1985) *Bringing the State Back In*. (Cambridge: Cambridge University Press).

Fagan, A. (2004) *Environment and Democracy in the Czech Republic*. (Cheltenham: Edward Elgar).

Fagan, A. (2005) 'Taking Stock of Civil-Society Development in Post-communist Europe: Evidence from the Czech Republic', *Democratization*, 12, 4, 528–547.

Fagan, A. (2006a) 'Neither 'North' nor 'South': The Environment and Civil Society in Post-conflict Bosnia-Hercegovina', *Environmental Politics*, 15, 5, 787–802.

Fagan, A. (2006b) 'Transnational Aid for Civil Society Development in Post-Socialist Europe: Democratic Consolidation or a New Imperialism?', *Journal of Communist Studies and Transition Politics*, 22, 1, 115–134.

Fagan, A. (2008) 'Global-Local Linkage in the Western Balkans: The Politics of Environmental Capacity Building in Bosnia-Herzegovina', *Political Studies*, 55, 1, 1–22.

Fagan, A. and Jehlicka, P. (2001) *The Impact of EU Assistance on Czech Environmental Movement Capacity since 1990* Workshop: Environmental Challenges of EU Eastern Enlargement. (Robert Schuman Centre for Advanced Studies, European University, Florence).

Falkner, G., Treib, O. and Holzleitner, E. (2008) *Compliance in the European Union. Living Rights or Dead Letters?* (Aldershot: Ashgate).

Falkner, G., Treib, O., Hartlapp, M. and Leiber, S. (2005) *Complying with Europe. EU Harmonization and Soft Law in the Member States*. (Cambridge: Cambridge University Press).

Fay, C. (2003) *Current Status of Water Sector Restructuring in Poland* Working Paper published by the EU Project Intermediaries.

Fernández, A. M., Font, N. and Koutalakis, C. (2008) 'Governance in the Environmental Sector: Specificites of Southern Europe', *EU NewGov Policy Brief*, 12.

Figueiredo, E., Fidélis, T. and Pires, A. d. R. (2001) 'Grassroots Environmental Action in Portugal (1974–1994)' in K. Eder and M. Kousis (eds.) *Environmental Politics in Southern Europe. Actors, Institutions and Discourses in a Europeanizing Society*. (The Hague: Kluwer Academic Publishers), 197–224.

Font, N. (ed.) (2001a) *La europeización de la política ambiental: desafíos e inercias*. (Madrid: Istmo).

Font, N. (2001b) 'La Política d'Espais Naturals' in R. Gomà and J. Subirats (eds.) *Polítiques públiques a Catalunya, 1980–2000*. (Barcelona: UAB-UB).

Font, N. and Morata, F. (1998) 'Spain: Environmental Policy and Public Administration. A Marriage of Convinience Officiated by the EU?' in K. Hanf and A.-I. Jansen (eds.) *Governance and Environment in Western Europe. Politics, Policy and Administration*. (Essex: Longman).

Fousekis, P. and Lekakis, J. N. (1997) 'Greece's Institutional Response to Sustainable Development', *Environmental Politics*, 6, 1, 131–152.

Franck, T. M. (1990) *The Power of Legitimacy Among Nations*. (Oxford: Oxford University Press).

Fritz, V. (2004) *State Weakness in Eastern Europe. Concept and Causes* EUI Working Papers.

Fülöp, S. (2003) 'A vízgyűjtő kerületi tervezéssel kapcsolatos jogharmonizáció problémái és a közösségi részvétel jelentősége a folyamatban' in MTVSZ (ed.) *A Víz Keretirányelv természetvédelmi vonatkozásai*. (Budapest).

Fundación Nueva Cultura del Agua (2007) *Análisis de la Implementación de la Directiva Marco del Agua en España*. 2005–2006 (http://www.unizar.es/fnca/ docu/docu171.pdf).

Gallagher, T. (2005) *Theft of a Nation: Romania Since Communism*. (London: Hurst & Company).

Gehring, T. and Kerler, M. (2008) 'Institutional Stimulation of Deliberative Decision-Making: Division of Labour, Deliberative Legitimacy and Technical Regulation in the European Single Market. ' *Journal of Common Market Studies*, 46, 5, 1001–1023.

Gehring, T. and Krapohl, S. (2007) 'Supranational Regulatory Agencies Between Interdependence and Control: The EMEA and the Authorisation of Pharmaceuticals in the European Single Market' *Journal of European Public Policy*, 14, 2, 208–266.

Gerhards, J. and Lengfeld, H. (2006) 'Das Ökologieskript der Europäischen Union und seine Akzeptanz in den Mitglieds- und Beitrittsländern der EU', *Zeitschrift für Soziologie*, 35, 24–40.

Ghellab, Y. and Vaughan-Whitehead, D. C. (eds.) (2003) *Sectoral Social Dialogue in Future EU Member States: The Weakest Link*. (Genf: International Labour Organization).

Gille, Z. (2004) 'Europeanising Hungarian Waste Policies: Progress or Regression?', *Environmental Politics*, 13, 1, 114–134.

Glenn, J. K. and Mendelson, S. E. (eds.) (2002) *The Power and Limits of NGOs: A Critical Look at Building Democracy in Eastern Europe and Eurasia*. (New York: Columbia University Press).

Goetz, K. and Wollmann, H. (2001) 'Governmentalising Central Executives in Postcommunist Europe: A Four-Country Comparison', *Journal of European Public Policy*, 8, 6, 864–887.

Goetz, K. H. (2005) 'The New Member States and the EU: Responding to Europe' in S. Bulmer and C. Lequesne (eds.) *The Member States of the European Union*. (Oxford: Oxford University Press), 254–280.

Gonçalves, M. E. (2002) 'Implementation of EIA Directives in Portugal. How Changes in Civic Culture are Challenging Political and Administrative Practice', *Environmental Impact Assessment Review*, 22, 3, 249–269.

Government of Romania (2004a) *Implementation Plan for Directive 98/83/EC on the Quality of Water Intended for Water Consumption*.

Government of Romania (2004b) *Plan Implementare pentru Directiva 2001/80/CE privind limitarea emisiilor anumitor poluanti in aer proveniti din instalatii mari de ardere.*

Government of Romania (2008) *Sectoral Operational Programme for the Environment 2007–2013. Annual Report* (Bucharest).

Grabbe, H. (2001) 'How does Europeanization affect CEE Governance? Conditionality, Diffusion and Diversity', *Journal of European Public Policy*, 8, 6, 1013–1031.

Grabbe, H. (2006) *The EU's Transformative Power – Europeanization through Conditionality in Central and Eastern Europe.* (Basingstoke: Palgrave Macmillian).

Grande, E. and Risse, T. (2000) 'Bridging the Gap: Konzeptionelle Anforderungen an die politikwissenschaftliche Analyse von Globalisierungsprozessen', *Zeitschrift für Internationale Beziehungen*, 7, 2, 235–266.

Greenspan Bell, R. (2004a) 'Further up the Learning Curve: NGOs from Transition to Brussels', *Environmental Politics*, 13, 1, 194–212.

Greenspan Bell, R. (2004b) 'Hungary: Developing Institutions to Support Environmental Protection' in M. Auer (ed.) *To Restore Cursed Earth. Appraising Environmental Reforms in Central and Eastern Europe and the Former Soviet Union.* (Boulder, Colorado: Rowman & Littlefield Press).

Grosse, T. G. (2005) *Democratization, Capture of the State and New Forms of Governance in CEE Countries.* (Warsaw: Foundation Institute of Public Affairs).

Grosse, T. G. (2006) 'New Modes of Governance in New European Union Member States. A Report on Social Dialogue in Selected European Union Countries', *NewGov Deliverable. European University Institute, Florence*, 17, D08.

Grosse, T. (2007a) 'Od czego zależy jakość dialogu społecznego? Koncepcja modelu państwa administracyjnego i państwa sieciowego na przykładzie instytucji dialogu społecznego', *Civitas*, 10, 121–152.

Grosse, T. G. (2007b) 'New Modes of Governance in Agencies Implementing EU Policies: Examples of Europeanization in Three New EU Member States', *NewGov Contract Deliverable. European University Institute, Florence*, 17, D08.

Grosse, T. G. (2008a) *Europa na rozdożu.* (Warsaw: Institute of Public Affairs).

Grosse, T. G. (2008b) 'Europeizacja a lokalne uwarunkowania administracyjne', *Zarządzanie Publiczne*, 1, 3, 69–90.

Haas, P. M. (1998) 'Compliance with EU Directives: Insights from International Relations and Comparative Politics', *Journal of European Public Policy*, 5, 1, 17–37.

Hajba, E. (1994) 'The Rise and Fall of the Hungarian Greens', *The Journal of Communist Studies and Transitional Politics*, 10, 3, 180–191.

Hall, P. A. (1999) 'Social Capital in Britain', *British Journal of Political Science*, 29, 3, 417–461

Hallstrom, L. (2004) 'Eurocratising Enlargement? EU Elites and NGO Participation in European Environmental Policy', *Environmental Politics*, 13, 1, 175–196.

Harper, K. (2005) "'Wild Capitalism' and 'Ecocolonialism': A Tale of Two Rivers', *American Anthropologist*, 107, 2, 221–233.

Haverland, M. (2000) 'National Adaptation to European Integration: The Importance of Institutional Veto Points', *Journal of Public Policy*, 20, 1, 83–103.

Hegedüs, J., Somogyi, E. and Tönko, A. (2003) *Current Status of Water Restructuring in Romania.* (Budapest: Metropolitan Research Institute).

Heinelt, H. and Smith, R. (eds.) (1996) *Policy Networks and European Structural Funds*. (Aldershot: Avebury).

Hellman, J. S., Jones, G. and Kaufmann, D. (2000) ' "*Seize the State, Seize the Day*" – *State Capture, Corruption, and Influence in Transition*' in T. W. Bank (ed.), Policy Research Working Paper.

Héritier, A. (2001) 'Differential Europe: National Administrative Responses to Community Policy' in M. G. Cowles, J. A. Caporaso and T. Risse (eds.) *Transforming Europe. Europeanization and Domestic Change*. (Ithaca: Cornell University Press), 44–59.

Héritier, A. (2002) 'New Modes of Governance in Europe: Policy-Making without Legislating?' in A. Héritier (ed.) *Common Goods. Reinventing European and International Governance*. (Langham: Rowman & Littlefield), 185–206.

Héritier, A. (2003) 'New Modes of Governance in Europe: Increasing Political Capacity and Policy Effectiveness?' in T. A. Börzel and R. . Cichowski (eds.) *The State of the European Union, 6 – Law, Politics, and Society*. (Oxford: Oxford University Press), 105–126.

Héritier, A. and Eckert, S. (2008) 'New Modes of Governance in the Shadow of Hierarchy: Self-Regulation by Industry in Europe', *Journal of Public Policy*, 28, 1, 113–138.

Héritier, A., Kerwer, D., Knill, C., Lehmkuhl, D., Teutsch, M. and Douillet, A-C. (2001) *Differential Europe. The European Union Impact on National Policymaking*. (Lanham: Rowman & Littlefield).

Héritier, A. and Lehmkuhl, D. (2008) 'Introduction. The Shadow of Hierarchy and New Modes of Governance', *Special Issue of Journal of Public Policy*, 28, 1, 1–17.

Héritier, A. and Rhodes, M. (eds.) (2010) *New Modes of Governance in Europe. Governing in the Shadow of Hierarchy*.

Hicks, B. (2004) 'Setting Agendas and Shaping Activism: EU Influence on Central and Eastern European Environmental Movements', *Environmental Politics*, 13, 1, 216–233.

Hille, P. and Knill, C. (2006) 'It's the Bureaucracy, Stupid'. The Implementation of the Acquis Communautaire in EU Candidate Countries, 1999–2003, *European Union Politics*, 7, 4, 531–552.

Hinoea, C. and Balogh, M. (2004) 'Managerial Reform in Romanian Public Administration', *Society and Economy*, 26, 247–261.

Hix, S. (1998) 'The Study of the European Union II: The "New Governance" Agenda and its Revival', *Journal of European Public Policy*, 5, 1, 38–65.

Hodson, D. and Maher, I. (2001) 'The Open Method as a New Mode of Governance: The Case of Soft Economic Policy Co-ordination', *Journal of Common Market Studies*, 39, 4, 719–746.

Homeyer, I. v. (2004) 'Differential Effects of Enlargement on EU Environmental Governance', *Environmental Politics*, 13, 1, 52–76.

Homeyer, I. v., Bär, S., Carius, A. and Deim, S. (2001) *Umweltpolitik in Mittel- und Osteuropa. Analyse der EU-Osterweiterung*. (Berlin: ecologic).

Honadle, B. W. (1981) 'A Capacity-Building Framework. A Search for Concept and Purpose', *Public Administration Review*, 41, 5, 575–580.

Hooghe, L. (ed.) (1996) *Cohesion Policy and European Integration: Building Multi-Level Governance*. (Oxford: Oxford University Press).

Hooghe, M. and Stolle, D. (eds.) (2003) *Generating Social Capital - Civil Society and Institutions in Comparative Perspective*. (New York: Palgrave Macmillan).

Howard, M. M. (2002) 'The Weakness of Postcommunist Civil Society', *Journal of Democracy*, 13, 1, 157–169.

Howard, M. M. (2003) *The Weakness of Civil Society in Post-Communist Europe.* (Cambridge: Cambridge University Press).

Howlett, M. and Ramesh, M. (2003) *Studying Public Policy: Policy Cycles and Policy Subsystems.* (Oxford: Oxford University Press).

Hughes, G. and Bucknall, J. (2000) *Poland. Complying with EU Environmental Legislation* World Bank Technical Paper (Washington D.C.).

Iankova, E. A. (2009) *Business, Government, and EU Accession: Strategic Partnership and Conflict.* (Lanham, MD: Lexington Books).

Iankova, E. A. and Katzenstein, P. J. (2003) 'European Enlargement and Institutional Hypocrisy' in T. A. Börzel and R. A. Cichowski (eds.) *The State of the European Union Vol 6: Law, Politics and Society.* (Oxford: Oxford University Press), 269–290.

Ijjas, I. and Botond, K. (2004) *Public Participation in the implementation of the WFD in the Middle Danube Subbasin in Hungary.* (Budapest: HarmoniCop).

IMAS (2000) *Opinions and Perceptions about NGOs in Romania.* (Bucharest: Institute of Marketing and Surveys in Romania).

Jachtenfuchs, M. (1995) 'Theoretical Perspectives on European Governance', *European Law Journal*, 1, 2, 115–133.

Jacobsen, H. K. and Weiss Brown, E. (1995) 'Strengthening Compliance with International Environmental Accords: Preliminary Observations from a Collaborative Project', *Global Governance*, 1, 2, 119–148.

Jacoby, W. (2000) *Imitation and Politics: Redesigning Modern Germany.* (Ithaca, NY: Cornell University Press).

Jänicke, M., Weidner, H. and Jörgens, H. (1997) *National Environmental Policies: A Comparative Study of Capacity-Building: with a Data Appendix, International Profiles of Change since 1970.* (Berlin; New York: Springer).

Jávor, B. and Németh, K. (2007) 'Kisebb állam, nagyobb baj?', *Társadalomkutatás*, 25, 4, 487–511.

Jehlicka, P. and Tickle, A. (2004) 'Environmental Implications of Eastern Enlargement: The End of Progressive EU Environmental Policy?', *Environmental Politics*, 13, 1, 77–95.

Jendroska, J. and Bar, M. (2005) 'Die jüngeren Entwicklungen des polnischen Umweltrechts' in H. J. Koch and J. Schürmann (eds.) *Das EG Umweltrecht und seine Umsetzung in Deutschland und Polen.* (Baden-Baden: Nomos).

Jerre, U. (2005) *Conflicting Logics? Implementing Capacity and EU Adaption in a Postcommunist Context* Department of Political Science. (Lund: Lund University).

Jessel, B. and Mackowiak-Pandera, J. (2004) 'UVP, SUP und FFH-Verträglichkeitsprüfung in Polen. Stand und Perspektiven der Entwicklung in einem neuen EU-Mitgliedstaat.', *UVP Report*, 5, 241–246.

Jiménez, M. (2001) 'Sustainable Development and the Participation of Environmental NGOs in Spanish Environmental Policy' in K. Eder and M. Kousis (eds.) *Environmental Politics in Southern Europe. Actors, Institutions and Discourses in a Europeanizing Society.* (The Hague: Kluwer Academic Publishers), 225–254.

Jordan, A., Wurzel, R. K. W. and Zito, A. (2005) 'The Rise of "New" Policy Instruments in Comparative Perspective: Has Governance Eclipsed Government?', *Political Studies*, 53, 4, 477–496.

Jordana, J., Levi-Faur, D. and Puig, I. (2005) 'The Limits of Europeanization: Regulatory Reforms in the Spanish and Portuguese Telecommunications and Electricity Sectors', *European Integration online Papers*, 9, 10.

Karpathaki, E. (2005) *Management Boards in National Parks. An Institutional Experiment Between the State and Civil Society* (National Centre of Public Administration and Local Government).

Katzenstein, P. J. (1984) *Corporatism and Change. Austria, Switzerland, and the Politics of Industry.* (Ithaca; London: Cornell University Press).

Katzenstein, P. J. (1985) *Small States in World Markets. Industrial Policy in Europe.* (Ithaca; London: Cornell University Press).

Katzenstein, P. J. (ed.) (1978) *Between Power and Plenty: Foreign Economic Policies of Advanced Industrial States.* (Madison: Wisconsin University Press).

Kaufmann, D., Kraay, A. and Mastruzzi, M. (2003) 'Governance Matters III: Governance Indicators for 1996–2002', *World Bank Policy Research Working Paper.*

Kaufmann, D., Kraay, A. and Mastruzzi, M. (2005) 'Governance Matters IV: Governance Indicators for 1996–2004', *World Bank Policy Research Paper.*

Kazakos, P. (1999) 'The "Europeanisation" of Public Policy: The National Environmental Policy between Domestic Factors and Supranational Commitments', *Greek Review of Political Science*, 13, 81–122.

Keller, J. (2008) 'Patterns of Sub-National Development Governance in the Case of Hungarian Micro-Regions. Case Studies on Programming, Implementation and Monitoring', *NewGov Contract Deliverable*, 15, D10.

Kelley, J. G. (2006) 'New Wine in Old Wineskins: Promoting Political Reforms through the New European Neighbourhood Policy', *Journal of Common Market Studies*, 44, 1, 29–55.

Kenis, P. and Schneider, V. (1991) 'Policy Networks and Policy Analysis: Scrutinizing a New Analytical Toolbox' in B. Marin and R. Mayntz (eds.) *Policy Networks: Empirical Evidence and Theoretical Considerations.* (Frankfurt a.M.: Campus), 25–59.

Kerameus, K. and Kremlis, D. (1988) 'The Application of Community Law in Greece', *Common Market Law Review*, 25, 1, 141–175.

Kerekes, S. (2000) *Environmental Policy Tools and Firm-level Management Practices in Hungary* (http://www.oecd.org/dataoecd/26/0/31686250.pdf Budapest University of Economic Sciences and Public Administration (BUESPA), Department of Environmental Economics and Technology in cooperation with OECD Environment Directorate).

Kerekes, S. and Bulla, M. (1994) 'Environmental management in Hungary', *Environmental Impact Assessment Review*, 14, 2–3, 95–105.

Kerekes, S. and Kiss, K. (eds.) (2003) *A megkérdöjelezett sikerágazat. Az EU környezetvédelmi követelményeinek teljesítése.* (Budapest MTA Társadalomkutató Központ).

Kerényi, S. and Szabó, M. (2006) 'Transnational Influences on Patterns of Mobilisation Within Environmental Movements in Hungary', *Environmental Politics*, 15, 5, 803–820.[ulc?]

Kiwa, N. (2002) *Synthesis Report on the Quality of Drinking Water in the Member States of the European Union in the Period 1996–1998.* (Nieuwegein).

Knill, C. (2001) *The Europeanisation of National Administrations. Patterns of Institutional Change and Persistence.* (Cambridge: Cambridge University Press).

Knill, C. and Lenschow, A. (eds.) (2000) *Implementing EU Environmental Policy: New Directions and Old Problems.* (Manchester: Manchester University Press).

Kohl, H. and Platzer, H.-W. (2007a) *Industrial Relations in Central and Eastern Europe. Transformation and Integration. A Comparison of Eight New EU Member States.* (Brussels: European Trade Union Institute).

Kohl, H. and Platzer, H.-W. (2007b) 'The Role of the State in Central and Eastern European Industrial Relations: The Case of Minimum Wages', *Industrial Relations Journal*, 38, 6, 614–635.

Kohler-Koch, B. (1996a) 'Catching up with Change: The Transformation of Governance in the European Union', *Journal of European Public Policy*, 3, 3, 359–380.

Kohler-Koch, B. (1996b) 'The Strength of Weakness. The Transformation of Governance in the EU' in S. Gustavsson and L. Lewin (eds.) *The Future of the Nation State. Essays on Cultural Pluralism and Political Integration.* (Stockholm: Nerenius & Santerus), 169–210.

Kohler-Koch, B. (1999) 'The Evolution and Transformation of European Governance' in B. Kohler-Koch and R. Eising (eds.) *The Transformation of Governance in the European Union.* (London: Routledge), 14–35.

Kohler-Koch, B. (2000) 'Framing the Bottleneck of Constructing Legitimate Institutions', *Journal of European Public Policy*, 7, 4, 513–531.

Kohler-Koch, B. and Eising, R. (eds.) (1999) *The Transformation of Governance in Europe* (London: Routledge).

Kohler-Koch, B. and Rittberger, B. (2006) 'The "Governance Turn" in EU Studies', *Journal of Common Market Studies*, 44, 1, 27–49.

Kolk, A. and Van der Weij, E. (1998) 'Financing Environmental Policy in East Central Europe' in S. Baker and P. Jehlicka (eds.) *Dilemmas of Transition. The Environment, Democracy and Economic Reform in East Central Europe.* (London: Frank Cass), 53–68.

Kooiman, J. (ed.) (1993) *Modern Governance. New Government-Society Interactions.* (London: Sage).

Kousis, M. (1999) 'Sustaining Local Environmental Mobilisations: Groups, Actions and Claims in Southern Europe', *Environmental Politics*, 8, 1, 172–198.

Kousis, M. (2001) 'Competing Claims in Local Environmental Conflicts in Southern Europe' in K. Eder and M. Kousis (eds.) *Environmental Politics in Southern Europe.* (Dordrecht, Boston, London: Kluwer Academic Publishers), 129–150.

Kousis, M. (2003) 'Greece' in C. Rootes (ed.) *Environmental Protest in Western Europe.* (Oxford: Oxford University Press), 109–135.

Kousis, M., Della Porta, D. and Jiménez, M. (2008) 'Southern European Environmental Movements in Comparative Perspectives', *American Behavioural Scientist*, 51, 11, 1627–1650.

Koutalakis, C. (2003) *Cities and the Structural Funds. The Domestic Impact of EU Initiatives for Urban Development.* (Athens: Sakoulas Publishers).

Koutalakis, C. (2004) 'Environmental Compliance in Italy and Greece. The Role of Non-state Actors', *Enviornmental Politics*, 13, 4, 754–774.

Koutalakis, C. (2005) Regulatory Effects of Participatory Environmental Networks. The case of the Seville Process. NEWGOV Deliverable, Project 14, D 02.

Koutalakis, C. (2007) 'Pharmaceutical Harmonization in Central Eastern Europe-New Modes of Governance in the Shadow of Conditionality', *Newgov Policy Brief*, 02.

Koutalakis, C. (2008) 'Regulatory Effects of Participatory Environmental Networks. The case of the "Seville Process"' in T. Conzelmann and R. Smith (eds.) *Multi-level governance in the European Union: Taking Stock and Looking Ahead*. (Baden-Baden: Nomos), 35–54.

Koutalakis, C. and Prange, H. (2006) 'Smoothing' Eastern Enlargement through New Modes of Governance?' in G. F. Schuppert (ed.) *Europeanization of Governance – The Challenge of Accession*. (Baden-Baden: Nomos), 133–152.

Koutoupa-Regakou, E. (2007) *Environmental Law*. (Athens-Thessaloniki: Sakkoulas Publishers).

Krónika (2008) '*Kelemen Hunor törvénymódosítást javasol, 2008. 09. 18.*' Krónika (Cluj-Napoca).

Krüger, C. and Carius, A. (2001) *Umweltpolitik und Umweltrecht in Rumänien. Eine Zwischenbilanz des Beitrittsprozesses*. (Berlin: ecologic).

Kutter, A. and Trappmann, V. (2010) 'Civil Society in Central and Eastern Europe: The Ambivalent Legacy of Pre-Accession', *Acta Politica*.

La Spina, A. and Sciortino, G. (1993) 'Common Agenda, Southern Rules: European Integration and Environmental Change in the Mediterranean States' in J. D. Liefferink, P. D. Lowe and A. P. J. Mol (eds.) *European Integration and Environmental Policy*. (London, New York: Belhaven), 217–236.

Ladi, S. (2005) 'The Role of Experts in the Reform Process in Greece', *West European Politics*, 28, 2, 279–296.

Lane, D. (2007) 'Civil Society Formation in the Post-Socialist EU Member States' in D. Obradovic and H. Pleines (eds.) *The Capacity of Central and Eastern European Interest Groups to Participate in EU Governance*. (Stuttgart: Ibidem-Verlag), 109–127.

Lane, D. (2010) 'Civil Society in the Old and New Member States: Ideology, Institutions and the Weakness of Democracy Promotion', *Acta Politica*.

Láng-Pickvance, K. (1998) *Democracy and Environmental Movements in Eastern Europe: A Comparative Study of Hungary and Russia*. (Boulder, Colo.: Westview Press).

Lavenex, S. (2008) 'A Governance Perspective on the European Neighbourhood Policy. Integration Beyond Conditionality?', *Journal of European Public Policy*, 15, 6, 938–955.

Lavenex, S. (2009) 'Intensive Transgovernmentalism in the European Area of Freedom, Security and Justice' in I. Tömmel and A. Verdun (eds.) *Governance and Policy-Making in the European Union*. (Boulder, CO: Lynne Rienner).

Le Galès, P. (1995) 'Introduction: Les réseaux d'action publique entre outil passe-partout et théorie de moyenne portée' in P. Le Galès and M. Thatcher (eds.) *Les réseaux de politique publique. Débat autour des policy networks*. (Paris: l'Harmattan), 13–27.

Lee, A.-R. and Norris, J. A. (2000) 'Attitudes Toward Environmental Issues in East Europe', *International Journal of Public Opinion Research*, 12, 4, 372–397.

Lehmbruch, G. (1982) *Patterns of Corporatist Policy-Making*. (Beverly Hills: Sage).

Lenschow, A. (2002) 'New Regulatory Approaches in "Greening" EU Politics', *European Law Journal*, 8, 1, 19–37.

Levy, J. D. (1999) *Tocqueville's Revenge: State, Society, and Economy in Contemporary France*. (Cambridge: Cambridge University Press).

Lijphart, A. (1998) 'Consensus and Consensus Democracy: Cultural, Structural, Functional, and Rational-Choice Explanations', *Scandinavian Political Studies*, 21, 2, 99–108.

Linz, J. J. and Stepan, A. (1996) *Problems of Democratic Transition and Consolidation: Southern Europe, South America, and Post-Communist Europe.* (Baltimore: Johns Hopkins University Press).

Lippert, B., Umbach, G. and Wessels, W. (2001) 'Europeanization of CEE Executives: EU Membership Negotiations as a Shaping Power', *Journal of European Public Policy*, 8, 6, 980–1012.

Luaces, P. (2002) 'Circumventing Adaptation Pressure? Implementing EU Environmental Policy in Spain', *South European Society & Politics*, 7, 3, 81–108.

Luif, P. (1995) *On the Road to Brussels. The Political Dimension of Austria's, Finland's and Sweden's Accession to the European Union.* (Vienna: Braumüller).

Magen, A. (2006) 'The Shadow of Enlargement: Can the European Union Neighbourhood Policy Achieve Compliance?', *Columbia Journal of European Law*, 12, 2, 495–538.

Magen, A. and Morlino, L. (eds.) (2008) *'Anchoring Democracy: External Influence on Domestic Rule of Law Development'.* (London: Routledge).

Magone, J. M. (1997) *European Portugal: The Difficult Road to Sustainable Democracy.* (London: Palgrave Macmillan).

Magone, J. M. (2003) *The Politics of Southern Europe: Integration into the European Union.* (Westport: Praeger).

Majone, G. (ed.) (1996) *Regulating Europe.* (London; New York: Routledge).

Makomaska-Juchiewicz, M. (2004) *'Cross Border Implementation and Coherence of Natura 2000 in Poland'* (http://www.ikzm-d.de/infos/pdfs/41_Poland_View.pdf) access date: 18.06.2009.

Mann, M. (1986) 'The Autonomous Power of the State: Its Origins, Mechanisms and Results' in J. A. Hall (ed.) *States in History.* (London: Blackwell), 109–136.

Mann, M. (1993) *The Sources of Social Power, Vol. 2: The Rise of Classes and Nation-States, 1760–1914.* (Cambridge: Cambridge University Press).

Manoleli, D. (2002) *Impactul implementarii Directivelor Habitate (92/43/CEE) si pasari (79/409/CEE), PHARE PROIECT PHARE RO 9907- 02- 01B, (The Implementation Impact of the Habitat (92/43/CEE) and Wild Birds (79/409/CEE) Directive)* (Bucharest: Institutul European din Romania).

Manoleli, D., Georgescu, L. P., Platon, V., Prisecaru, P. and Stanescu, R. (2002) *Impactul acquis-ului European de mediu asupra unor sectoare industriale în Romania* E. I. Romania (ed.), STUDII DE IMPACT PRIVIND PROCESUL DE PREADERARE (Bucharest).

Maraveyas, N. (1994) 'The Common Agricultural Policy and Greek Agriculture' in P. Kazakos and P. C. Ioakimides (eds.) *Greece and EC Membership Evaluated.* (London: Pinter), 56–73.

Marin, B. and Mayntz, R. (eds.) (1991) *Policy Network: Empirical Evidence and Theoretical Considerations.* (Frankfurt a.M.: Campus).

Markou, C., Nakos, G. and Zahariadis, N. (2001) 'Greece: A European Paradox' in E. Zeff and E. B. Pirro (eds.) *The European Union and the Member States.* (Boulder, CO: Lynne Rienner), 217–235.

Mayer, Z. (2002) *Az Integrált szennyezés-megelőzés és szabályozás irányelv (IPPC), és magyarországi megvalósítása: az egységes környeszethasználati engedélyezés.* (Budapest).

Mayer, Z. and Dragos, T. (2005) *Az IPPC irányelv végrehajtásának alakulása az Európai Unióban és Magyarországon.* (Budapest: Magyar Természetvédők Szövetsége).

Mayntz, R. (1993) 'Modernization and the Logic of Interogranizational Networks' in J. Child, M. Crozier and R. Mayntz (eds.) *Societal Change Between Market and Organization*. (Aldershot: Avebury), 3–18.

Mayntz, R. (1995) 'Politische Steuerung: Aufstieg, Niedergang und Transformation einer Theorie' in K. v. Beyme and C. Offe (eds.) *Politische Theorien in der Ära der Transformation. PVS Sonderheft 26*. (Opladen: Westdeutscher Verlag), 148–168.

Mayntz, R. (1997) *Soziale Dynamik und politische Steuerung. Theoretische und methodologische Überlegungen*. (Frankfurt; New York: Campus).

Mayntz, R. (2004) 'Governance im modernen Staat' in A. Benz (ed.) *Governance - Regieren in komplexen Regelsystemen. Eine Einführung*. (Wiesbaden: Verlag für Sozialwissenschaften), 65–76.

Mayntz, R. (ed.) (1983) *Implementation politischer Programme II. Ansätze zur Theoriebildung*. (Opladen: Westdeutscher Verlag).

Mayntz, R. and Scharpf, F. W. (eds.) (1995a) *Gesellschaftliche Selbstregulierung und politische Steuerung*. (Frankfurt a.M.: Campus).

Mayntz, R. and Scharpf, F. W. (1995b) 'Steuerung und Selbstorganisation in staatsnahen Sektoren' in R. Mayntz and F. W. Scharpf (eds.) *Gesellschaftliche Selbstregulierung und politische Steuerung*. (Frankfurt; New York: Campus), 9–38.

Mbaye, H. A. D. (2001) 'Why National States Comply with Supranational Law. Exlaining Impementation Infringements in the European Union 1972–1993', *European Union Politics*, 2, 3, 259–281.

Mény, Y. (1988) 'France' in D. C. Rowat (ed.) *Public Administration in Developed Democracies. A Comparative Study*. (New York: Marcel Dekker, Inc.), 273–292.

Meyer-Sahling, J.-H. (2006) 'The Rise of the Partisan State? Parties, Patronage and the Ministerial Bureaucracy in Hungary', *Journal of Communist Studies and Transition Politics*, 22, 3, 274–297.

Migdal, J. S. (1988) *Strong Societies and Weak Sates. State-Society Relations and State Capabilities in the Third World*. (Princenton: Princeton University Press).

Ministerio do Ambiente & Ministerio de Energia e Innovaçao, *Plano Nacional de Redução das Emissões das Grandes Instalações de Combustão*, Diario de la República, n°122, 27 June 2006.

Ministerio de Obras Públicas y Transportes (1992) *Medio Ambiente en España. 1991*, (Madrid).

Ministerio de Obras Públicas, Transportes y Medio Ambiente (1993) *Medio Ambiente en España. 1992*, (Madrid).

Ministerio de Obras Públicas, Transportes y Medio Ambiente (1994) *Medio Ambiente en España. 1993*, (Madrid).

Ministerio de Obras Públicas, Transportes y Medio Ambiente (1995) *Medio Ambiente en España. 1994*, (Madrid).

MKIK (2004) *A környezetvédelmi hatóság tevékenységével kapcsolatos ipari vélemény és javaslat a munka javítására. Összefoglaló értékelés*. (Budapest Magyar Kereskedelmi és Iparkamara).

MMGA/ANAR (2007) *Planurile de management ale bazinelor hidrografice din Romania. Probleme importante de gospodărirea apelor*. (Bucuresti: Ministerul Mediului si Gospodariri Apelor).

Mocsári, J. (2004a) 'Environment Policy in Hungary' in A. Ágh (ed.) *Europeanization and Regionalization: Hungary's Preparation for EU-Accession*. (Budapest: Hungarian Center for Democracy Studies).

Mocsári, J. (2004b) 'Missing Details behind the Big Picture: The Delayed Implementation of the Habitats Directive in Hungary', *Budapest Papers on Europeanization* 18.

Molina Álvarez de Cienfuegos, I. (2000) 'Spain' in H. Kassim, G. Peters and V. Wright (eds.) *The National Co-ordination of EU Policy. The Domestic Level.* (Oxford: Oxford University Press).

Molina Álvarez de Cienfuegos, I. (2001) 'La Adaptación a la Unión Europea del Poder Ejecutivo Español' in C. Closa (ed.) *La Europeización del Sistema Politico Español.* (Valencia: Tirant lo Blanch), 162–197.

Morlino, L. (2002) 'The Europeanisation of Southern Europe' in A. Costa Pinto and N. Severiano Teixeira (eds.) *Southern Europe and the Making of the European Union.* (New York: Columbia University Press).

Mudde, C. and Kopecky, P. (eds.) (2002) *Uncivil Society: Democracy and Extremism in Postcommunist Societies.* (London: Routledge).

MVTSZ (2003) *Kapcsolatépítés a vállalati szféra és a környezetvédő társadalmi szervezetek között. Környezetvédő társadalmi szervezetek felkészítése az EU vállalati környezetvédelemmel kapcsolatos szabályozásának megvalósítására* A HU0010-01-01-0035 számú Phare ACCESS Mikro-projekt zárótanulmánya (Budapest).

Neagu, I. (2006) *Fraude sub ape.* (Curierul National).

Neves Sequeira, T. (2001) *Crescimento Económico no Pós-guerra: os Casos de Espanha, Portugal e Irlanda.* Texto para Discussão DGE-05/2001 (Covilhã: Universidade da Beira Interior).

Noutcheva, G. and Bechev, D. (2008) 'The Successful Laggards: Bulgaria and Romania's Accession to the EU', *East European Politics and Societies*, 22, 1, 114–144.

Novac, C. and Auer, M. (2004) 'Forestry Resources in Transition: The Romanian Experience' in M. Auer (ed.) *Restoring Cursed Earth: Appraising Environmental Policy Reforms in Central and Eastern Europe and Russia.* (Boulder: Rowman & Littlefield), 93–117.

Nunberg, B. (1999) 'Modernizing the Romanian State: The Go-Slow Administrative Transition' in B. Nunberg (ed.) *The State After Communism Administrative Transitions in Central and Eastern Europe.* (Washington, DC: World Bank), 53.

Nunberg, B., Barbone, L. and Derlien, H.-U. (1998) *The State After Communism: Administrative Transitions in Central and Eastern Europe.* (Washington, DC: World Bank).

Obradovic, D. and Alonso Vizcaino, J. M. (2007) 'Good Governance Requirements Concerning the Participation of Interest Groups in EU Consultations' in D. Obradovic and H. Pleines (eds.) *The Capacity of Central and Eastern European Interest Groups to Participate in EU Governance.* (Stuttgart: Ibidem Publishers), 67–108.

Obradovic, D. and Pleines, H. (eds.) (2007) *The Capacity of Central and Eastern European Interest Groups to Participate in EU Governance.* (Stuttgart: Ibidem-Verlag).

OECD (1993) *Environmental data. Compendium 1993.* (Paris: OECD Publications).

OECD (1997) *Environmental Performance Reviews: Spain.* (Paris: OECD Publications).

OECD (1998) *Economic Surveys: Spain.* (Paris: OECD Publications).

OECD (2004) *Environmental Performance Reviews: Spain.* (Paris: OECD Publications).

OECD/DANCEE (2003) *Models of Water Utility Reform in the Central and Eastern European Countries.* (Paris: OECD Publications).

O'Hagan, E. (2004) 'Too Soft to Handle? A Reflection on Soft Law in Europe and Accession States', *Journal of European Integration*, 26, 4, 379–403.

Olearius, A. (2006) 'Zwischen Empowerment und Instrumentalisierung: Nichtstaatliche Akteure der Umweltpolitik während des Beitrittprozesses' in A. Kutter and V. Trappmann (eds.) *Das Erbe des Beitritts: Europäisierung in Mittel- und Osteuropa.* (Baden-Baden: Nomos), 339–359.

Olson, M. (1982) *The Rise and Decline of Nations: Economic Growth, Stagflation, and Social Rigidities.* (New Haven: Yale University Press).

O'Toole, L. J. and Hanf, K. (1998) 'Hungary: Political Transformation and Environmental Challenge', *Environmental Politics*, 7, 1, 93–112.

O'Toole, L. J., Jr. (1994) 'Local Public Administrative Challenges in Post-Socialist Hungary', *International Review of Administrative Sciences*, 60, 2, 291–304.

Padgett, S. (2000) *Organizing Democracy in Eastern Germany: Interest Groups in Post-Communist Society.* (Cambridge: Cambridge University Press).

Palincsar, S. A. (1998) 'Social Constructivist Perspectives on Teaching and Learning', *Annual Review of Psychology*, 49, 345–375.

Papp, T. (2006) 'Contribuţia Grupului Milvus la realizarea reţelei de arii protejate europene "Natura 2000" din România', *Migrans*, December, http://www.milvus.ro/English/Migrans/2006dec_ro.pdf.

Paraskevopoulos, C. J., Panagiotis, G. and Rees, N. (eds.) (2006) *Adapting to EU Multi-Level Governance. Regional and Environmental Policies in Cohesion and CEE Countries.* (Aldershot: Ashgate).

Partidario, M. d. R. and Nunes Correira, F. (2004) 'POLIS - The Portuguese Program on Urban Environment: A Contribution to the Discussion on European Urban Policy', *European Planning Studies*, 2, 3, 409–424.

Pasti, V. (2006) *Noul capitalism romanesc.* (Iasi: Polirom).

Pavlinek, P. and Pickles, J. (2000) *Environmental Transitions: Transformation and Ecological Defense in Central and Eastern Europe* Routledge.

Pavlinek, P. and Pickles, J. (2005) 'Environmental Past/Environmental Futures in Post-Socialist Europe' in J. Carmin (ed.) *EU Enlargement and the Environment. Institutional Change and Environmental Policy in Central and Eastern Europe.* (London: Routledge), 237–265.

Penu, O.-D. (2004) 'Romanian NGOs and NATURA 2000' in H. Korn, R. Schliep and C. Epple (eds.) *Report of the International Workshop 'Capacity-Building for Biodiversity in Central and Eastern Europe'.* (Isle of Vilms German Federal Agency for Nature Conservation), 25–30.

Péter, J. (2004) *Public Service International Research Unit – WaterTime National Context Report – Hungary.* (Budapest: Eötvös József College).

Péter, J. (2007) 'Law and Sustainability: The Impact of the Hungarian Legal Structure on the Sustainability of the Water Services', *Utilities Policy*, 15, 2, 121–133.

Petrova, T. and Tarrow, S. (2007) 'Transactional and Participatory Activism in the Emerging European Polity', *Comparative Political Studies*, 40, 1, 74–94.

Pierre, J. and Peters, B. G. (2000) *Governance, Politics and the State.* (Basingstoke: Palgrave-Macmillan).

Pinho, P. (1997) 'Local Planning and National Environmental Assessment Procedures: The Developer's Mitigated role in Disjointed Negotiation Processes', *Urban Studies*, 34, 1, 2037–2052.

Popa, A., Matei, G., Ciomos, V., Dumitrescu, A., Giosan, V. and Mendes, K. (2001) 'Romania' in G. Péteri and M. T. Horváth (eds.) *Navigation to the market.* (Budapest: LGI Open Society Institute), 389–437.

Pralong, S. (2004) 'NGOs and the Development of Civil Society' in H. Carey (ed.) *Romania since transition.* (Lexington: Lanham), 229–247.

Presidential Decree (404/1989) *'Reorganization of Regional Directorates of the Ministry of Environment, Spatial Planning and Public Works'.* (Greek Government Official Gazette 173/A/1989).

Pridham, G. (ed.) (1991a) *'Encouraging Democracy: The International Context of Regime Transition in Southern Europe'.* (Leicester: Leicester University Press).

Pridham, G. (1991b) 'The Politics of the European Community: Transnational Networks, and Democratic Transitions in Southern Europe' in G. Pridham (ed.) *Encouraging Democracy: The Institutional Context of Regime Transition in Southern Europe.* (Leicester: Leicester University Press).

Pridham, G. (1994) 'National Environmental Policy-Making in the European Framework: Spain, Greece and Italy in Comparison', *Regional Politics and Policy,* 4, 1, Special Issue, 80–101.

Pridham, G. (1996) 'Environmental Policies and Problems of European Legislation in Southern Europe', *South European Society and Politics,* 1, 1, 47–73.

Pridham, G. (2007) 'The Effects of the European Union's Democratic Conditionality: The Case of Romania during Accession', *Journal of Communist Studies and Transition Politics,* 23, 2, 233–258.

Pridham, G. and Cini, M. (1994) 'Enforcing Environmental Standards in the European Union: Is There a Southern Problem?' in M. Faure, J. Vervaele and A. Waele (eds.) *Environmental Standards in the EU in an Interdisciplinary Framework.* (Antwerp: Maklu), 251–277.

Przeworski, A. (1990) *East-South System Transformation.* (Chicago: Chicago University Press).

Putnam, R. D. (1988) 'Diplomacy and Domestic Politics: The Logic of Two-Level Games', *International Organization,* 42, 3, 427–460.

Putnam, R. D. (1993) *Making Democracy Work. Civic Traditions in Modern Italy.* (Princeton: Princeton University Press).

Queiros, M. (2003) 'Le système productif local d'Agueda et la responsabilité environnementale', *Géographie, économie, société,* 5, 2, 203–222.

Radaelli, C. M. and Kraemer, U. S. (2008) 'Governance Areas in EU Direct Tax Policy', *Journal of Common Market Studies,* 46, 2, 315–336.

Raik, K. (2004) 'EU Accession of Central and Eastern European Countries: Democracy and Integration as Conflicting Logics', *East European Politics and Society,* 18, 4, 567–594.

Ramus, C. A. (1991) 'The Large Combustion Plant Directive: An Analysis of European Environmental Policy', *Oxford Institute for Energy Studies,* EV7.

Randeria, S. (2003) 'Cunning States and Unaccountable International Institutions: Legal Plurality, Social Movements and Rights of Local Communities to Common Property Resources', *European Journal of Sociology,* 44, 1, 27–60.

REC (1997) *Problems, Progress and Possibilities. A Needs Assessment of Environmental NGOs in Central and Eastern Europe* (Szentendre).

REC Romania (2005) *Institutional and practical barriers to public access to environmental and water-related information to support public involvement for the implementation of the EU's Water Framework Directive in Romania Regional*

Environmental Center - Romania (ed.), Danube Regional Project - Componenta 3.4 'Imbunatatirea Accesului la Informatii si Participarea Publica in Luarea Deciziilor pentru Mediu' (Bucharest).

REC Romania (2007) *Analiza chestionarelor completate de membrii Comitetelor de Bazin (Analysis of the survey among members of the RBMCs)* (Bucharest).

Rhodes, M. (2005) 'Employment Policy' in H. Wallace, W. Wallace and M. A. Pollack (eds.) *Policy-Making in the European Union.* (Oxford: Oxford University Press), 279–304.

Rhodes, R. A. W. (1997) *Understanding Governance: Policy Networks, Governance, Reflexivity and Accountability.* (Buckingham; Philadelphia: Open University Press).

Richardson, J. J. (ed.) (1982) *Policy-styles in Western Europe.* (London: Allen & Unwin).

Risse, T. and Lehmkuhl, U. (2007) 'Regieren ohne Staat? Governance in Räumen begrenzter Staatlichkeit' in T. Risse and U. Lehmkuhl (eds.) *Regieren ohne Staat? Governance in den Räumen begrenzter Staatlichkeit.* (Baden-Baden: Nomos), 13–40.

Risse, T. and Lehmkuhl, U. (eds.) (2010) *Governance in Areas of Limited Statehood.* (New York: Columbia University Press).

Rodrigues, R., Coutinho, M., Lopes, M., Ferreira, J. and Borrego, C. (2004) *Revision of the Legislation of Atmospheric Pollutants Emissions in Portugal.* (Durham: CEM).

Rose, R. (1994) 'Rethinking Civil Society: Postcommunism and the Problem of Trust', *Journal of Democracy*, 5, 3, 18–30.

Rose-Ackermann, S. (2005) *From Elections to Democracy. Building Accountable Government in Hungary and Poland.* (New York: Cambridge University Press).

Rose-Ackermann, S. (2007) 'From Elections to Democracy in Central Europe. Public Participation and the Role of Civil Society', *East European Politics and Societies*, 21, 1, 31–47.

Rosenau, J. N. and Czempiel, E.-O. (eds.) (1992) *Governance Without Government: Order and Change in World Politics.* (Cambridge: Cambridge University Press).

Rotariu, V. (2007) *Mediu: Veolia: Regretam ca nu mai sunt licitatii.* (Ziarul Financiar).

Roy, J. and Kanner, A. (2001) 'Spain and Portugal: Betting on Europe' in E. Zeff and E. Pirro (eds.) *The European Union and the Member States. Cooperation, Coordination and Compromise.* (London: Boulder), 236–263.

Royo, S. (2003) 'The 2004 Enlargement: Iberian Lessons for Post-Communist Europe', *South European Society & Politics*, 8, 1–2, 287–313.

Royo, S. (2007) 'Lessons from the Integration of Spain and Portugal to the EU', *Political Science & Politics*, 40, 4, 689–693

Rozgonyi, T. and Toarniczky, A. (2007) 'Szervezeti kultúra a magyar vízügyi igazgatóságok példáján', *Társadalomkutatás*, 25, 1, 21–43.

Ryall, A. (2007) 'EIA and Public Participation: Determining the Limits of Member State Discretion', *Journal of Environmental Law*, 19, 2, 1–11.

Sapelli, G. (1995) *Southern Europe since 1945. Tradition and Modernity in Portugal, Spain, Italy, Greece and Turkey.* (London, New York: Longman).

Sardamov, I. (2005) 'Civil Society and the Limits of Democratic Assistance', *Governance and Opposition*, 40, 3, 349–402.

Saro, G. (2001) 'La Política Industrial' in C. Closa (ed.) *La Europeización del Sistema Político Español.* (Madrid: Istmo), 421–440.

Saurugger, S. S. (2007) 'Differential Impact: Europeanizing French Non-state Actors', *Journal of European Public Policy*, 14, 7, 1079–1097.

Scharpf, F. W. (1978) 'Interorganizational Policy Studies: Issues, Concepts and Perspectives' in K. Hanf and F. W. Scharpf (eds.) *Interorganizational Policy Making. Limits to Coordination and Central Control*. (London: Sage), 57–112.

Scharpf, F. W. (1991) 'Die Handlungsfähigkeit des Staates am Ende des zwanzigsten Jahrhunderts', *Politische Vierteljahresschrift*, 32, 4, 621–634.

Scharpf, F. W. (1993) 'Positive und negative Koordination in Verhandlungssystemen' in A. Héritier (ed.) *Policy-Analyse. Kritik und Neuorientierung. PVS Sonderheft 24*. (Opladen: Westdeutscher Verlag), 57–83.

Scharpf, F. W. (1997) *Games Real Actors Play. Actor-Centered Institutionalism in Policy Research*. (Boulder: Westview Press).

Schimmelfennig, F. and Sedelmeier, U. (2004) 'Governance by Conditionality: EU Rule Transfer to the Candidate Countries of Central and Eastern Europe', *Journal of European Public Policy*, 11, 4, 661–679.

Schimmelfennig, F. and Sedelmeier, U. (2005) *The Europeanization of Central and Eastern Europe*. (Ithaca, NY: Cornell University Press).

Schimmelfennig, F., Engert, S. and Knobel, H. (2006) *International Socialization in Europe. European Organizations, Political Conditionality and Democratic Change*. (Houndsmills: Palgrave Macmillian).

Schmidt, V. A. (1996) *From State to Market? The Transformation of French Business and Government*. (Cambridge: Cambridge University Press).

Schmidt, V. A. (2006) *Democracy in Europe. The EU and National Polities*. (Oxford: Oxford University Press).

Schout, A. and Jordan, A. (2005) 'Coordinated European Governance. Self-Organizing or Centrally Steered?', *Public Administration*, 83, 1, 201–220.

Schreurs, M. (2004a) 'Environmental Protection in an Expanding European Community: Lessons from Past Accessions', *Environmental Politics*, 13, Supplement 1, 27–51.

Schreurs, M. (2004b) 'EU Enlargement and the Environment: Institutional Change and Environmental Policy in Central and Eastern Europe', *Environmental Politics*, 13, 1, 27–51.

Scott, J. and Holder, J. (2006) *Law and 'New' Environmental Governance in the European Union*, NewGov Deliverable, European University Institute, LTFIa/D3d.

Servos, A. (2003) *European Policies for Drinking Waters. The case of Greece*. (Athens: National Centre of Public Administration and Local Government, unpublished thesis).

Sidjanski, D. (1991) 'Transition to Democracy and European Integration: The Role of Interest Groups in Southern Europe' in G. Pridham (ed.) *Encouraging Democracy. The International Context of Regime Transition in Southern Europe*. (Leicester: Leicester University Press), 195–211.

Simmons, B. A. (1998) 'Compliance with International Agreements', *The Annual Review of Political Science*, 1, 75–93.

Sissenich, B. (2007) *Building States without Society: European Union Enlargement and the Transfer of EU Social Policy to Poland and Hungary*. (Lanham: Lexington Books).

Sissenich, B. (2008) 'Cross-National Policy Networks and the State: EU Social Policy Transfer to Poland and Hungary', *European Journal of International Relations*, 14, 3, 455–480.

Sissenich, B. (2010) 'Weak States, Weak Societies: Europe's East-West Gap', *Acta Politica*.

Smismans, S. (2006) 'New Modes of Governance and the Participatory Myth', *European Governance Papers*, 1, N-06-01, http://www.connex-network.org/eurogov/pdf/egp-newgov-N-06-01.pdf.

Somlyódy, L. (2000) 'A magyar vízgazdálkodás', *Magyar Tudomány*, 6.

Sommer, J. and Rotko, J. (1999) 'Umweltrechtsprechung in Polen – aktueller Stand und künftige Entwicklungen' in K. Matthias and H.-C. Brauweiler (eds.) *Internationales Umweltrecht. Ein Vergleich zwischen Deutschland, Polen und Tschechien.* (Wiesbaden: Deutscher Universitätsverlag).

Soran, V., Bíró, J., Moldovan, O. and Ardelean, A. (2000) 'Conservation of biodiversity in Romania', *Biodiversity and Conservation*, 9, 8, 1187–1198.

Spanou, C. (1995) 'Public Administration and the Environment' in M. S. Skourtos and K. M. Sofoulis (eds.) *Environmental Policies in Greece.* (Athens: Dardanos, Tipothito), 115–175.

Spanou, C. (1998) 'Greece: Administrative Symbols and Policy Realities' in K. Hanf and A.-I. Jansen (eds.) *Governance and Environment in Western Europe. Politics, Policy and Administration.* (Essex: Longman), 110–130.

Spanou, C. (2000) 'Greece' in H. Kassim, G. Peters and V. Wright (eds.) *The National Coordination of EU Policy. The Domestic Level.* (Oxford: Oxford University Press), 161–181.

Stark, D. and Bruszt, L. (1998) *Post Socialist Pathways. Transforming Politics and Property in Eastern Europe.* (Cambridge: Cambridge University Press).

Stark, D., Vedres, B. and Bruszt, L. (2006) 'Rooted transnational publics: Integrating foreign ties and civic activism', *Theory and Society*, 35, 3, 323–349.

Stefan, G. (2007) 'Normele UE lasa mii de prahoveni fara apa potabila (EU norms leave thousands of Prahovans withouth drinking water)' (Gandul: UrbanNews).

Støle, Ø. (2003) *Europeanization in the Context of Enlargement. A Study of Hungarian Environmental Policy,* Oslo: ARENA Report. No 07/*2003*.

Streeck, W. and Schmitter, P. C. (eds.) (1985) *Private Interest Government. Beyond Market and State.* (London et al.: Sage).

Syrett, S. (1997) 'The Politics of Partnership. The Role of Social Partners in Local Economic Development in Portugal', *European Urban and Regional Studies*, 4, 2, 99–114.

Talberg, J. (1999) *Making States Comply. The European Commission, the European Court of Justice and the Enforcement of the Internal Market.* (Lund: Studentlitteratur).

TERRA Mileniul III and ALMA-RO (2008) *Viziunea organizatiilor neguvernamentale de mediu asupra Protectiei Mediului in Romania Urbana - analiza primara a datelor* Asuma-ti responsabilitatea. Gandeste politici verzi. Barometru ONG (Bucharest TERRA Mileniul III).

Thiel, A. (2004) *The Role of the European Commission in Restructuring the Institutional Framework of Water Services: The case of the Algarve.* Presented at: IV Congreso Ibérico sobre Gestión y Planificación de Aguas (Tortosa).

Tilly, C. (1975) *The Formation of the Nation State.* (Princeton: Princeton University Press).

Toole, Laurence J. O. (1997) 'Networking requirements, institutional capacity, and implementation gaps in transitional regimes: the case of acidification policy in Hungary', *Journal of European Public Policy*, 4:1, 1–17.

Tovias, A. (2002) 'The Southern European Economies and European Integration' in A. Pinto Costa and N. Severiano Teixeira (eds.) *Southern Europe and the Making of the European Union, 1945–1980s*. (New York: Columbia University Press), 159–207.

Trenz, H.-J. (2008) 'European Civil Society: Between Participation, Representation and Discourse' in U. Liebert and H.-J. Trenz (eds.) *Reconstituting Democracy from Below. New Approaches to Civil Society in the New Europe*. (Oslo: Arena).

Tsebelis, G. (2002) *Veto Players: How Political Institutions Work*. (Princeton: Princeton University Press).

Tulmets, E. (2005) 'The Management of New Forms of Governance by Former Accession Countries of the European Union: Institutional Twinning in Estonia and Hungary', *European Law Journal*, 11, 5, 657–674.

Turnock, D. (2001) 'Environmental Problems and Policies in East Central Europe: A Changing Agenda', *GeoJournal*, 54, 485–505.

Turnock, D. (2002) 'Romania ' in F. W. Carter and D. Turnock (eds.) *Environmental Problems of East Central Europe*. (London: Routledge), 366–393.

Turnock, D. (2007) *Aspects of independent Romania's Economic History with Particular Reference to Transition for EU Accession*. (Aldershot, England; Burlington, VT: Ashgate).

UNECE (2001) *Environmental Performance Review of Romania* (New York/Geneva: United Nations Economic Commission for Europe).

United Nations Environment Programme. (1999) *Environmental Impacts of Trade Liberalization and Policies for the Sustainable Management of Natural Resources: A Case Study on Romania's Water Sector*. (New York: United Nations).

USAID (2008) *2007 NGO Sustainability Index for Central and Eastern Europe and Eurasia*. (Washington, D.C.: USAID).

Vachudova, M. A. (2005) *Europe Undivided: Democracy, Leverage and Integration after Communism*. (Oxford: Oxford University Press).

Vari, A. and Caddy, J. (eds.) (1999) *Public Participation in Environmental Decision-Making: Recent Developments in Hungary* (Budapest: Akademiai Kiado).

Vari, A. and Kisgyorgy, S. (1998) 'Public Participation in Developing Water Quality Legislation and Regulation in Hungary', *Water Policy*, 1, 2, 223–238.

Vaughan-Whitehead, D. C. (2003) *European Union Enlargement Versus Social Europe?* (Cheltenham, Northampton: Edward Elgar).

Vieira, J. M. P. (2003) 'Novos paradigmas e desafios para a gestao da água em Portugal' in L. d. Moral and P. Arrojo (eds.) *La Directiva Marco del Agua: realidades y futuros*. (Zaragoza: Fundación Nueva Cultura del Agua).

Voigt, R. (ed.) (1995) *Der kooperative Staat*. (Baden-Baden: Nomos).

Wasilewski, A. (2005) 'Die Entwicklung des Naturschutzrechts in Polen' in H. J. Koch and J. Schürmann (eds.) *Das EG Umweltrecht und seine Umsetzung in Deutschland und Polen*. (Baden-Baden: Nomos).

Weale, A., Pridham, G., Cini, M., Konstadakopulos, D., Porter, M. and Flynn, B. (2000) *Environmental Governance in Europe. An Ever Closer Ecological Union?* (Oxford: Oxford University Press).

Weiss, L. (1998) *The Myth of the Powerless State Governing the Economy in a Global Era*. (Cambridge: Polity Press).

White, S. (2005) 'A Progressive Politics of Responsibility: What would it Look like?', *Public Policy Research* 12, 1, 7–14.

Whitehead, L. (1991) 'Democracy by Convergence and Southern Europe: A Comparative Perspective' in G. Pridham (ed.) *Encouraging Democracy. The International Context of Regime Transition in Southern Europe.* (Leicester: Leicester University Press), 45–61.

Wolf, K. D. (2000) *Die neue Staatsräson – Zwischenstaatliche Kooperation als Demokratieproblem in der Weltgesellschaft.* (Baden-Baden: Nomos).

Woolfson, C. (2006) '"Working Environment and "Soft Law" in the Post-Communist New Member States', *Journal of Common Market Studies*, 44, 1, 195–215.

WWF-HELLAS (2003) *Progress on Preparation for Natura 2000 in Future EU Member States. Synthesis and Country Rreports for Bulgaria, Czech Republic, Estonia, Hungary, Latvia, Lithuania, Malta, Poland, Romania, Slovakia, and Slovenia'.*

Yoder, J. (2003) 'Decentralisation and Regionalisation after Communism. Administrative and Territorial Reform in Poland and the Czech Republic', *Europe Asia Studies*, 55, 2, 263–286.

YPEXODE (2006) *General Secretariat for Administrative Affairs, Department of Human Resources* (Athens: Ministry of the Environment).

Zimmer, A. and Priller, E. (eds.) (2004) *Future of Civil Society: Making Central European Nonprofit-Organizations Work.* (Opladen: VS Verlag).

Zinnes, C. (2004) 'The Environment in Transition' in H. Carey (ed.) *Romania since 1989. Politics, Economics and Society.* (Lanham: Lexington Books), 439–460.

Zinnes, C., Tarhoaca, C. and Popovici, M. (1999) 'Enforcement, Economic Instruments, and Water Pollution Abatement Investment in Romania', *Water Resources Update.*

Zubek, R. (2001) 'A Core in Check: The Transformation of the Polish Core Executive', *Journal of European Public Policy*, 8, 6, 911–932.

Zürn, M. (1997) '"Positives Regieren" jenseits des Nationalstaates', *Zeitschrift für Internationale Beziehungen*, 4, 1, 41–68.

Zürn, M. (1998) 'Global Governance and Legitimacy Problems', *Governance and Opposition*, 39, 2, 260–287.

Żylicz, T. (2000) *Costing Nature in a Transition Economy.* (Cheltenham: Edward Elgar).

Żylicz, T. and Holzinger, K. (2000) 'Environmental Policy in Poland and the Consequences of Approximation to the European Union' in K. Holzinger and P. Knoepfel (eds.) *Environmental Policy in a European Union of Variable Geometry?* (Basel: Helbing & Lichtenhahn).

Index